It's Gonna Get Messy
Copyright © 2025 by Rebecca Eve Young
All rights reserved.

No part of this publication may be reproduced, distributed, or transmitted in any form or by any means, including photocopying, recording, or other electronic or mechanical methods, without the prior written permission of the publisher, except in the case of brief quotations embodied in critical reviews and certain other noncommercial uses permitted by copyright law. For permission requests, write to the publisher at the address below.

Published with Wandering Words Media
www.wanderingwordsmedia.com

Cover typography and illustration by Tiffany Lastrucci
Author photograph by Ani Madueño
Interior design and layout by Rina Alhadeff
Manufactured in the United States of America
First edition

ISBN: 979-8-9994028-0-6 (pbk.)
Library of Congress Cataloging-in-Publication Data has been applied for.

This is a work of creative nonfiction. Some names and identifying details have been changed to protect the privacy of individuals. While the author has made every effort to ensure the accuracy of the information contained herein, any mistakes or omissions are unintentional.

For more information, contact:
Rebecca Eve Young

www.rebeccaeveyoung.com

It's Gonna Get Messy

An Unfiltered True Story of Heartbreak, Healing, and Reinvention

Becca Eve Young

"We delight in the beauty of the butterfly but rarely admit the changes it has gone through to achieve that beauty." - Maya Angelou

For Dad.

Why, hello there.

Take a breath with me. A deep one. Let the noise around you soften for a moment. Maybe you don't believe in synchronicity. I didn't either, once upon a time. But life has a wild way of showing us what we weren't ready to see. We'll get to that.

For now, imagine we've both ended up at the same little cosmic bus stop, out in the middle of nowhere—or everywhere, depending on how you see it. You and me, on a worn bench beneath a vast, star-filled sky in some quiet corner of the Universe, à la *Forrest Gump*.

What story, you might wonder, am I about to share with you as we sit here together on our cozy little bench? It's about one of the most tender, gritty, and universal quests in this wild human experience: the journey of remembering your worth and reclaiming self-love. Not as a concept. Not in a self-help book kind of way. Not with perfectly written affirmations and a vision board (though they absolutely have their place). I'm talking about the kind of lived truth that happens when everything falls apart, and you're left staring into the mirror, wondering who the hell you are.

If you've ever felt lost in life—in love, in grief, in trying to prove your worth, in people-pleasing, in bad decisions, in unhealthy relationships, or even just trying to make sense of what the hell you're here *for*—you might just find something in these pages that speaks to you. Maybe even a compass.

Sharing this much of myself is equal parts liberating and terrifying. But something from the depths of my soul tells me it's time. So here we are. And I have one humble request: try to leave judgment—okay, *most* of it—right here on this page.

Judgment has a way of blocking the very thing we all crave the most: connection. Trust me, I've seen firsthand how it erodes compassion and dims joy. I know this because I've been the one pointing fingers, thinking I had it all figured out. But really, I was just afraid. I found out the hard way that making overly critical comments about others only reflects our own insecurities. Judging others never made me feel more secure—it only made my world smaller. Compassion fosters understanding, while judgment slams the door shut.

If you're still here, still willing to settle in, let your edges soften. Keep an open heart, even when parts of this story feel unfamiliar, messy, or hard to love. Especially then.

Because to be honest, you might not like the version of me you meet in the beginning. That's fair. I didn't like her much either. Still, I hope you'll give her a chance. She's got a few heartfelt things to share.

So grab a chocolate, perhaps a tasty beverage, and let's settle in for a cozy visit. This won't be polished. It won't be perfect. But it *will* be honest. And hopefully, it'll feel a little bit like you're not alone in this messy human experience.

What's ahead is the unvarnished true story of my life based on my memories—names changed for privacy, sure—but the mess? That's all real. Because, well... healing never happens in the tidy version. It happens in the unraveling.

And this is mine.

Chapter One

Shit. My pants are wet.

I awaken to the sensation of my head having a pulse of its own. If I could pinch off the blood supply north of my collarbone to soften the throb for even a single second, I would. That shortsighted impulse would naturally end my life, but currently, I feel as if it would be worth the relief from the pounding agony steadily growing worse with each breath.

Without parting my eyelids, I shuffle deeper into my cocoon of sheets and am startled to realize they feel far too crisp for my typical lazy bi-weekly washing schedule. Quite questionably crisp, in fact. I slowly breathe in and out deeply several times, which feels like a monumental task. My lungs fill with remarkably familiar yet foreign, stale, somewhat mechanically scented, excessively dry air. I detect hotel vibes. I wonder if I should even risk subjecting my already thumping skull to the tiniest speck of light with a glance at my surroundings. In the end, I do. Blink, blink, blink, as rapidly as I possibly can. *Where in the actual fuck am I?* Blink, blink, blink again, with an ever-so-subtle head tilt southward. Alright, let's take inventory. It appears I'm currently swaddled within a nest of excessively crisp white linens. Definitely not my place. Quite likely a hotel. Wonderful. However, there seems to be a marked raw connectedness with said linens south of my personal midline border. A quick gander under the sheets reveals a distinct lack of pants or underwear. And, why, pray tell, am I wearing a midnight black silk blouse paired with absolutely nothing? My father always said I was a curious child.

I dare to lift my head further to see beyond my starched white cotton nest, taking quick note of excessively patterned carpet with a kaleidoscope of unnecessary colors, the standard mini bar with a sprawl of tiny, single serving bottles, and a half-devoured can of sour-cream Pringles. Ugh, that explains the crusty film of salt covering my tongue like leaked battery acid. My surroundings begin to spin, so I ever so gently roll my head back to its desired horizontal haven.

Flashes from the night before begin flooding my mind—massive steaks, seemingly endless bottles of rich burgundy wine, glasses sloppily clinking together, cheers after cheers after cheers. Blackjack dealers surrounded by a menagerie of giddy, furious, horny, and lonely guests trapped on a tiny island of hope together. Free excessively large screwdriver planes landing in succession in front of me like O'Hare during the holidays. A blur of a…roller coaster? Co-workers exchanging a slew of cautiously optimistic one-liners: "Looks like we're *working* on our hydration levels tonight!" Tequila shots burning my throat and misdirected lime squirts burning my eyes. Holding a friend's head while they vomited down the side of a shimmery and glitzy tower of endless glass, randomly tarnishing the sparkly glass on the way down. Vegas.

It's starting to piece together in sloppy, sporadic remembrances. And then—I remember.

I'm in Vegas for a weekend-long business trip to a travel industry conference. Apparently, I chose to mix every flavor of alcohol available and get absolutely obliterated. I hated to say it, but I wasn't surprised. At least in my stumbling haze I still had an internal compass functioning well enough to help me locate my hotel room, and plop my sloppy self safely into this pristinely bleached bed. The precious moments of peace and quiet are unfortunately spent unconscious before waking, rallying to do it all again today. Socializing in large groups is so terribly exhausting, especially when it comes to keeping up the filter required to remain at least somewhat professional boozing with co-workers.

There is a sudden unexpected reverberation across the bed. I startle, gripping the sheets with my fingertips and pop my right eye wide open, left eye squeezed tightly shut, stealing a peek in the direction from which the disturbance rumbled my way.

Ohhhhh shit. There is another human in my bed. All I can see above the clouds of starch are short blond locks and hints of facial hair stubble, features that do not at all resemble my husband. *Shit. No. No. No. No. No. NO. NO!* My face flushes and my heart beats so fast I fear there isn't sufficient space in my body to contain it. Luckily, there are a few feet between us in this sprawling king size bed. I'm perched precariously close to the left edge with nothing but obnoxiously patterned commercial-grade carpet below me to break my fall. I can't recall a damn thing about how I ended up here. Not getting to the hotel, the room, the bed. *Jesus.* This simply can't be happening. It just cannot be.

I squeeze both my eyes shut and suddenly feel nauseous from the tips of my toes to the split ends of my surely disastrous hair. I wish it all away. The being next to me coughs loudly, and I slowly peek at him again, needing answers. *Gawd, please don't be a stranger. Errr—scratch that. Maybe do be a stranger.* The last thing I need is a co-worker in my bed. The corners of our eyes meet.

Shit.

Still no glimmers of familiarity. He pulls the sheets down to his chest to reveal a baby blue dress shirt with splotches of orange splatter on the collar dancing around the buttons chaotically like funfetti, then he turns his head fully toward me.

"Robert! What in the actual fuck?!" I yell, the sound turning into a stab to my head. He shakes his head from side to side, groans and then manages a single muffled chuckle. My mind races and I once again struggle to embrace the fact that I'm still lying here—peeks under the covers—in my silk dress shirt but completely without underwear and pants. I can barely get the words out of my battery-acid filled, desert-scorched, disgusting mouth.

"Did we uhhhh...did umm...oh my God, did we...?" My mouth starts to water and I'm fighting the dread bubbling within my stomach.

"No. We. Didn't." He delivers the good news, giving multiple seconds between each word.

"Are you beyond-a-glimmer-of-a-doubt positive?"

"I am remarkably crystal clear on this one." The relief is sublimely overwhelming. I feel it might have the power to cure my hangover right here and now. This sleepover-mate is at least a familiar co-worker I've had small talk with roaming the office halls, albeit not familiar enough to be considered an office friend. That doesn't diminish the casualness of my questions given the precarious situation.

"Well, that's a relief. Might you have any useful knowledge as to why I'm currently lacking my pants and underwear?" I whisper, in hopes of making the situation less real.

"Zero clue. You followed me up here to make sure I didn't, in your own words, 'choke on my own vomit' after you helped hold my non-existent hair while I relieved myself of all the unnecessary OJ and vodka over the side of New York, New York. Yeah, that roller-coaster ride was a terrible idea." He pauses his recall and slowly raises both palms of his hands to his eyes, rubbing both his eyes with palms like windshield wipers, likely trying to scrub these events from his memory. "I came out of the bathroom last night after spending most of the night passed out on the floor, to find your pants at the foot of the bed and you, passed out cold, under the covers."

"Huh. Really? I seriously have zero clue why I didn't just go back to my own damn room. The last thing I remember is playing Blackjack and downing those insanely large screwdrivers. Ugh. Then nothing. Zilch for recall. I don't think I've even had a screwdriver since I was…twenty-one? Never. Ever. Again."

"You said you needed *kindred company*."

"*Whaaaat?*" my tone balances precariously somewhere between curiosity and disbelief with a finishing splash of bitter annoyance at myself. I'm genuinely not sure what I found 'kindred' about sleeping next to a virtual stranger.

I was starting to emerge out of its hangover fog when I was hit with the realization it must be relatively late in the morning. I had to get the hell out of there immediately or I was going to be late to stroll the showroom floor with my co-workers. *Fuck*. All I wanted was to be utterly alone, something nearly impossible to accomplish in the endless swirling human soup that is Las Vegas.

"Hey, Robert, do you mind, um, tugging those sheets up over your mug so I can grab my pants and underwear with a little dignity? I need to nurse this hangover with a hot shower and a bucket of coffee before I head to work."

His smile is more of a nauseous grimace. "Sure thing, Becca."

He vanishes below the blankets, and I slowly slide out the side of the bed, glancing back his way to ensure he wasn't taking a machismo peek. Luckily, he was lost to the turbulent sea of frothy white bedding. I hastily grab my black lace thong—*what the hell...it's wet?* I reach for my cactus-colored jeans, also incredibly wet. *For fucks sake.* I hold the thong and pants out, staring in utter disbelief and confusion at the ceiling. *Why in the world are these so fucking wet? At least this explains why I took them off.*

I don't want to linger any longer, so I say nothing and step one reluctant leg then the other, into my cold, wet thong. I shift my attention to my skinny jeans and attempt to shove in one athletic leg at a time, tugging with all my might. *Holy hell.* I might as well be attempting to get into a wetsuit that was at least a size too small. I continue to tug, twisting my ankle, and shaking my leg until I am finally able to pull the suddenly stretchless fabric up to my knees. *Stretchy jeans, my ass.* I am genuinely afraid the fabric might tear, and then where would I be? Stuck here, in a quasi-stranger's hotel room, with only a black-lace thong attempting to cover my goods. With one final push, pull, and deep breath, I manage to button myself in. Sealing my cold, damp, taught wet fate. *Fuck me.* I shuffle over to the corner of the room, grab my bag, and head for the door.

I quickly spit out, "See you downstairs."

An inaudible reply drifts from somewhere within the tousled bed.

I put my hand on the doorknob, my mind seems to be barely humming along questionably like an old refrigerator on its last leg, I take a deep breath, steeling myself. *Shit.* The hallways are sure to be swarming with co-workers and colleagues by now. My company had made a point of booking us all on the same few floors, so the chances of me encountering someone I knew were far higher than those of my winning a jackpot downstairs. I dig in my purse and find the keycard to my room, 1410.

I grab the door handle and poke my head out the door and look quickly to the left at the room number placard to enlighten myself on my current location, 1003. *Shit.* So much for slinking down the hall. My trek was going to require either an elevator ride or four flights of stairs, wearing the same clothes from dinner last night, albeit now mysteriously soaking wet from the waist down. I am too scared to look in the mirror, knowing there wasn't much I'd be able to do to fix this. I throw my disastrous mess of long, brown, bedraggled hair into a bun atop my head and boldly step into the hallway.

I think briefly about tossing my sunglasses on; being Vegas, that would be acceptable at this hour; however, it would also be a clear sign to any coworker I ran into that I was indeed, beginning the day, in a literal disaster-pants status. The stairwell sign is forty feet away. I hustle that direction, keeping my eyes locked on the floor, not daring to make eye contact with a single soul. Before I could get to safety though I sense someone coming my way.

"Hey! Becca!" came a very chipper voice from down the hallway, just as I reach for the stairwell door and dart inside. I don't dare look back. I'll deal with making excuses or apologies with whoever that was later, after I've showered and rejoined the living. I double-time it up the stairs with a renewed sense of purpose and some unwelcome chafing where my wet jeans are rubbing against my thighs. I plow ahead without stopping and reach the fourteenth floor, panting like a dog in the desert. My head feels like it is going to explode.

I burst through the stairwell door and am deliriously thankful to see my hotel room just a few doors away. I hustle that way fumbling with the key card, slamming it up against the sensor with so much power that I drop it onto a more aggressively artistic carpet. *Pants. So. Tight.* I attempt to bend down but the jeans are my iron maiden. I'm forced to lean down, sticking one straight leg up high into the air in order to grab at my key to sanctuary with the tips of my fingers. *Never mind me, just doing my morning yoga triangle pose.* I desperately fumble and then snag it, teetering back up to hungover wilting tree pose. I slap the card on the sensor again. Finally, I am rewarded with the blinking green light and permission to enter.

I step into the beautiful darkness of my own empty room, letting the door slam heavily behind me. I lean backward fully into it with a thud, slowly sinking down to the floor, my hair sticking straight up onto the door above me as I slide down, as if to cheer, *Yay! You made it!*

I don't cry. I don't feel relief. I don't feel a damn thing at all besides ridiculously tired and uncomfortable. I am numb. Knowing I'm already running late, I just allow myself one moment of rest before reluctantly drag myself up off the floor and begin the process of struggling to peel my jeans away from my flesh. When I finally manage to get them off, I bring them up to my face, call it stupid curiosity, and inhale deeply. I immediately gag. *Oh gawd, they smell utterly of piss.* I barely make it to the bathroom sink and vomit a myriad of fluorescent colors that should never come out of the human body.

That's when everything comes back in a brain-cracking flash. Stumbling into the hotel room last night, just behind Robert, pushing him inside. Far too much wine and too many screwdrivers slushing in our stomachs, aching to be released. He rolls into the bathroom and immediately lands on the tile floor, snuggling up to the toilet for the night. I didn't see a reason to end the night just yet, so I dove into his mini bar shoveling Pringles, peanut M&M's, and a mini bottle of vodka into my mouth. I remember wrangling open a can of Sprite as well as a bottle of water and guzzling them both in a drunken attempt to keep my head from spinning off its axis.

And now I'm safely in my own room, peering back into the toilet, vomiting up all the blurry memories and salty snacks galore. With every flush of the loo, the memories of the night before graciously fading again. *Oh, dear God.*

I flashback again to last night.

After guzzling all the liquid in Robert's room, I found Robert still totally passed out, curled up, and cozy around the base of the toilet. My drunken self swayed in the doorway, tilting my head, blurry vision contemplating my options. And then my memory goes blank. *Fuck me.* I likely desperately needed to pee but was afraid he would wake up to see me sitting half naked on the toilet above him, so I must have done what any intelligent, resourceful, utterly wasted corporate woman would do to keep herself decent in these circumstances...I pissed myself. I fucking pissed myself then removed my urine-soaked pants and underwear, left them on the floor, and then tucked my wasted ass into my co-worker's bed. Alone. I must not have wanted to be seen stumbling out of his room in the wee hours of the morning searching for a bathroom, or my own damn room. So, my drunk ass decided to stay. For 'connection.' For 'kindred company.' This my friend is nearly the peak of my living that sweet, sweet corporate-climbing dream. Unfortunately, we're not even close to the top of that deliriously endless ladder, just yet.

Chapter Two

I do, I don't, I do.

I shower quickly, preparing myself mentally to dive into the sea of bodies drifting around the Vegas conference-room floor. The final few days of the conference are spent in a numbed-out blur, wandering aimlessly through a sea of vendor booths that all seem to say the same thing. Lots of fluorescent lights and rows upon rows with no windows. Lots of big, eager smiles attempting to camouflage exhausted eyes. I continue to drink far too much at the company-organized dinners to propel myself through trying to earnestly and excitedly chat with co-workers and vendors, but at this point, I can't pause for even a second to tune into the thoughts and feelings swirling in my own head.

Thankfully, I manage to avoid running into Robert again. My work environment, with its lack of empathy or compassion, keeps me firmly disembodied from my emotions for self-protection. I am so deeply out of alignment with what brings me joy. I don't even know what brings me joy. Hell, I don't think I even know *me* anymore.

The thought flashes like a flashlight in my eyes. I blink. I push it aside.

I stay out of any more trouble and next thing you know I'm hopping off a plane and back in my Portland office on Monday sans a break. I roll right into another week and fourteen straight days of

IT'S GONNA GET MESSY

work after attending the disaster pants Vegas travel conference for the short-term vacation rental management industry.

Not familiar with the industry? Think people who want to Airbnb their home but need someone to manage it for them while still taking a nice slice of their profits. I'm currently in my post MBA career-climb as the Director of Marketing for the largest company in that space. The company is nearing their IPO: Initial Public Offering, which is when a company goes live as an official publicly traded company on Nasdaq. At this stage they've raised a total of over $800M in funding over seven rounds from capital investment firms. I've been with the company nearly two years and the brand spanking new office I work at in downtown Portland is undoubtedly the nicest office I've ever worked in.

Picture entire floors styled like West Elm showrooms, Four floors of comfy sofas, lounge chairs, and desks mostly used for just dropping your coat and bag. A full blown café in the lobby with baristas whipping up matcha lattes, cold brews, and chai with every milk under the sun. Floor-to-ceiling glass conference rooms, smart TVs, ergonomic chairs. A basement filled with bike racks and showers so you can ride in and get ready on-site.

Upstairs, a fully stocked kitchen with endless snacks, ping-pong tables, kombucha and beer on tap. And then—the crown jewel—a rooftop deck nestled in the heart of the business district, surrounded by glass towers and warehouse lofts, where workers sip afternoon beers among manicured greenery, while eyes from neighboring buildings peer down at the curated calm of our urban ant farm worker haven.This is what the corporate dream looks like in every single piece of popular culture and societal narrative I've ever taken in. Hell, I'm pretty sure this was on the cover of my MBA 'this pricey paper will prove your worth' brochure. Except as we're all having meetings on this splendid rooftop we love, we simultaneously complain about the disbanded leadership, poor pay, long hours, mediocre communication, and general lack of cohesion around company purpose. Our purpose seems to equate to hitting a certain dollar amount of revenue determined by leadership come hell or high water, and not much else. This is what I'm trading the limited hours of my life for. PowerPoints with arbitrary goals and continuously climbing green chart lines symbolizing human life hours for cash. *Is this all life is really about?*

I didn't hate my job, I wasn't dying for each day to end. But did I stroll to work each morning with passion and hunger firing inside of me? Not so much. I tell myself I'm happy just checking the success boxes. On the plus side, everyone at the company is incredibly kind, intelligent, and true experts in their disciplines, plucked from other tech companies on the West Coast and throughout the world. Leadership is interesting. Family owned and bootstrapped from inception almost ten years ago, they've built it all up from their own kitchen table with just three people working insane hours and hustling for cash for half a decade until earning funding.

Today, the company has nearly 6,000 workers and operates in eighteen countries. The CEO is sharp on the business building front but operates in a 'Steve Jobs management' style of straight to the point, no bullshit, no compliments, fairly emotionless. The meeting commentary is mostly heartless, regardless of goals attained. It's a continual dizzying cycle of new campaign action, action, action. More, more, more content. Test, test, test a zillion channels and customer messaging. All with terribly limited analytics to properly test our theories, so the hoop jumping, and random pivots never end. I am rooted in continual pleasing for acceptance and approval. There is no gratitude, no recognition, no trophy. All of this makes it insanely hard to keep a team motivated and clear on our current goals.

I roam this shiny new symbol of corporate achievement daily, hustling between meetings, shoving a granola bar into my face as I swing open another massive, heavy glass door with an audible vacuum sealed *whoosh* to signal the beginning of my next meeting in another corporate fishbowl conference room. I move from one fishbowl meeting to another, typically running a few minutes late because I either have to catch up in the hallway with a team member for just a second to answer a question or because I have to pitstop in the bathroom so my bladder doesn't burst.

The irony is, I'm too busy to even enjoy my surroundings. Except the café. My caffeine consumption is through the roof, and I go there at least three to four times a day. I typically send a text message to the barista to have my drink ready so I can swoop in, grab it, and go. Oh, and the beer on tap. I manage to pause and use that lovely benny too when I'm still at the office at 6pm and the stress and exhaustion of my body promptly asks me, *why haven't you begun drinking yet? Haven't you noticed the sun is nearly gone through the tinted windows enveloping you?* 'No actually, I hadn't.' Le sigh.

My husband of the last eight years understands this is a new gig with a 'great on the resume' company, so he frequently has a glass of wine and food waiting for me when I get home. I'm so grateful for his support and the delicious dinner awaiting me because it means I can continue to burn the candle at both ends. To earn the money and eventual recognition of my worth I'm positive that one day will arrive if I just hustle a bit more, earn a bit more, produce a bit more. Without fail, the glass of wine turns into a whole bottle, with several hours of mindless Netflix binging until it's time for me to pass out for dessert. No kiddos in the home front equation. I never experienced a strong pull to have kids. It didn't help that having a career was always positioned as a prize ambition for my latchkey Gen X/Millennial cusp generation.

I guess a subtle pull of considering kids came up in my early 30s but my husband's occasional quick-triggered temper random outburst over the years led me to believe we'd have very different parenting styles. During a heated discussion he mentioned once that if anyone messed with our potential future children on the playground, or hurt them deeply in any way, he'd 'murder them.' No, he wouldn't have murdered them, I mean...*likely not?* But the anger in this expression was so deeply visceral, I could feel the potential for rage underneath if Papa Bear had to defend the cubs. I feared this vastly complicated additional relationship layer of having kids would lead to monumental relationship heartache, so I moseyed along from the thought of having kids, or at least kicked the can as hard as I could. I kept my goals deeply career focused, but at this point I feel like I've barely blinked and somehow it's now nearly fifteen years later from when we first met and our marriage is on a rapid descent into implosion and there is barely time for either of us to put our face masks on, let alone check in with the other.

Let's hop back in time for a moment to help you see how we met, and how I've managed to land myself here.

Chapter Three

Roots run deep.

Back in my super senior year of college, I was playing water polo, oh-so-badly wanting to linger on campus for just one more year before my inevitable indoctrination into the real world. I was on the brink of graduating with a degree in interior design, interning at one of the most nationally recognized architectural firms in town to boost my resume.

One day, my best friend Paige peeked her cute, curly, dirty-blonde bob over the cubicle wall, her eyes twinkling mischievously. "Bex, come check this out," she said, pointing at her computer screen with a sly smile.

I moseyed around the sad, dull, gray fabric-paneled wall separating us and found myself staring at a cringingly optimistic site: Yahoo Personals. Online dating was just beginning to gain popularity, and Paige had set up a profile, her cursor hovering over the "publish" button.

Intrigued and deliriously bored at work, I decided to set up my own. In a moment of truly regrettable creativity, I chose the world's worst profile headline: *Man's Best Friend.*

We both hit publish at the same time, giggling at the absurdity of it all. We made a pact right then and there—to be each other's wing-women on any dates, ensuring neither of us ended up abducted or murdered. Online dating felt foreign, taboo, and just a little bit unsafe. But mostly, it felt like an adventure.

My future husband, Luke, was date number two. We met at a local sports bar downtown for a few friendly games of pool. It wasn't love at first sight, if you believe in that sort of thing, but we enjoyed each other's company and hit it off enough to keep hanging out regularly. Before I knew it, he was moving into my simple, ever-so-slanted college house next to the campus football stadium with my roommate and me a few months later.

We partied our asses off and romped around town happily blind in our new love bliss. Days were lost to the warm vibration of someone else's hand wrapped tightly around mine, the ending and beginning of each other's hands still wonderfully undetectable. When two eyeballs staring back at you across the pillow blind you to anything but the hum of new love pumping through your dazed, confused, still-pretty-clueless-about-how-the-real-world-actually-works college student veins. We chose to drink, dance, play, and have obliterated drunk sex on the regular

I graduated in the spring, and four months into our whirlwind romance, we decided to take the plunge and move into our own teeny, closet-sized studio apartment. With heartfelt promises to stay close, I hugged my college roommate goodbye and embarked on this first big adult-relationship leap with my new boyfriend. As we locked eyes while I waved farewell, an unspoken understanding passed between us—this decision felt both exhilarating and precarious.

Those early years after college were a blur of adventure and indulgence. We explored Wisconsin's lakes and state parks, hit the slopes snowboarding, partied with abandon, and drank far too much. Our relationship was a cycle of highs and lows—wild nights, heated arguments, passionate reconciliations, and, ultimately, an inevitable breakup due to our constant fighting.

I witnessed a bar fight or two, instigated by my future husband, all brushed off as youthful, alcohol-fueled bravado. But deep down, I knew his occasional outbursts of anger weren't something I could ignore forever. For someone as sensitive and emotional as I was, his temper hinted at a storm I wasn't sure I could weather in the long run.

Eventually, I felt the need to escape the Midwest and the gravitational pull of our volatile love, so we decided to break up so I could accept my first 'real job' out of state in Denver at twenty-five. It was my first time leaving my hometown of Madison, Wisconsin.

Like many in my generation—heck, in *most* generations—I was raised by parents who grew up in the era of 'children should be seen and not heard.' My dad had been beaten with a belt by his own overly aggressive father, which left grandpa's heavy bootprint on his heart. My mom, the youngest of nine, grew up with modest means on a farm with little access to healthcare. She rarely speaks of her childhood, but from the fragments I've gathered, it seems it was decent yet often tinged with heavy hardships.

This, of course, meant that as a pair, my parents were terribly ill-prepared to have any sort of open, honest, emotional communication with me because they hadn't received that themselves.

What I didn't realize at the time was that this upbringing meant *I* wasn't prepared for it in adulthood either. I will say, though, that they certainly did better than their parents had—which, in the end, is really all one can ask.

I was only spanked once as a kid, for missing the school bus after getting lost in play. As if missing *The Price is Right* with Bob Barker wasn't punishment enough, my dad, all 6'3" and well over 200 pounds of him, gave me a firm smack on the rear. But when he saw my big pouty brown eyes fill with tears, it became clear: one spanking was enough for both of us.

Growing up, my dad was the fun-loving, adventurous, and chatty one, overflowing with "I love yous," playfulness, and positivity galore. While my dad excelled at discussing sports, current events, and the weather, we didn't talk much about my feelings. Instead, we bonded deeply through countless weekend swims at the lake, snorkeling for "treasures" (aka rocks), racing each other in the water, and indulging our shared addiction for massive cones of Blue Moon ice cream. We practiced our dives from the outcropped granite rocks along the lake shore every summer, played hoops in the driveway, and hit softballs in the backyard after supper until dusk.

I was a daddy's girl through and through.

We had so much fun playing together, and I'm eternally grateful for that wonderful part of my childhood. But emotionally, I had to raise myself—like so many other children of emotionally distant parents. I knew my parents loved me, but I never truly felt seen or understood. My questions and curiosities about the deeper meaning of life were left to my own imagination, forming thoughts and opinions in solitude.

My parents never kissed in public, never hugged, and never displayed affection in front of my brother and me. I never once heard them say 'I love you' to each other. Yet, my dad clearly adored my mother—writing her little notes and cards regularly. His office displayed a large, hand-drawn framed portrait of my mom, an artist's rendering from when they married in their twenties.

They were dapper and beautiful, a picture-perfect couple from a bygone era. My mom bore a striking resemblance to a classic 1920s actress—porcelain skin, a perfectly oval face, stunning dark eyes, and a coy, subtle smile. My dad, with his crew cut, dimples for days, and an incredible beaming grin, could spread sunshine on the cloudiest of days.

My dad was the absolute sweetest, with the tender heart of a poet—but exhaustion and overwork sometimes brought out his temper. He worked the midnight shift at a juvenile detention facility, and we were young and rowdy, desperate for his attention when he needed sleep. We'd hear him leap out of bed, the floor creaking in warning as he stomped down the hall, bellowing, "Be quiet!" Which always got my little heart racing. I found my mom's even temperament comforting, even if she wasn't expressive.

Growing up as a young girl, I longed for a bond with my mom—a connection that hovered like a dream I couldn't quite touch. I had no strong emotional attachment or real conversations with her, which was difficult for an emotional child yearning for closeness. When she wasn't working as a school psychologist, she was praying, reading, or drifting elsewhere in her own thoughts. I often asked if I could have a hug, a request that became a routine plea. Dad likely caught on that I wasn't getting my fill of hugs from my mom, so he made it a daily practice to ask, "Have you had your hug today?" Of course, I always said no multiple times a day, just to stock up on my extra quota of hugs and fill the silent needs of my sensitive young heart.

I never heard the words 'I love you' from my mom, and kisses were simply not a thing in our household. That's not to say she didn't care. I knew, in her own way, that she did. Her love was expressed through acts of service like cooking dinner, making sure I got to my endless swim lessons and meets, but never through words of affirmation and rarely with physical affection. She was an introverted Midwesterner, embodying the Scandinavian way of being—reserved, proper, and emotionally contained.

But there's another layer to my relationship with my parents that left me feeling untethered and uncertain.

You see, I was raised a Christian Scientist. This is very much not the same thing as Scientology, though some people tend to confuse the two. In a nutshell, Christian Scientists are a sect of Christianity that believe your true essence is that of a perfect spiritual being. While matter and our material existence appear real to our physical senses, they are ultimately an illusion. The belief is that if we embrace the understanding that we are perfect spiritual beings, our physical bodies won't be sick. It's a religion that teaches one must rely solely on "spiritual sense" to discover what is ultimately real.

The religion was founded by Mary Baker Eddy, an American author, teacher, and religious leader in the late 1800s. She also founded the Church of Christ, Scientist. Christian Scientists believe that prayer brings about a change in spiritual understanding, which in turn brings healing to the body. As a result, followers are discouraged from using medicine or seeking health care from a doctor. They are taught that prayer is the most effective defense against illness, rather than traditional medicine.

Seeking medical treatment is generally frowned upon in the Christian Science community, and those who do so may find themselves ostracized. Members often forgo most medical interventions, choosing instead to rely solely on Christian Science treatment—prayer—for themselves and their children. While some families may go to hospitals for childbirth, it is widely discouraged by devout followers, who insist on home births. Growing up, I often wondered what would happen in the case of a serious accident.

Over the years, there have been varying opinions on medical care within the church. Today, church leaders say that healthcare is not strictly forbidden, leaving it up to individuals and families to decide. However, that wasn't my understanding growing up. In Sunday school and into adulthood, I distinctly remember being told that Christian Science healthcare facilities do not allow pain medication. If a patient requested it, they would be asked to leave. Only prayer was considered an acceptable form of treatment.

My mother was introduced to Christian Science in high school by her own mother, who turned to the religion as a way to cope with their lack of their financial ability to access healthcare growing up. My mom embraced it fully and completely into adulthood, and eventually converted my father about a decade before my birth. I was born in a hospital but never visited a doctor, never swallowed a single pill, never had a single test, or even entered a hospital until I was eighteen. The religion was responsible for establishing state medical exemption statutes when medical treatment for a child conflicted with the religious beliefs of parents.

Fortunately, I was never severely injured as a child. Looking back, I believe my parents would have taken me to a hospital if my life were in danger. But as a kid, that never felt like a possibility. I recall suffering through an awful ear infection, screaming in pain throughout the night while my mom sang hymns and prayed for my healing. I also remember a roller-skating crash that left my knees bloody and raw. A Band-Aid was the only medical treatment I received.

The church's beliefs also shaped my education. At my parents' request, I was excused from several health and biology classes to avoid exposure to what they considered misinformation. While my classmates attended these lessons, I sat in the hallway reading for leisure, an odd arrangement that inevitably led to teasing.

Another peculiarity of my childhood was the concept of birthdays. Age was considered irrelevant in our religion since our physical bodies were not seen as real. I never once said 'happy birthday' to my mother, and I was deeply confused and upset as a child when I didn't get birthday celebrations like my friends. To soften the disappointment, my dad created a loophole, calling our birthdays 'special days.' I tried to pretend it didn't bother me, putting on a bold face and telling my classmates to mind their own business. But deep down, I knew my family was different. I made a mental note to mention doctors, science, and anything non-religious as often as possible around my friends—anything to prove I wasn't part of something... unusual.

I recall being about six years old in Sunday school, and I asked my Sunday school teacher, "If our bodies aren't real, and we can't go to the doctor, then why do I have to brush my teeth every night before bed?" He stared blankly at me, mouth agape, stuttered a bit, and then completely ignored me. He simply asked me to read the next part of the lesson out loud as if I hadn't asked anything.

At that moment, I distinctly remember thinking, *Ahhhh, I see! The jig is up, guys! This is all a web of lies.* And from that point on, humor aside, I felt like I was being deceived. I no longer felt safe with my very caretakers. The religion, the teachings, everything—I saw it as a carefully constructed illusion.

I decided the best way to protect myself was to pretend I was completely onboard. I became the perfect pupil. Every Sunday, I put on my cute dresses, acted cheerful, and enthusiastically chatted with everyone after church. I knew that playing along meant ice cream and french fries after church as my reward for being good, so I played the part flawlessly. In essence, I was rewarded for abandoning myself. If someone had truly talked to me—really listened to my worries—it might have changed my experience. But that was not the environment I was raised in. Questioning the origins of our beliefs simply wasn't an option.

There were also strange loopholes in the religion that left my young mind rather perplexed. For example, we were allowed to see the dentist. I was even taken to get glasses in middle school. If our bodies were perfect spiritual beings and illness was an illusion, why were my teeth and eyes different? No one ever answered me.

Hell, even the cat I rescued when I was ten years old visited the veterinarian regularly. He got all the necessary annual visits and medicine for heartworms, but I never saw a doctor. I remember thinking, *Are pets somehow more valuable than humans? The cat gets medical care, and I don't?!* The contradictions baffled me. It was a confusing way to grow up, and I know this is where I learned to ignore my intuition and simply play the part of the happy, enthusiastic young girl. I pushed down my internal warning signs and never voiced my concerns about the religion. Speaking up would mean I wasn't the perfect child, and I desperately wanted to be good—to please my parents, to please this God they spoke of.

I'd never met Him, but I certainly didn't want someone of that rank against me.

By eighteen, I considered myself vaguely spiritual but entirely non-religious. The moment I could, I went to a doctor for a full check-up and was relieved to be deemed fit as a fiddle. When I needed medication to be approved for my first trip abroad to China for college, I took it without hesitation—but I didn't mention it to my parents. Even into adulthood, I still wanted to please them and avoid rocking the religious boat.

Throughout my adult life, my parents were very much aware I was not a Christian Scientist, yet they still occasionally sent me articles from the *Christian Science Monitor*, signaling their hope that someday I'd find my way back and discover the healing power of the religion. I found this not only deeply annoying but infuriating. I told them I respect their views and expect them to respect mine. I didn't entirely fault them for their choices or for how I was raised—okay, maybe just a little bit. But I was so damn tired of feeling like I wasn't good enough or that something was lacking within me simply because I didn't subscribe to their religion.

They never said it outright, but their actions spoke volumes—at least in my mind—throughout my entire childhood and well into adulthood. They weren't accepting me for who I was.

I'm sure you can understand that this type of upbringing leaves a person just a smidge desperate for that first taste of secure love. And let me tell you, that first big relationship—living together for the first time—is a doozy for anyone who grew up in a mess like mine. When I left home at eighteen for college, everything seemed fine on the surface between me and my parents. I never vocalized all these worries growing up; they remained internal. So by my mid-twenties, I had zero realization that my upbringing was negatively affecting me in the slightest. I honestly thought it was pretty darn decent.

That realization, my friend, comes just a wee bit later.

As I found my footing living alone for the first time in the big, exciting, mountainous city of Denver at the age of twenty-five, I was so damn desperate to be seen and loved that I pushed past the red flags. I ignored the signs that the relationship with Luke I was just brave enough to leave behind in Wisconsin wasn't right for me. Missing a connection to my Wisconsin roots, not yet comfortable in my own skin, and unsure of who I really was, I clung to what was familiar. Just two months after I moved, Luke followed me out to Denver to give our relationship another shot. I should have been finding my own way, yet I held tight to the comfort of the past and clung to the comfort of the deepest love I had known.

The job I had landed in Denver was in the flourishing new home-building and construction industry in Colorado. The position offered a generous six-figure salary comprising base pay and commissions. Embracing the allure of the American Dream, I indulged in acquiring material possessions that symbolized success. Opting for a nearly new car—thanks to my frugal Midwestern upbringing—I proudly made it my first major purchase. I also invested in a pristine home situated within a picture-perfect subdivision full of fancy recreation centers, immaculate sidewalks, and charming restaurants.

Luke and I hiked most weekends, played softball, joined an adult kickball league, and ventured out to snowboard nearly every mountain in Colorado. We attended baseball games, tried amazing restaurants, explored state parks, and traversed every inch of our new mountainous home. Our relationship felt solid—we talked earnestly about our days each evening, supported each other, and snuggled every night before falling asleep. I found my nook of security nestled in his chest, our hands intertwined at every available moment. We encouraged and uplifted one another through life's daily obstacles.

Sure, we had our fights—what passionate couple doesn't? But what I knew with certainty in my heart was that we were a team, committed through thick and thin.

We were flying high on good times for quite awhile and then the Great Recession hit us deliriously hard in the early spring of 2009. I was working in the epicenter of the recession crisis, new home building. I was laid off right in the middle of an appointment, which ended abruptly with my boss escorting the clients out of the showroom and locking the office doors in the middle of the day. The severity of the recession sunk into my bones. I was in total shock. Everything was uncertain and up in the air, not only for my present, but I had no idea what this was going to mean for my future. I was scared shitless. Period.

Sadly, they don't properly cover the protocol or action steps for emotionally handling shocking career moments such as these in college. So, without any income coming my way for the foreseeable future, I got nervous and quickly sold the first new home I had scrimped and saved to purchase just two years earlier. Luke and I had been living there together, although I did snag the loan on my own in my name with my salary, he was helping out by paying a little bit of rent and working on countless house projects in sweat equity, but now, I was jobless, and it seemed like there were far less jobs available than people who needed them.

I felt utterly directionless and I panicked.

I was almost thirty, and we'd been dating for nearly seven years. There was absolutely a deep love between us, but there was also a lot of fighting. We had zero emotional maturity—arguing often, constantly swaying between being deeply in love and blaming each other for the shadows of inner pain from our upbringings that we didn't know how to manage. Even though we spent so much time together, we communicated so poorly. Our fights dragged on because we both focused on winning. Neither of us had the patience or presence to be the bigger person. Were we tender in the face of our vulnerabilities? Hell no—we attacked. What I didn't realize then was that we weren't intentionally trying to hurt each other; we were both just trying to keep ourselves safe in the only way we knew how.

Despite our love, our struggles took a toll. But with a recession looming and years of history between us, I felt we had too many sunk costs. So, I made a decision: it was time to get married or move on. His choice, but if we can't commit to each other forever, I can't continue. And just like that, despite the highs and lows, despite our unconscious mutual dependency, we got engaged. Love can be such a twisting maze at times.

Just a few months later, at a weekend wedding bash, I watched—through a drunken haze—as Luke erupted in a violent outburst, swinging fists at a dear friend over a misunderstanding. It shattered my sense of security. For the first time, I was forced to see the warning signs I could no longer ignore. I was deeply embarrassed by the fight. I was hurt by his reaction and angry at the way he treated someone we both cared about.

The next morning, hours later, I was *this close* to telling him I was calling off the engagement. But then, he sincerely apologized—to me, to our friends. While part of me knew we should be completely done, another part clung to the fact that we were good 89.4 percent of the time.

Surely that's enough to sustain a relationship?
Surely other people feel this way too?
Surely relationships are hard?
Surely random brawls happen?
Surely we can work through this?
Surely *I* can fix this and make it all better.

Our adventures were fueled by plenty of booze—not just a glass of wine with dinner, but copious drinking most nights and weekends, which didn't help our volatility. I had my outbursts too. After one particularly spirited argument in Denver, I kicked my heel through a bathroom door, thinking he'd locked me in. The door was just jammed. After he helped me out, I passed out naked on the living room floor. He covered me with a blanket and went to bed. Classy, right?

We had so much built-up resentment after nearly a decade together, and neither of us knew how to communicate our feelings without blowing up. We numbed ourselves with distractions—constant social plans, weed, binge-watching TV, and plenty of booze. The truth was, we barely even knew what our feelings were anymore.

Throughout our relationship, there had been countless moments where I tried to push Luke to be a better person—to be less reactive, to find a job that I believed better suited his capabilities, to earn more money. I had always carried the financial load for us in Denver, as my salary had been considerably higher than his which was a constant point of tension between us. I resented my role as the provider. So I'd push him to expand his education, to apply for that next role, to bridge the gap.

At times, he thanked me for pushing him to be better. But somehow, over the years, I had promoted myself from partner to coach, to trainer—and, well, he wasn't a *damn dog*.

I can tell you right now, that's a surefire way to squash romance in a relationship.

No adult wants to be nagged or trained into becoming something they're not.

I was mixing love and coercion—a *toxic* cocktail.

I knew he was deeply intelligent, that was what initially attracted me to him, and I believed he was capable of so much more than he gave himself credit for. But in truth, I didn't accept him for who he was. Instead, I was convinced I could "help" him.

In my mind, relationships were about continual improvement, about pushing each other to be better. But at that time in my life, "better" only meant achieving more in the eyes of society—more money, a better job, more material success. Luke, on the other hand, was far happier with comfort and stability. He dreamed of living in a small town, having a steady, middle-of-the-road job, and simply sticking with it. There was absolutely nothing wrong with that, but we lacked the communication skills to work through our differences, to truly understand the fundamental gap between our core desires.

Looking back now, I can clearly see that my urgency to get married wasn't driven by a burning desire of my own, but rather by a need to check the box on society's script for what we were *supposed* to be doing at that age. It wasn't a lifelong dream of marriage, I just wanted to feel securely attached, to be chosen. I was never the girl who fantasized about her wedding day, the flowers, the cake, or gliding down the aisle in a big, poofy dress. But I did long to be deeply loved.

We decided to move back to Madison from Denver a year into the recession, drawn back to our comfort zone by fear, ongoing financial struggles, and the desire to be near family as we prepared for our upcoming wedding. I found a basic, unfulfilling job specifying flooring that paid decently, and we got hitched while still living under his father's roof to save money. Thankfully, my parents were remarkably cool and understanding about it.

We both agreed how much people spent on traditional weddings was insane. How was it a great idea to start a marriage buried in debt for a single day? Determined to keep things simple and frugal, we saved throughout the summer and opted for an unconventional celebration, even sending digital evites—practically unheard of at the time—instead of traditional paper invitations to cut costs.

The fall ceremony was a joyous occasion, a simple waterfront gathering beneath a large oak tree on the edge of a beautiful Madison, Wisconsin lake. Technically, the spot wasn't designated for weddings, but we figured if we kept things short and sweet, no one would have time to notice. Besides, there weren't any posted rules against quick gatherings of family and friends. We set up a few folding chairs on the grass at the water's edge for our elderly guests, while the rest of the group stood cozily around us.

A classic 1950s car dropped me off, and I chose to walk down the nonexistent grassy aisle on my own. To this day, I'm not entirely sure why. I love my dad dearly, but I think, deep down, I knew I didn't want to be 'given away.' I wasn't a thing or possession to be handed off, symbolically or otherwise. He fully supported my decision, how could he not? He knew I was still the same little six-year-old girl he used to boost into the air to help her reach the basketball hoop, only for her to demand he put her down so she could make the shot on her own.

My mom seemed to enjoy the day, socially awkward as she was. I had hoped she would tell me I looked beautiful. Instead, she said the dress was nice—which, I suppose, was as close as I would get to having that dream fulfilled.

We exchanged heartfelt vows through tears at the edge of the lake and celebrated with our seventy guests on a boat ride around the lake, indulging in delicious appetizers, hearty enough to double as dinner, and of course, an open bar. The festivities ended with the entire boat belting *Livin' on a Prayer* at the top of our lungs. I was happy. My husband seemed truly happy.

As a nightcap to our unconventional reception, we ended up at a polka bar—because, Wisconsin—clearly, three hours of open-bar drinking on the boat wasn't quite enough.

Before we even made it home, we got into a fight on our wedding night. We were both quite drunk, and things escalated. I wish I could tell you what it was about, but I have zero recall—which says a lot about how much I'd indulged in the open bar by that point.

I escaped into a bathroom stall, burying my face in the curls of my best friend Paige as I sobbed, admitting that I thought I was making a mistake. We talked it out, though to this day, I don't remember what she lovingly said to stop my tears. But whatever it was, it worked. I wiped my face, pulled myself together, and reminded myself of the obligation I felt to check the marriage box and make sure everyone beyond the bathroom door was still having a wonderful time. I pinched my cheeks, smiled into the mirror, and stepped back out to finish the night.

When I stepped back out, I found myself alone just as someone announced it was time for us to take the dance floor for the final dance of the night. I would later learn that, at that very moment, my new husband was walking down the block, away from the venue, after getting into an argument with one of his closest friends—who was apparently utterly wasted and yelling profanities in the parking lot.

I'm glad I missed witnessing that incident...or am I? Maybe I would have listened to my intuition. Maybe it would have screamed a little louder. But clearly, I wasn't ready to hear it yet.

So, I stood there on the empty dance floor in my wedding dress, alone, waiting for him to appear. He eventually thought better of his actions and returned, but not before I had to awkwardly sway by myself for a few minutes, smiling brightly at the crowd staring back at me. "Well...maybe he's just in the bathroom?" I joked, my forced grin working overtime to distract them.

He appeared with a cheer from the crowd and walked toward me, I breathed deeply, surrendered to the image that the eyeballs on us should see, and I allowed him to wrap me up in his arms, just grateful not to be embarrassed further. Clinging to this person who loved me, we swayed to the music. Feeling his warmth envelope me, I shook it off. What I mean to say here is, I literally deleted it from my mind and decided it was just a drunken blur that didn't really happen. Poof, gone.

We'll chat more on this control-alt-delete, coping mechanism later.

All was fun and joyous again. I smiled giddily over his shoulder at all our friends and family. I do want to reiterate here, there was most certainly a love between us, but something was also off deep in my very core, poking me subtly in my gut, and back then, I simply didn't have the instincts to realize my intuition that was screaming at me. I refused to listen—hell, I didn't know *how* to listen. Back then, I naively thought marriage could fix all our woes since we were now committed to each other in love for life.

Truth be told, I was totally blind to my own trauma that had me all upside down, inside out, and backward about what it means to love and be loved.

Chapter Four

Ready player one.

A few months before the wedding I had proposed a wild idea to Luke for our honeymoon. He had heard about the Camino de Santiago from a customer at the BMW car dealership he was a service advisor for back in Denver, and mentioned it to me. I did a little research on it and fell in love with the idea of completing it, for our honeymoon, naturally. There's nothing quite like hiking from the border of France over the Pyrenees Mountains and across the entire northern region of Spain to the western coast over a five-week period to challenge a new marriage, right?

Did I mention that I love travel, growth, and personal betterment? I do. I do. I do!

Growing up, I never ventured beyond state lines, but once I got to college, I developed a fierce desire to see the world. For my first adventure abroad I desired something exotic, so I proposed a trip to China and Tibet to study Feng Shui for a summer my junior year in college as part of my undergraduate Interior Design program. It took quite a bit of convincing, and extra hours of waitressing, but my parents gave into my pleading to support my adventurous side and they scrimped and saved to help me out with the tuition.

That trip was the catalyst for my first-ever visit to a doctor's office to get the necessary checkup to travel abroad, although admittedly I never told my parents about that prerequisite. The visit felt oddly easy—I was actually eager to care for my body's safety in a way that had once felt so elusive and even sinful growing up. I remember thinking, *What's the big deal?* They may not have seen or heard me emotionally in the way I longed for, but I was grateful they always wanted the best for me and supported even my wildest, most adventurous goals.

That trip sparked my love for navigating challenges, embracing the unknown, and learning through travel. Luke had never been abroad before, let alone backpacked for an extended period. Just before I met him, I'd been lucky enough to backpack through England, Scotland, Ireland, and Wales with my brother the summer after college. I scrimped and saved every penny to make it happen and even maxed out my first credit card, but the experience was unforgettable.

Neither of my parents had ever traveled abroad or even been on a plane. My parents' primary means of escape was through *National Geographic*, Rick Steves' countless travel shows, movies or *Islands* magazine.

My dad was especially captivated by *Islands* magazine. Each month, when it arrived, he would pore over the pages, mesmerized by the turquoise waters and swaying palm trees, talking about snorkeling, exploring, and the tropical destinations he hoped to see someday. Yet, in reality, he had never stepped on a plane or traveled anywhere—except for one visit to see me in Denver. They never explicitly said why they never traveled; it simply wasn't a passion or calling for them. They liked staying close to home.

Perhaps for my dad, envisioning and experiencing those places in his mind was enough. But not for me—I needed to see them in person, to smell, touch, and fully immerse myself in them. I was incredibly grateful that my parents supported my adventurous spirit in any way they could.

For that reason, the hubs and I didn't ask for traditional wedding gifts. Instead, we used a website that allowed guests to contribute to our honeymoon in the form of gear, dinners, and experiences—things like "buy us a massage in Barcelona" or "buy us new hiking poles."

Our honeymoon adventure hiking the Camino de Santiago challenged us right from the start. We arrived in Paris two days after our wedding and took a train to the border of Spain to begin our journey. The reality of our intensely long days set in immediately—hiking about eight hours a day, each of us carrying a forty-pound pack on our backs. We stayed in simple *albergues*, or hostels—sometimes in a tiny private room if we were lucky, other times in vast repurposed churches-turned-pilgrim bunkhouses with up to a hundred other travelers.

Luckily, by the end of each day, we were so wiped that we didn't care too much about where we slept or whether the showers were chilly. We were just grateful for a bed. The countryside and small towns we passed through were breathtaking. Strolling through farm fields, quaint hilltop villages, wine country, and even a few larger cities, we met incredible people from all over the world—some traveling with friends, others walking alone in deep reflection and solitude.

It was such a gorgeous experience—until it wasn't.

My left knee began to give me trouble several days into our thirty-five-day journey. I felt stiffness and pain later in the afternoon after hours of hiking each day. I tried stretching it, wrapping it, applying Tiger Balm, and massaging it, but the long muscle leading into the right side of my knee—my IT band—kept tightening so severely that it caused relentless pain.

Things came to a head two weeks later, halfway through an eight-hour hike in the middle of nowhere. I sat down and started sobbing—sobbing from the pain, the frustration, and the reality that after all the planning and the time off I had begged for at work to make this once-in-a-lifetime opportunity happen, I was now here, sidelined by a stupid tight muscle.

I had been talking about the pain for a week, and although Luke patiently waited while I stretched throughout the day, he offered little in the way of the emotional empathy I needed—but wasn't expressing. Frustrated, I took it out on him, telling him he wasn't being compassionate enough and needed to show more care for what I was going through. All I wanted was the occasional *Hang in there, honey. This isn't your fault. Take all the time you need.*

He did acknowledge this was indeed a sucky situation, but he was also over my complaining. Two weeks into the hike, as I once again lamented my pain, my new husband responded pragmatically: he grabbed my pack, added it to his own, and marched off ahead.

Left sitting alone on the trail in the middle of the Spanish countryside, I sobbed some more and questioned everything—what was I *doing*? Was this even a good partnership? Was he emotionally soft enough for me? I loved him so much, yet there was friction from misalignment, too.

Eventually, I got up and hobbled along for the next few hours until I found him waiting at the edge of the next town. We both apologized, agreeing that exhaustion had gotten the better of us. We decided to rest and regroup. After all, we weren't even halfway through the Camino.

I woke up the next morning to a subtle itch around my midsection. Then my neck. And then my ankles. I headed to the hostel bathroom to investigate what the heck was happening and saw large, splotchy red bumps—about the size of mosquito bites—rapidly forming all over my body. By midday, I looked like a leper, and the itchiness was relentless. The red bumps covered my stomach, ran up and down my legs, wrapped around my neck, and even crept onto my face.

The hubs agreed that my appearance was rather alarming, so we started searching for a clinic, only to find ourselves starring in a Goldilocks-esque comedy.

You remember—three beds, and none of them were quite right?

The first clinic we found was full, the next one was far too pricey, and the third had a waitlist around the block. Mind you, this was back when international cell phone data plans weren't really a thing, the horror, which meant that locating a clinic required asking around for recommendations from locals and other travelers.

After hearing that the wait to see a doctor would be a day or more, I started sobbing again. I could barely see through my tears. Not knowing what else to do, I sat down on the steps outside the clinic to continue my cry more comfortably, much to the hubs' dismay, who found the whole display overly dramatic. But I simply couldn't hold the tears in.

There were quite a few times in our relationship when I was told I was overly emotional, that my tears were too much or that I used them as a weapon to manipulate a fight, so I always did my best to restrain them. In this moment, though, I simply couldn't.

While he was sympathetic to my current plight, there was an underlying vibe of deep annoyance in his growing impatience, his tone sharpening, his sighs deepening. I felt like a burden. What I really needed was a big bear hug and for him to say, *Well, this is a bit rough and unplanned, isn't it? How can I help you feel more at ease?* I needed him to genuinely see me, to hear my frustration about this stressful situation. Instead, I felt so terribly alone.

Finally, the nurse at the third clinic took pity on me and said she could sneak me in for a quick appointment. My Spanish skills were average after four semesters in high school and one in college, but I managed to get out, "Haz lo que necesitas hacer." *Do what you need to do.*

The doctor explained that she suspected bed bugs but thought it was more likely some kind of bizarre allergic reaction. To this day, I'm still not sure. She then produced an excessively large needle and motioned for me to pull down my hiking pants. I bent over, and before I had a chance to steady myself, she plunged it into my ass so deeply and painfully that I found myself sobbing all over again.

She handed me a tube of cream for the angry red bumps covering my body and sent me to another small room to pay for my visit. I was in pure panic mode, convinced that this emergency medical visit was going to cost me thousands of dollars and completely blow through our honeymoon budget, forcing us to go home sooner than planned. The woman in charge of billing looked up and said, "Sesenta euros."

Thank gawd. Seventy euros. I breathed a sigh of relief and gratitude. Crisis averted—for now.

On the way back to the hotel, we spotted the oddest little contemporary black sign on the side of an old stone building. Completely out of place, it didn't fit its surroundings at all. It simply read, "...Plan B."

We looked at each other and, with stupid, cheesy grins, had a *duh* moment—realizing that even in chaos, there can always be a Plan B.

Back at the hotel, as I lay in bed lathered from head to toe in cream, we briefly contemplated going home. But then I said, "Fuck that. We're here, we already have the time off work, let's design a Plan B!"

We pulled together in solidarity, apologized for our outbursts, and admitted that we were both just tired, overwhelmed, and still deeply in love. There was no one else I would have wanted to be on this messy adventure with, this was genuinely true in my heart at that moment. So, instead of continuing our hike on the Camino, we promptly hopped on a bus and headed south to Madrid to dive into Plan B.

In Madrid, we got hosed on a last-minute rental car, found a cute boutique, and picked up a couple of stylish outfits—ditching our REI hiking gear so we could feel transformed before setting off on our new Euro road trip adventure. We explored and savored our way through southern Spain, Barcelona, and the south of France, then roamed into Italy, making our way down to Pisa and Rome, up and over to Venice, and onward into Austria and Switzerland, before ultimately looping back to Spain to catch our pre-planned return flights home.

It was an epic and joyous adventure filled with breathtaking scenery, incredible food, and unforgettable experiences. We blew past our original Camino budget but compensated by frequently sleeping in the car rather than spending money on a bed for the night. We agreed we'd work it off later in life and that seizing the adventure in front of us was well worth it. It was such a grand trip, and we told each other how grateful we were to experience every second of it—the struggles, the fights, the sights, the whole wonderful, hot mess of our adventure.

Oddly enough, that sentiment still holds true, even now, looking back through the rearview mirror of our eventual marital collapse.

When we returned home, the constant battles over how and when to spend our hard-earned savings during our honeymoon solidified something in me: I needed to earn more, produce more, and climb the corporate ladder faster. I convinced myself that more money would mean more fulfillment: the bigger house, the nicer car, the fancier wardrobe, the better vacations, where perhaps we wouldn't have to sleep in the car as often as we had on our honeymoon.

And so, after a year of working in Wisconsin, I went back to school for my MBA.

IT'S GONNA GET MESSY

I was raised to believe in the academic marketplace, with both of my parents earning college degrees and my mom holding a master's degree from Berkeley. I didn't want to lose momentum in my career by quitting my job to go back to school full-time—that was so terribly inefficient for this Virgo—so I opted to get my MBA in the evenings.

I attended classes late into the evening after a full day's work, two nights a week for the next two and a half years, coming home at 9:30 or 10 p.m., utterly exhausted. My drive for perfection and growth couldn't be satiated, I was never satisfied with what I had. I was on the treadmill of achievement at Level 10, maximum incline.

We worked, we saved, we partied, we adventured, we bought our first home together as a married couple. We grew as a couple, but we also fought mightily a good amount of the time. Usually after drinking too much. Usually when we really needed to release some of our pent-up, unexpressed needs and desires, so highly charged that it always turned into a battle of who could win, rather than both of us being heard. Rather than both of us winning.

Our resentment and lack of emotional connection would build until one of us finally attempted to voice how unsettled we felt, and things would erupt into a massive argument. He hadn't gone to college, and I was getting my master's degree, which only widened our perceived societal divide.

Things culminated in our worst fight ever during the summer after I completed my MBA program. The origins are fuzzy, but the argument was rooted in the shadow of the misalignment mountain standing between us—my relentless pursuit of betterment versus his desire for comfort.

It was the Fourth of July. We were on the lake in our amazing $2,500 Craigslist find—our 1979 Bayliner, complete with electric blue carpeting, blue and white puffy vinyl cushions, and fuchsia pinstriping.

We had been watching the fireworks and drinking heavily, making our way back to our resort on the lake in the boat when the fight started. He upset me about something, and I tore into him verbally in a way I'm sure was positively ruthless. Furious, he decided he'd had enough of my verbal lashing—but there was nowhere to escape on our little boat, rocking in the thick darkness of the endless unseen horizon of Green Bay swaying beneath us.

So, to shut me up, he swiftly struck the back of my head with his open hand, so quickly and abruptly that my face nearly hit the tilted windshield in front of me. I saw stars. I fell into numbed silence, unable to process that what had just happened had *actually* happened. I was in shock.

We arrived back at the dock in silence. After securing the boat, he simply walked away without a word. I wandered over to the resort's outdoor fire pit to cry alone for a while, but guests were staring at me, so I eventually returned to our simple lakeside cabin. I curled up on the floor in front of the fireplace, lying there long into the night, inhaling the smoke while tears streamed down my face. It's terrifying how the line between being in love and being completely lost is sometimes just a misplaced hair away.

The next morning, we were both still livid. No one apologized. I told myself it wasn't about me, that the bulk of his anger stemmed from long before I ever entered the picture. It had always been there. And the moment it reared its head, I immediately blamed it on the drinking and ignored it. I didn't calmly ask him what had made him react that way. I didn't hold space to hear him. I was just ready to be done. *Again.*

He was angry that I constantly nagged about ways to make our lives "better" and that I wasn't nurturing or attentive, but his anger only made me harden and pull away from him even more. In truth, I had been unconsciously pulling away for years because I didn't feel safe in our partnership—his outbursts of anger had slowly stripped that away.

What would cause an intelligent MBA earner who had managed large teams and budgets in the hundreds of millions to stick around after a slap to the head? That's called a deep *fear of abandonment*, my friend.

At first, I made him out to be the bad guy. But what I didn't see right away was that we were *both* out of line. Words can create irreversible damage too. Although society tells us that physical harm is what crosses the line, and it does, verbal abuse is no less brutal.

We talked things through, yet again. I forgave the slap because I realized that my words had been just as painful to him as his physical hit had been to me. In truth, the pain of my words cut just as deeply and would last even longer than the physical harm he had caused me. Tearing into someone the way I did, verbally, is also a form of abuse. When something is said with the intent to wound, the damage rarely fully heals, leaving behind a silent but lingering scar.

The hit to my head, the physical pain, dulled within minutes. But what I didn't realize was that it had left an unseen wound, terribly deep in my trust and sense of safety. What we didn't know then was that our untreated wounds from that night would fester beneath the surface, eventually spreading into every branch of our relationship until it became impossible to see where to amputate in order to save the tree. The damage had already been done.

Instead of closing the rift this episode created by becoming a more nurturing partner, I unknowingly began to build a cocoon around myself. I started to withhold the full extent of my capacity to love in an attempt to protect myself from further hurt. I was numbing myself, shielding myself so much that I could no longer feel the soft pulse of my own heart.

He wasn't fundamentally good as a partner—not objectively—but if I looked at myself in the truest light, I wasn't either. Somehow, I saw my own faults reflected back at me in him, and that mutual recognition must have been the glue that kept us together. Neither form of abuse was any less cruel or unacceptable when used against someone you're supposed to love.

It may not seem obvious from what I've shared, but at this moment, it was as if I had blinked and suddenly found myself in a relationship where I was tolerating actions and behaviors completely misaligned with my core beliefs and values. Deep down, I knew it. I was sacrificing my morals and dissolving my boundaries in a desperate attempt to salvage what was left of our marriage—just five years in. I ignored my feelings and lashed out constantly with the only weapon I had: my words.

I coped by frequently calling him names, like an asshole, when his intensity made me feel unsafe. He, in turn, responded with even more intensity, using his anger as a shield. He had always carried quite a bit of repressed anger, but now he was also reacting to the fact that his wife didn't accept him as he was. Anger was a way for him to feel strong and powerful. And what I couldn't see then was that it was also his way of coping with—and expressing—the helplessness we both felt, silently and not so silently, as we existed in this union.

I felt as though I couldn't breathe, desperately trying to hold on to something that, deep down, wasn't meant for me. I was scared to be alone. I was scared to lose the closest love I had ever known. I was scared to admit failure. I was scared that taking steps to end this would mean eventually putting my heart out there again. I was drawn to the chaos, a reflection of my own insecurity and lack of self-confidence. Outwardly, I exuded confidence—I *did* feel completely confident in my work life—but in my close personal relationships? I felt unsteady.

The routine of our committed relationship felt secure, so we decided the solution was to dive in even further.

We both agreed to commit to therapy. He got a therapist. I got a therapist. We met with our own individual therapists—who, as it happened, were longtime friends. Then, for additional context and insight, we brought the four of us together for group sessions. Our *fucking therapists* had therapists to talk about our therapy.

I was convinced we could make this work, that we could heal this. Despite the outbursts, there was undoubtedly love underneath, and I thought love could fix this. People in my family didn't get divorced. Society told us we were failures if we got divorced. If you didn't slug it out through thick and thin and all the twists and turns life threw at you, you were a *fucking* failure.

What the hell was that?

Legally and ethically, society makes it *terribly* difficult to leave a partnership that should have been anchored in freedom and love at its core—not shame and guilt.

In therapy, deep childhood trauma surfaced for the hubs. I could feel how profoundly it ran for him, and I knew in my core that healing would take a monumental effort over years and years and years—if it could be healed at all. But I was still completely oblivious to my own trauma.

We also didn't have the emotional intelligence, tender communication, or compassion needed to change our deep-seated patterns at home, outside the safety of a refereed therapist's office. By that point, we were too mad at each other. Too hurt. Too wounded.

Our relationship was a disaster—we criticized each other regularly, existing in contempt, defensiveness, and silent stonewalling. All words synonymous with *ego*. Neither of us listened intently. Our gut reaction was to become defensive, to fight to be right. In other words, neither of us felt safe, but we didn't know how to articulate that.

We were failing to connect when all we wanted was so desperately to be seen and heard. We were hiding the deepest parts of ourselves, and without vulnerability, without acceptance, how could there be love? The mountain in front of us was too steep, too overwhelming. Instead of addressing the issues head-on, I chose distraction. I ran from the resentment, the anger, the childhood trauma. I chased money as a source of fulfillment instead.

In the fall of 2015, we moved to Seattle to be back in the mountains we loved, but also to accept a fifty percent salary increase for myself post-MBA. I told myself that more money and a city that better fit our outdoor lifestyle would make things more copacetic between us.

I could tell that parts of him wanted to stay, but he also seemed excited about the idea of getting the hell out of dodge—about kicking the can down the road on the *immense* amount of work we needed to do on our relationship. We told ourselves that with some therapy under our belts, surely we had the tools to guide us on the right path.

Instead, we distracted ourselves from the work we *so* desperately needed to do, with house shopping and discovering every inch of another new state.

And somehow, for a time, we found a rhythm again—a rhythm of joy, love, and exploration.

We were forced to lean on each other and come together in this new environment far from home. We left the mountain of emotional trauma in the rearview mirror, exploring, camping, and truly falling in love with the Pacific Northwest. I dared to think that perhaps this had done the trick.

But of course, my resentment continued to grow over the fact that I was contributing considerably more financially to our partnership.

He didn't feel like he was fulfilling his duty as a male partner, and I didn't feel like I had someone holding their own in our relationship because all I focused on was dollar signs. Money continually caused tension and resentment between us.

I kept pushing him to apply for bigger jobs, to broaden his career goals, and in doing so, I refused to accept where he was—and likely never would. I was subconsciously following a roadmap that told me continual improvement and career growth were the keys to happiness.

I made the fatal mistake of falling in love with someone's future potential instead of accepting them exactly as they were. Neither of us could be unapologetically ourselves, which made us friends, not life partners.

Life wasn't easy for him either. Imagine desiring comfort but never feeling like enough because, once something had been achieved, there was no time to celebrate—just the next move onto the next goal. My way of feeling alive was exhausting to him. The truth was, I wanted a partner with the same career drive and earning potential that I had, and I kept trying to mold my husband into that vision when all he wanted was a simple life in a rural town.

You simply can't change anyone. It's odd how much we all *know* this, yet we still try, against our better judgment. That desire to change has to come from within. My fix-it mindset was also helping me avoid my own feelings of sorrow, fear, and lack of control over my chosen circumstances.

What I couldn't see at the time was that, because I hadn't been emotionally seen as a child, I was desperate to be chosen. To please my parents growing up, I had to suppress my fears and true emotions and become another version of myself to earn love. So at this point, I was willing to be *any* version to be loved. Christian Science had placed unrealistic expectations of perfection on me, so I learned to place them on myself—and on my partner. I was looking for perfection. In other words, I was looking for the impossible.

Healthy relationships invite us to be *more* of who we are, not less. I was trying to change him. I was judging him against what I wanted him to be, rather than seeing him for who he was. Real love isn't something you control, construct, or imagine in the future. Love is something you recognize in real time—it feels reciprocal and honest, even in the smallest, most unglamorous moments.

This new city discovery distraction miraculously lasted three years, until my company was acquired. The new ownership began layoffs immediately; one by one, my colleagues disappeared. But the powers that be *promised* me my position was secure and proceeded to use me up until the very end. Then, once they had all the information they needed from me post-acquisition, they laid me off—along with the few remaining original employees—a few weeks before Christmas.

Delightfully devious bastards.

We were in full flail. We'd been here before, but this time, I was finally acknowledging that I was tethered to someone I no longer wanted to be with. And I could see that the feeling was mutual. We were just so deeply dependent on each other's company, on the identity of *us*—so afraid to be alone, so afraid to admit to society, and to my terribly religious Midwestern family, that my marriage had failed.

Heaven forbid I become the Scarlet Letter of the family. Heaven forbid I'm still not the perfect child.

This was when we *should* have called it quits, but instead, I pulled out our well-worn survival playbook one last time: *Hey, let's distract ourselves again and move to Portland.*

I had a great job opportunity there with an amazing company and a higher salary. I knew from experience that moves like this brought us closer together—so we repeated the cycle, forcing ourselves to lean on each other in a new state and unfamiliar environment.

I know. It's all so exhausting and obvious, isn't it?

Maybe you've been here before too—with someone you love?

Oddly enough, when you're in the thick of it emotionally, it simply *isn't*.

Chapter Five

The Earthly escape.

So now, my friend—you're all up to speed. Thanks for bearing with me for a hot minute. I needed to give you the full backstory before we dive into what comes next.

I currently find myself returning to work on this dreary Monday morning in Portland after my disastrous pants-pissing Vegas work trip, wondering why everything in life feels so terribly empty. I started this new job in the spring, but here I sit just six months later, in the fall of 2018, feeling completely exhausted by my job and, yet again, by our relationship.

I don't say a damn thing to Luke about the trip upon my return. Although nothing physical happened in Vegas, waking up next to a virtual stranger in bed was *most definitely* wrong. But things had been so tense between us, and I didn't want to rock the boat.

Three short weeks later, we are up in the mountains of Oregon, celebrating the holidays, trying to carve out some quality time to rekindle a spark—when we get a call on Christmas Eve morning.

Our dear mutual friend, and my best guy friend, John, has committed suicide.

The holidays suddenly come to a screeching halt. It's like a bomb has gone off. My ears are ringing, the room tilts, and while I can see his mouth moving from across the room, I can't hear a damn thing. I simply can't process the news.

We come together on the bed, and he wraps his arm around me. But something feels *terribly* off now. I don't feel consoled by my husband in the slightest. His arm around me doesn't feel truly sincere.

He cares deeply for John, but this was also a friend he had once accused me of having feelings for, something that couldn't have been further from the truth. Under the surface, we are both holding onto anger, assumptions, and now, a layer of profound sadness.

I flash back to the month before, when we were in Wisconsin visiting family and saw John. I knew something wasn't right the moment I looked at him. Something in the light and energy of his face was *off*, I had never seen him that way before. But I didn't bring it up. I assumed he was just tired, so instead, I pushed through, talking about upcoming travels, his work, and other superficial things.

Now, I know.

Now, I recognize that look—the look of someone who has fallen to a new level of despair. I'll never forget the way his spirit looked and felt only a month before he planned to take his own life. His face already reflected the life beginning to drain from him, simply by carrying the weight of his decision. There was an unmistakable energy radiating from him that I will never, *ever* forget as long as I'm on this planet.

After his passing, I learned that John had been planning and considering his escape from this world for quite some time. I didn't know it when he was alive, but I later found out that he had previously attempted suicide as a college freshman by carbon monoxide poisoning, and then again not long after by driving his car into a bridge abutment. He had expressed feeling crushing anxiety and depression all his life.

He confided that work was a major contributing factor—he hated his job. Constant changes in management left him in a perpetual state of fear that he would be terminated at any moment. The Wednesday before his death, over his lunch break, he bought the gun. A large-caliber gun.

John placed a banker's box on the passenger seat of his car, neatly filled with all his financial information and a few letters. On top of the box, in clear, deliberate writing, were the words: *For my family.*

In his suicide letters, he wrote, *I have tried everything to overcome the anxiety and depression, and nothing has worked...* He didn't see a way out of his suffering. Yet, in the same breath, he said he had lived a good and fulfilling life.

Some of us pack a lifetime into just a few years. John *did* this. The cruel irony is that he was the life of every party he ever walked into. His smile, humor, heart, and charisma lit up every room.

Looking back, I realize every chapter of our friendship was special—not in some profound, poetic way, but in his ability to show up consistently, every time. He was the kind of friend who always had your back, who listened intently, who brought 110 percent laughter and enthusiasm to every single hangout. Every time was *magic*.

But no one—no one—saw the depths of his suffering.

I so desperately wish he could have lifted himself up with the brilliance we all felt in his presence.

Losing him shook me to my core. Somehow, it numbed me while also *waking me the fuck up*—cracking my entire perception of existence wide open. It felt like a slap across the face, screaming:

You have one life, Becca. For fuck's sake, please live it.

How many more days will I have?

A handful?

Hundreds?

Thousands, if I'm fortunate?

His death felt unbearable in the moment, but as time passed, in an odd way, I became immensely grateful for that soul-shattering loss because it jolted me awake to the gift of this one precious life. The walls of my world had already been forming catastrophic cracks, and his death sent a massive chunk crashing at my feet, the impact so sharp and painful that the impending disaster finally caught my attention.

Much like Andy Dufresne in *The Shawshank Redemption*—my favorite movie of all time—it suddenly occurred to me that there *might* be a way out of the prison I had found myself in. John's loss put a crack in my heart, but it also ignited a deep, newfound desire for happiness and freedom.

The profound weight of losing our friend quickly seeped into our usual marital survival tactics. Our tried-and-true method of distracting ourselves from despair by moving cities was losing its effectiveness. This time, the Band-Aid stayed on for less than a year.

I was preparing to leave for my company ski and snowboard trip when I heard that a coworker visiting from out of state wanted to join us but didn't have any gear. I asked the hubs if we could lend him his snowboard boots, jacket, and pants since they were the same size.

He was deeply annoyed and told me that he preferred not to lend his stuff out.

I was just as annoyed in return and snapped back, "It's just sitting there collecting dust, and he'll be wearing his own base layers and socks. Why is this such a big deal? Why can't you help a friend of mine out?"

This, my friend, is called a *boundary*.

He didn't want to lend out his gear, which I viewed as deeply unreasonable because *I* would have lent mine without hesitation. But *he* was not *me*. I challenged him: "How can you be so selfish?" Eventually, he gave in to my pressures.

Upon reflection, *I* was the one being selfish. He had every right to set that boundary with his personal belongings, even if I didn't view lending out sporting gear the same way. It wasn't my job to find my coworker gear to use.

The day after the trip, my coworker returned the gear, but the snowboard boots weren't laced up correctly, and my husband told me there was an odor coming from them. Then he looked me dead in the face and said: *"I could put my hands around your throat and watch your face turn blue, and it would feel so good."*

I stared back at him, feeling the visceral hatred he had for me—and at that same instant, I felt my own calm, visceral hatred for him.

The continual feeling of not being safe, combined with my dismissive disregard for his boundaries, sat there in the room between us like a dense fog. One we couldn't see through and one that would never lift.

We had left so much unsaid for so long. We had no idea where the other was truly coming from. *Shit, we were too fucking scared to ask.*

We were deeply entrenched in the stories of our minds, firmly in our egos, convinced that the *other* was to blame.

There were no counterbalances.

The resentments we carried were completely one-sided. We had been in *Ready Player One* mode for so long that the game had become a battle where only one of us could win.

So many unspoken feelings, so many buried emotions—years of silence had formed into a looming tsunami above us, a shadow too great to escape.

There was no rescuing this boat's passengers. The tsunami that had been blocking our light for so long finally struck and plummeted us to the depth of darkness, with such immense pressure that finally forces change, in the only way that tragedy can sometimes. All the way to the bottom of the dark encompassing sea where there was no sense of direction. We didn't know how to sit with our difficult emotions, we hadn't learned how to meet each other with compassion. We were heavy in ego, anger and unprocessed trauma on both sides.

All of this was created and cultivated slowly by micro disconnections, held back difficult communications, and culminated in insurmountable disagreements over the years. Only resentment, blame, and desperation remained between us.

Would you believe me if I said we didn't end it here? Well, my friends, sadly we didn't. Instead, we moved one last time. The farthest we could muster was to a new place in Portland. At this point, I recognize being alone is better than being lonely with someone.

Just two months later, over Sunday breakfast, we look at each other, and I simply say to him, "This is so done, isn't it?"

He looks at me, pauses with sad eyes, and agrees. "It so is."

Another long pause.

"Would you like more coffee?" I offer sincerely.

"Yes, please." And he drinks what is left in his cup, before I offer some fresh brew.

There is no more anger. No yelling. No blame. We sit here in surrendered silence. We are finally utterly exhausted down to the core of our beings. We are done in every single cell of our bodies. There is no choice at this point, it simply is. No, love just isn't enough. There has to be open, safe, and vulnerable communication to make things work. This should have been our path years ago, yet we didn't know how to let go.

And so, we finally, *finally* do. One can only wait, until one can simply fucking wait no longer.

Chapter Six

Table for one?

We begin the painful process of untangling our physical, financial, familial, and emotional lives.

Physically, we are so enmeshed that even though our intimacy is basically nonexistent, we still share almost every moment outside of work. Hell, we still brush our teeth side by side every night. We shower together most of the time. We always have dinner together. At home and on weekends, we are like Siamese twins—together, always. Terribly reliant on each other.

Emotionally, our communication as a couple is horrendous, but when we look at our relationship objectively, we are basically best friends. We begin a process that, though deeply painful, is one of the moments I am most proud of in our marriage. In our mutual fear of the unknown, we somehow find solidarity in our impending dissolution, allowing us to consciously uncouple in the most loving way possible. We lean on each other. Our relationship's origins—friendship—begin to emerge again, carrying the fresh scent of relief in the air, the sky clearing from the storm clouds of expectation.

With a chance at freedom in front of us, the anger and hate fade rather quickly.

Funny how expectations vanish when there's no longer a contract binding you together, with just that teeny-tiny bit of pressure always looming underneath: *"Till death do us part."*

What kind of contractual union is that?

We continue living together for a while, letting the finality sink in. It takes two full months, but then, one long weekend while I'm away on a work trip, he quietly packs up his things and moves into an apartment across town.

I return from my trip to an empty home.

We amicably file for divorce without legal assistance and are notified by the courts that our divorce will be final in September, right around what was supposed to be our nine-year wedding anniversary.

Don't you think it's rather odd that you can get married in a quick fifteen-minute ceremony, but it takes half a year, a mound of potential legal fees, and hefty financial setbacks to undo that decision?

Isn't it strange that it's the only license on the planet you *don't* have to do a little work to renew?

My only real point of contention was that Oregon is a fifty-fifty state, so we agreed to split all assets evenly, including my 401(k)s. I had started saving early, in my twenties, while Luke didn't begin until his thirties. I had considerably more saved, thanks to my two degrees and higher salaries, but he argued that fifty-fifty was the law and that he had contributed to our relationship in many ways beyond finances.

In that regard, I agreed, relationships aren't just about money. I appreciated his efforts in our marriage outside of financial contributions: house projects, yardwork, car fixes. But the truth is, in retrospect, I didn't fully value them.

I still didn't quite agree on splitting the 401(k)s, since I had started saving before we were married. But I was in deep surrender mode by then, so I simply said *fine*—and dipped into my only cash reserves to avoid pulling from the 401(k)s to complete the settlement.

We sit in the living room and lay out all our adventure gear, camping equipment, and mutual keepsakes accumulated over fifteen years together. That afternoon, we turn the painful process into a game: *You pick one thing, I pick one thing,* dividing our once-shared belongings until everything is agreeably separated.

Each piece we grab represents a moment in time, a trip, an adventure, a city explored together. It is simultaneously gut-wrenching and freeing.

Emotions fly in every direction, unpredictable and chaotic. I know there are a myriad of feelings to process, but there are so many—moving at different speeds, crashing into each other—that all I can do is bob and weave, trying to function without getting hit. I feel like one of those tiny PowerBalls bouncing around inside a glass bin, waiting to be plucked out.

At the same time, it becomes apparent that my father back in Wisconsin is growing sicker by the day. He is diagnosed with a rare autoimmune disease, and at this juncture, he can barely get out of bed most days. We speak frequently on the phone, but it's a lot to process.

I feel guilty admitting that I'm thankful for the distance out on the West Coast because, deep down, I know I wouldn't have the strength to watch him suffer firsthand.

And as if life isn't unraveling fast enough, work begins collapsing as well.

As my husband moves out, an implosion at my Portland job hits—more layoffs for my team, nearly half the department eliminated. I had been warned that marketing was the toughest department to find stability in, as the CEO had a particular passion for tearing it down. The department had already been built and dismantled several times before I arrived. I watch as my boss and dear girlfriend is let go, followed by my counterpart and most of her team.

Now, for the first time in my life, I am living alone.

I am running a shattered department for a brazen company trying to go IPO.

And it is becoming more and more evident that my dad is dying.

I go into survival mode. The weight of everything is too much. I am drastically losing weight. The department is in shambles. Team morale is in the shitter. My life is falling apart, and I simply *do not* have the strength to lead a department the way I should.

Not even close.

I force myself to shift into protection mode, trying to cheer up myself, and the crumbling marketing team, as best I can. I fight to get my team raises, failing repeatedly despite our department being nearly half the size and still carrying the same workload. When I *do* finally secure some meager compensation bumps for my team, I inherit the entire department and don't see a single penny more for myself.

Then, I learn that my male counterparts—holding similar titles, managing far fewer employees—are making 20–35 percent more than I am.

I am beyond livid.

Of course, a little extra compensation for my team is fleeting in an environment like this. I encourage them to enroll in continuing education courses and certifications, siphoning funds from project budgets to help them feel prepared for the inevitable next round of layoffs. We take on volunteer work to feel some small moments of purpose.

Eight weeks into my new role, my new boss pulls me into his office one morning to tell me he has also been let go.

I notice a mini bottle of Bailey's sitting on his desk, a small anniversary gift from someone in the office. Without hesitation, I crack it open, pour it into my coffee, and stare straight at him, cool and collected, nodding as I take in the news.

He looks at me, stunned.

I think, he suddenly realizes I am worse off than he is.

Now, I am reporting directly *one level* below the CEO.

Conveniently, the CEO's little brother.

Keepin' it in the family.

As I'm sitting in his office I get a text that Dad is back in the hospital. I leave his office without saying a word to duck into the stairwell as the tears well up. I begin to sob. I'm shaking, gripping the wall, my mind floods with fears of Dad dying in the hospital while I'm 2,000 miles away. Or maybe it's my vision that's swirling. The ground feels like it's shattering beneath me, and I grab the rail in the stairwell, collapsing onto one of the pristine cement steps that have barely been tread upon.

Lucky stairs.

Movement is impossible. It's 10 a.m. and I stare at the Bailey's still swirling in my coffee as I sit on the stair. I take a slow sip—lip quivering, hand shaking.

Living the corporate dream.

What do you think, young lady? Was this worth the sacrifices?

Shut up. Please shut up right now, I just... I can't.

I can't keep it together anymore. This path—the path of the accomplishment junkie, where my worth came from achievements—was crumbling. I had no clue who I was at my core.

Work had indeed become a four-letter word.

I bike home in the middle of the day along the riverfront, barely able to see through my tears. I arrive at an empty home, living alone for the first time in my entire life, at the age of 38. I crack open a bottle of wine and sit on my porch, staring blankly at the river until night falls.

It's hard to believe it, but we actually did it.

After a decade and a half of cohabitation, we're *actually* done.

I stare, barely moving, utterly exhausted.

I shuffle inside and drop into bed.

The next morning, I sign myself up for therapy and add it to my weekly routine—every Monday morning before heading into work. A defense mechanism against the *Sunday Scaries*, which now begin creeping in by mid-afternoon. As I anticipate returning to work, my heart starts racing, like that instant when you're speeding over a hill and suddenly spot a cop.

I hit snooze at least six times every morning in defiance of the inevitable.

The following particularly gloomy, rainy Monday, after hitting snooze an ungodly number of times, I step into the slow, steady, old-school elevator with its green marble walls and shiny golden metal buttons and take the ride towards delving into my pain.

Up, up, up to the top floor of a high-rise office building overlooking the city of Portland.

I sleepwalk down a narrow hallway, find the office, and knock before entering. A desk sits just inside with a handwritten sign: **Take a seat.**

I find myself thinking of *Alice in Wonderland*—and if there were a little bottle labeled *Drink Me*, I most certainly would.

The waiting area is small, with a few magazines proposing all sorts of ideas for healthy living, healthy homes, and a positive mindset. I sink into one of the six simple chairs against the stark white walls, staring at the courtesy corner plant.

Then, I just sit.

Alone.

A few minutes later, my new therapist opens the waiting room door and invites me to follow her back to her lovely corner office.

I walk in and see not one sofa, but three—plus two comfy chairs—forming a menagerie of seating options. It feels more like a cozy living room or a funky coffee shop than an office, with books, lamps, art, and a few scattered tables.

I hesitate. "Where should I sit?"

She simply raises her arm, glides her hand around the room, palm up, and looks at me kindly, saying nothing—implying, *wherever you'd like, dear.*

I spot a velvety, forest-green tufted sofa in the far corner and make my way over. Settling into the corner, I kick off my black high heels, tuck my pleated dress-pant-adorned legs under me, and get comfortable. I tie my hair back into a loose ponytail, adjust my white blouse, grab my coffee, and take a sip.

It's the week after my newest boss's layoff. I've been drinking and numbing my way through most things and can't really recall the details of the past few days. I blink, trying to focus on her, to be present.

My therapist is a kind, plump woman in her early fifties, with rosy cheeks. She wears a cute floral oversized shirt from Ann Taylor Loft and light pink pants. She sits just a few feet away on a simple cream sofa perpendicular to mine, with bright floral *Anthropologie* pillows cheerfully joining the conversation.

Maybe she's hiring, I think to myself. *Maybe I can work here. Maybe I can just fetch coffee, offering everyone walking in a warm, knowing smile—Yep, I've been there too.*

She says something, but I'm too deep in thought about how to pitch my credentials as an overqualified candidate for a psychologist's office coffee-fetcher.

I blink back at her. "Sorry, what was that?"

She looks at me with kind eyes, radiating a grandmotherly patience—steady, warm, but direct in a way I immediately respect.

"What brings you in today?"

I stare at her.

"My best guy friend recently committed suicide, my office is in ruins with constant layoffs and excessive passive-aggressive over-management, and I'm in the process of filing for divorce after fifteen years with a partner I loved deeply but was also terribly angry with and, occasionally, scared of."

I take a sip of coffee.

I stare back blankly.

"Oh, and I still had access to an old email account of his, so a random ping showed me an epic trail of emails expressing his love to a new interest just two months after moving out. I don't think he cheated physically, but emotionally? Yeah, that was hard to read. And yet, at this stage, it also wasn't. You know? We were emotionally done years ago. That about covers it."

I take another sip of coffee, smiling tiredly.

She looks at me with such warmth, such gentle reassurance. "You know, you don't have to hold it all together, dear. You don't have to be perfect. You can let a bit of that hurt out."

Oh, I think, *She sees me.*

Why has no one in my life—none of my closest humans—ever summed up the pressure I've felt my entire life so perfectly?

Well.

I suppose I would've had to *tell* someone how I felt first.

I begin to sob. And sob. And sob.

For the rest of the hour, I don't say another word.

I release. And release. And release some more.

I try to stop, try to bring up something else, but I can't.

I *almost* pull it together.

She nods toward the clock. "Time's up."

Gawd, you have no idea.

On the way to the door, she hands me a tissue for the road. "Next week?"

I sigh heavily. "Sure."

I give an exhausted head nod and make my way to the brilliantly planned rear exit—designed so I don't have to showcase my puffy-eyed face to her next eager guest. No need to squash anyone's hopeful mojo.

I stop in the bathroom to adjust my face before heading into the office and stare at my reflection—the exhausted eyes, the black mascara trailing down my cheeks. I don't recognize myself.

And, in truth, I don't really *see* myself either.

I'm just going through the motions.

I allow myself quick pressure releases here and there, like in the therapist's office just now, but there's so much beneath the surface that I am simply ignoring.

I am numbing my way through the days.

And while I *should* feel relief that I've taken this massive step toward dissolving my marriage, I haven't really begun to process much of it.

Fine.

None of it.

I have begun to process *absolutely nothing*.

Chapter Seven

Light the match.

My exciting new city move is backfiring. I'd been here only a year and had thrown myself into work straight out of the gate, so I really didn't have any friends to lean on besides my co-workers. And while it was painfully obvious to them that I was in the middle of a life spiral, I couldn't fully verbalize it. I couldn't let them know that the person running the show in our shitshow of a department was also deep in shitshow survival mode.

I mean, they knew I was stressed out of my mind in the office, but they didn't fully grasp how badly my personal life was disintegrating. I showed a few of my cards when I asked a fellow single co-worker for text support before heading out to dinner alone—after, no joke, Googling "How to dine alone."

It's one thing to travel solo in a place where you don't know anyone, but sitting alone in your *own* city feels like a whole other thing for a grown-ass woman who has never lived on her own.

To ease my discomfort, I still find myself spending a fair amount of time with my future Former—dinners, drinks, hanging at each other's places. Hell, in late July, we even attended a wedding together, where I still wore my wedding ring because we hadn't told anyone about the separation yet. We wanted to get ourselves grounded before the inevitable barrage of questions and explanations from friends and family.

Oddly, under this new umbrella of freedom and zero expectations, arguments are nonexistent. We are getting along better than we have in years.

I silently wonder what it is about the absence of a ring on a finger that makes one feel like ceasing to give the middle finger.

And so, spring and early summer roll by. The months of dreary rain covering the city begin to lift as we slowly learn to uncouple.

My days consist of therapy, attempting to keep myself together, trying to keep my department from falling apart, working late hours to avoid going home, and drinking—a *lot*—to numb myself from feeling anything at all.

I get random meeting invites from the CEO with descriptions like: "I've been unimpressed with the details on our recent direct mail creative samples (I'll bring examples). Let's review what's coming next." I defend myself and the department, showing with statistics that our leads and deals are *way* up over last year. But creative work in marketing is so often subjective. Like trying to debate art.

Meanwhile, my dad is back home from the hospital, but his decline is accelerating. He's getting out of the house less and losing more strength from the autoimmune disease. And yet, even as his body fails, whenever we speak on the phone, he is always so loving, positive, optimistic. He marvels at the intense blue of the sky. The colorful birds outside his window. The deliciousness of the lunch he just ate. The excitement of the baseball game earlier that day.

That's the way of my dad—eternally optimistic, finding joy in the smallest of things.

I am such a daddy's girl. I just wish I could channel even a *glimmer* of his optimism right now.

With our wedding anniversary looming, we finally let everyone know—via a mass text message sent individually—that we are calling things good. That the divorce is entirely mutual. That we are very much still friends.

There's a lot of shock from our friends, given that there was never an inkling we weren't happily married. Very few ever saw his angry outbursts or my swearing and name-calling.

Ah, the torture of the human ego that is social media.

So many people keep up appearances rather than openly sharing their struggles. Such is the human condition, and I was no better—always posting our happy travel adventures, always professing our love. Those moments *were* real, but they were a heavily filtered version of the truth.

Luke and I naturally have all of our friends intertwined after a decade and a half together, so our mutual friends invite us up to their cozy cabin outside of Seattle for the upcoming Fourth of July holiday. When we arrive, they acknowledge the separation for a moment but reassure us it's obviously for the best since it's a mutual decision.

And because we're gliding right into best-friend land, oddly, it strangely feels like nothing has changed. As if no relationship loss has occurred at all.

We dive headfirst into celebrating—gleefully floating on the river outside their cabin, laughing over epic bonfires, toasting copious amounts of marshmallows for s'mores, drinks flowing, weed abundant enough to fuel a joyful haze.

My dad suffering in bed doesn't exist. My marriage ending doesn't exist.

My emotions are locked in an iron chest, parked at the bottom of the ocean, blissfully lost at sea.

We're deep into the revelry on this sunny Fourth of July afternoon when I get an email from the CEO directly about the "useless fluff" content my team is producing. Mind you, this is the same CEO who hires top-tier talent from amazing companies—only to stop by my desk to micromanage *the color of the envelope* on a direct mail piece.

"We need cream, not white," was a favorite go-to. Or, "We need the printed handwritten font to look more human."

He is constantly in the weeds, trying to control each micro-decision—things that should be entrusted to the meticulously selected executives. A leader who *cannot* let go.

I fling myself onto the riverside cabin bed and begin to sob.

I've got a good solid buzz going, and I'd hit a joint just before reading his message—so I draft a zinger of an email reply to the CEO. The general vibe? Passive-aggressively calling out his impossible leadership and his inability to lean on the key talent and leadership right in front of him.

I save it to Drafts, where all my emotionally charged masterpieces go to die and feel a tiny bit of relief from the throbbing anxiety in my chest.

Maybe an hour goes by. I'm staring at the mountains before me, the rush of the stream roaring just forty feet ahead, the magnificent eagle's nest across the river.

Becca, what in the actual fuck are you doing?

I feel like a caged animal. Exhausted from powering through life. Exhausted from trying to please everyone. I quickly open the email draft, staring at it. A massive smile spreads across my face as I hit send.

I know, at this moment, that my job is likely gone.

I don't give two fucks.

I give *zero* consideration to the fact that I have no backup income. No one to lean on.

Everything is burning around me, so I might as well douse it in gasoline and grab some popcorn for the show.

I can't tell if I'm crazy or if this company has made me that way. All I know is—it's *Shawshank Redemption* time, and my tunnel isn't progressing fast enough. Andy took nineteen years to dig his way to freedom with a miniature rock hammer, and I sure as hell don't have that kind of patience. It's time for the bulldozer.

The first thing I do when I get back to town is walk into the office of the CEO's little brother—my direct boss. He has me sit down and close the door. He stares at me, half amused, half thrilled to deliver the news, his underhanded eyes resting just slightly lower than my own gaze across his sprawling desk. He informs me that what I wrote is "irrevocable."

I stare back blankly. "Yeah. I figured." Super. Now I'm out of a job.

A few days pass, and strangely, I don't hear much of anything about my exit.

I tell my boss I should probably talk to the CEO face-to-face to determine next steps.

He pushes back, *hard*, saying that I should work through him alone. This is the same boss who frequently makes comments about random budget allocations with no basis, no plan.

I decide to cut out the little narcissistic middleman, because I never truly believed he had my best interests at heart anyway, and I send an invite for a fifteen-minute one-on-one with the CEO. He accepts immediately.

I walk into the huge fishbowl aquarium of a conference room. The *swoosh* as the door closes feels like I've entered an airlock on a spaceship. My heartbeat quickens. My breath catches.

To this day, the exchange is a bit of a blur.

I sit down and speak quickly, getting ahead of whatever he's about to say. I tell him that his email was inappropriate, that I was doing my best, that it's impossible to keep running on this never-ending task wheel of never enoughness and continual layoffs.

He looks me in the eye, pauses, and actually says, "Sorry."

I'm *shocked*. I didn't even know he knew that word. I've never heard it—or any of its many linguistic apologetic cousins—exit his mouth before. We talk back and forth, a bit optimistically at first, but then I hear the same musings creeping back in.

We need to try this creative. Try this content. Target this audience. Test this offer. Say these things.

And suddenly, I can feel it happening, we are right back in *Groundhog Day*. He just desires too much control. He doesn't trust me or my team. I have to give it to him, he has no shortage of ideas, but deep down I know this isn't working. This is a sinking ship.

Then, something inside me—some deep, undeniable *knowing*—makes me toss out a completely random idea. I know our International Marketing team is struggling to gain traction without centralized leadership. I also know we need growth in multiple countries (we're present in eighteen) but I especially know that Mexico is a hot topic, ripe for expansion. And something about Mexico tugs at my core.

So, I propose that I take what I've learned leading North America's marketing to drive international growth. A six-month, boots-on-the-ground assignment in Mexico, focused on expanding our short-term rental presence in Baja California Sur. This is not a position that exists.

He looks back at me, his face perking up. "I like it."

Blink, blink, blink. *You DO?* "Fantastic," I reply, a smile spreading across my face.

I immediately leave the conference room and message my contact in HR to draft the position and paperwork before the moment slips away—before I lose my grip on this life raft in the storm.

"Huh, what do you mean you're going to Mexico? What role? Reporting to who?"

"I'll get that to you shortly," I reply, already scrambling to conjure up the deliverables, structure, and goals of this position that *does not exist*. "Let's just get the ball rolling. Use my current job description as the baseline."

***

Little did I know, asking my CEO to export me to Mexico would lead me down the wildest, grueling, absolutely epic, forever life-altering path I could have imagined. Something deep within me had been bellowing RUN, and although I wasn't yet fully conscious of it, I had finally listened to my inner knowing.

Something deep within was screaming—*this fucked-up shit will not be my story.*

I'm ready to douse everything in gasoline, toss a match, and just see what the hell happens.

Goodbye, marriage. Goodbye, pristine office. Goodbye, country.

Hello, *freedom.*

Chapter Eight

Viva la Mexico.

I can hardly believe it. Just two and a half months later, everything I own is in storage, and I'm about to hit the road with my 4Runner, lightly packed with what I think I'll need. It's the fall of 2019, a little over two weeks after my 39th birthday and only three days shy of what would have been my wedding anniversary. However, two weeks ago, I received official notification from the state court—our divorce is now final. Just days short of being married a decade.

My company has agreed to place me abroad for a six-month assignment in La Paz, Baja California Sur, Mexico, with the option for an extension depending on how the next half-year unfolds. I give up my apartment, unsure of how long I'll actually be away, and put everything I own into a massive storage POD.

I sit my team down and, through tears, explain that at this point, I have to put my own mask on before assisting others. I don't say it *that* cheesily, but they understand. They can tell just by looking at me. I've lost weight. I barely have time for lunch. I have massive bags under my eyes. I'm not leading. I'm surviving.

I feel guilty for abandoning the team, for contributing to yet another leadership change—pure insanity at this point. I've already had *three* bosses in three months, and most of my team is in similar boats.

I hold one final team meeting before heading out the next day.

"Look, obviously this is an insanely tough department to be in," I tell them. "Please don't take the constant changes and shifting direction as a reflection of your capabilities. The broader vision needs dialing in, as well as leadership that's willing to actually stay the course for a moment, as I'm sure you've keenly noticed. I'm here via phone, Slack, email—if you ever need me. But hopefully, my replacement can finally bring some stability to the department."

They can hear the lie in my voice. We *all* know there isn't much to be done about it.

After the meeting, I speak with each of them individually, making sure all concerns are heard. Then we all go out for an epic night of drinks and jello shots to celebrate our wins—in *our* eyes—before I promptly begin unplugging myself, emotionally and physically, from the mothership the next morning.

I had my escape pod. And not a moment too soon.

***

It's a sunny fall day as I begin my 2,030-mile southerly road trip adventure. I head out of Portland, driving toward the coast, when I get word that my dad is in the hospital again. I hold my breath and listen, but thankfully, it's confirmed that it will be a short stay. I exhale deeply, feeling the stress in my bones.

I give him a call, and he assures me in his usual chipper voice that he's okay and going home soon. "Keep me updated on your adventures with Facebook Messenger," he says.

Although the platform is terrible for society's mental health, I'm grateful that it at least keeps my dad social and forming new connections, and sharing his bird photos. The man posts a bird photo *every single day* and has built quite the following, he informs me.

"That's awesome, Dad. I'll be sure to click over and like a few." I feel guilty. I've been so wrapped up in my own life spiral that I haven't been engaging or reaching out enough. I have to do better.

Sitting shotgun is my curly-haired, dirty blonde bestie, Paige—bringing this full circle, since she also sat shotgun when she egged me on to put my dating profile online to meet Luke. She was my wingwoman the night we met on our very first date. She flew out from Minneapolis to join me on this journey, riding by my side as we make our way to the coast and, ultimately, San Diego over the next six days, swapping drive time along the way.

A week was as long as she could get off work, so Luke is planning to meet us in San Diego and drive with me the rest of the way to La Paz. Like I said, we're really enjoying each other's company again without the tether of marital expectations lingering in the air. With space, we can finally see so clearly—we were always better as friends. In truth, it had mostly been that way all along, but we ignored the signs, mistaking the joy of companionship for *true* love.

Paige and I head southwest, eager to put some distance between us and the city. We drive down the coastal highway, passing through charming Pacific City, lovely Depoe Bay, quaint Newport, and beautiful Yachats, hugging the coastline as we go. We stop along the way to soak in the breathtaking natural beauty of the Oregon coast—stunning rock formations nestled within the rugged, radiant emerald landscape.

As we roll down the simple two-lane highway, the sound of the waves crashing against the rocky shoreline begins to seep into my being. Slowly, a sense of serenity replaces the endless days of staring at white plaster walls, gray metal beams, and rows upon rows of artificial fluorescent lights. The misty salt air is mesmerizing, soothing, *calling me home.*

We stop for a day to wander among the magnificent giants of the Redwood Forests, breathing in the crisp, pine-scented air. We laugh, we cry, we talk about everything—our journey from college until now, how much has changed, yet how some things remain the same. *Work for money, save the money, get better jobs, travel when we can. Repeat.*

We're both just relieved this next phase is finally unfolding.

After a final delicious meal together, we stroll out of a restaurant, arms linked, when something bright yellow catches my eye. It's distinctly out of place. I tilt my head sharply, the way a dog does when it's trying to understand what the hell you're saying.

A classic bright yellow Post-it sits on the ground, thick black lettering in remarkably nice handwriting scrawled across it: **Crossroads.**

***

Well, damn. Yes. Yes, that's certainly where I find myself. I smile to myself, saying nothing, simply appreciating the moment as we wander back to the hotel under a sky full of stars.

The next day is a final sprint to San Diego. The trip has been a beautiful, slow roll down the West Coast—salty sea air, nourishing sun, bestie bonding time, occasional rainbows, delicious food. I begin to see a hopeful light at the end of the traditional office untethering tunnel.

I drop Paige off at the airport and give her a gigantic squeeze, thanking her for her companionship.

"I'm so excited for you. You've got this, woman. I love you." She hugs me tight. I fight back tears as I watch her walk toward her terminal. In my heart, I'm excited—yet nervous. But I know I'm ready for this. Okay, maybe not ready, exactly. But I know there's no other way but *through*.

I don't sit alone in the airport for long before Luke arrives, and, honestly, I'm so excited to see him.

He lands, and I collect him in baggage claim (*oh, the irony*) before we head out for one last night on the town before crossing the border into Mexico the next morning.

Over dinner, we both shed a few tears reminiscing about the beautiful times and adventures we've shared over the years.

Then, we head back to the hotel to rest for the long drive ahead. Same room. Different queen beds. Not a single thought or ounce of sexual energy between us after fifteen years together. Crazy, yet perfectly sane.

In the morning, we hit the road south toward Tijuana, the Former at the wheel for the first shift. I refuse to call him my ex when speaking of him to others, it carries such a negative connotation.

The excitement is palpable as I see signs for the Mexico International Border.

"It's happening! ¡*Viva México!*" I can't help but feel like a giddy teenager breaking the rules, escaping the typical routine to go on an adventure and color my life just a little outside the lines.

We approach the border at the San Ysidro Port of Entry—the largest land border crossing between San Diego and Tijuana, and the fourth-busiest land border crossing in the world, with 70,000 northbound vehicles and 20,000 northbound pedestrians crossing each day. We see the zillion lanes ahead, pick one, and get comfy waiting, but surprisingly, traffic is moving at a decent pace. We're only in line for about 45 minutes before making our way through the primary crossing. A slew of cameras are pointed at the truck, but no one is checking identification. We keep rolling forward, passing quite a few border control agents and multiple inspection points off to the right, but no one stops us or waves us to pull over.

We look at each other, shrug, and beam. "Yaaaas, we're in Mexico!"

So, we keep rolling through Tijuana and onto the major highway heading south. I glance to my right and see two rusty, towering metal mesh walls, at least 20 or 30 feet high, winding over the terrain—designed to keep anyone from entering unlawfully, allowing nothing through but their fingertips and a few stolen glances. Against the wall, dozens of makeshift tents are scattered, with hundreds of migrants standing by the gate. They appear to be waiting for Border Patrol to let them in and transport them to processing centers, hoping for a chance to enter the United States and make a living there.

It's funny how the grass is always greener, depending on life experiences and perception. By much of the world's standards, I was deemed fortunate to be born in the U.S.—the *land of opportunity*—yet here I was, feeling like I couldn't get outside its borders fast enough.

Just 30 minutes south of Tijuana, the immense, chaotic energy of the city fades into the vast openness of northern Baja. To my right, nothing but the Pacific Ocean. To my left, sparse desert hills dotted with cactuses. The intense Baja sun glares back at me.

The primary reason for Luke coming along was to expedite the drive. I'm terrible at long spans behind the wheel, I max out at about four or five hours, but he can drive 21 hours straight if he has to. Like any long road trip, though, there are always precautionary tales. The secondary reason was the safety narrative surrounding Mexico.

IT'S GONNA GET MESSY

I had read blog posts and travel sites warning of carjackings, robberies, and gas shortages, painting this stretch as potentially unsafe. But I'd also read accounts describing it as effortless, incredibly safe, and breathtakingly beautiful. Of course, there was also the American media's portrayal of Mexico as a dangerous, underdeveloped country. Some friends questioned my decision to go alone, thinking I was *nuts* to drive it solo.

But me? I've traveled extensively. I know any country or city is capable of its dangerous moments, and I wanted to form my own opinion from firsthand experience. Still, a road trip is always more fun with a friend, and I wanted to kick things off with company, just to make the trip extra safe and enjoyable.

As we reach our first rest stop for the night, the roads have proven to be excellent, and we have never once felt unsafe. That said, I admit having someone with me is more comforting than going it alone. Northern Baja is quite remote, we go for hours without seeing another car as we drive deeper into the central peninsula.

The most action we get is about halfway through the drive, when we're stopped at a highway inspection point. National Guardsmen in desert camo stand in trucks, gripping assault rifles—an alarming sight at first, especially as the *very first* people we encounter on the road. In the U.S., police typically have their guns holstered and to the side, but here, the brazen display of large weaponry is a standard defense.

We pull up, and they ask where we're headed in Spanish. I rely on my four semesters of high school Spanish, plus the semester I took in college. During our honeymoon in Spain, my Spanish improved a decent amount, so I'm able to make conversation and reply.

"Estamos en camino a La Paz para visitar amigos." *We're on our way to La Paz to visit friends.*

The guard looks at me, a bit surprised that my Spanish pronunciation is actually fairly decent. I hope this earns us some brownie points, even though we're carrying nothing illegal and are very much in Baja legally. I decide not to even bring up the temporary work thing, that's considerably harder to explain.

He asks us to step out, and they do a thorough inspection of all the bags in the car, looking under seats, in glove boxes, and inside center consoles. I don't love them rifling through all my things, but we sit patiently, and about twenty minutes later, we're heading south once more.

We travel about seven hours and stay in a cute little two-star hotel about three hours north of the border to the southern Baja peninsula as the sun is setting. We're greeted by a wonderfully chipper front-desk woman, her round face beaming over the colorful tiled counter. She seems genuinely happy to see some guests in the otherwise sleepy roadside motel.

We promptly ditch our bags and make our way to the bar for chips, salsa, and Pacificos. Okay, and maybe a few shots of tequila too—I do love tequila. We're grateful for our little desert oasis, the friendly staff, and the tasty beverages. We both agree it's simultaneously hard *and* not hard to process that we're here—as friends—that our divorce is now final, and that we're truly embarking on our own unique journeys. Still, we're happy for it.

We pass out early, so we're fresh-ish to hit the road at sunrise.

We wake early to the warm Baja sun illuminating our cute and simple room in a golden glow. We mosey out to the courtyard to grab some breakfast burritos filled with cheese, rice, and beans, along with some burnt coffee, then roll out to fuel up my truck just across the street.

A lot of travel blogs had warned about limited gas stations along the way, but that hasn't been the case so far. Still, we make a habit of filling up whenever we drop below half a tank, just to be sure. We've got an eight-hour drive ahead to our next stop, a beautiful little mountain town on the Sea of Cortez.

As we leave the hotel and head south, the landscape begins to shift—rolling hills, towering cactuses, and unexpected bursts of turquoise sea come into view. I'd never considered myself a desert person, but Baja slowly wins me over with its quiet, rugged beauty. By the time we reach the quaint little town at sunset, I'm completely enchanted. That night, we fall asleep full and content, sea breeze drifting through the open windows. The next morning brings sunshine, strong coffee, and a balcony view that makes it hard to leave, but our final stop still lies a few hours ahead.

IT'S GONNA GET MESSY

Since this role was entirely made up by me, there wasn't a specific city I was required to be in—so I selected the capital of Baja California Sur, La Paz. I hadn't done a ton of research. Friends said it was a great option for expats who wanted to live by the beach in Mexico without being in an overly touristy resort town.

I'd only been to Baja once before for our one-year wedding anniversary—to Cabo San Lucas, ironically, which is packed with resorts and pool parties galore.

It's funny—after always chasing opportunities in big cities like Denver, Seattle, and Portland for more earning potential, action, and outdoor adventures, all I wanted now was slow and simple.

We hit one more National Guard stop, a quick conversation, and a less invasive inspection than the first, then we're back on the road, rolling into our final destination La Paz, in the early afternoon.

We waste no time, eagerly setting out to explore the beautiful malecón promenade along the sea, stretching for nearly four miles, from the central marina all the way past the city. We check out the stunning beaches north of town, stopping into cafés and charming little bars for fresh ceviche caught that very day and ice-cold Pacificos overlooking the water.

"Dang," Luke says, "I'm pretty jealous, nice choice." I smile broadly in agreement.

An epic sunset rolls over the town, streaking the sky with incredible purples and pinks. The water absorbs the colors, infusing them into its very essence, turning into a rich, flowing liquid ink.

The next morning, we grab coffee at a charming little French café, and just like that, our adventure is done. We drive two hours south to the international airport in Baja, so Luke can head back north.

I drop him off, and as we hug goodbye, the tears flow. The moment has come.

My 2,600-mile journey has come to an end—it's all real. I now *live* in Mexico. And I'm totally on my own. I don't know a single soul here.

I wipe away my tears, watching as he disappears with his backpack through the security line and slowly out of sight. It truly is the end of an era. My emotions are a swirling mix of excitement and anticipation.

Heading to the bathroom, I splash some water on my face before making the drive back north to La Paz. I look in the mirror and say out loud, "Well, amiga, are you ready?"

A Mexican woman next to me tilts her head and gives me a strange look—*okay, odd lady talking to herself*—before quickly turning away from the sink to dry her hands.

I can tell from the sound of my voice and the look in my eye in the mirror: I *am* ready.

But also… I'm really not ready at all.

Chapter Nine

Girl on fire.

As I drive home alone, heading back north to La Paz, I'm booking it. I'm not even twenty minutes outside the airport after dropping off Luke when I spot a truck at the top of a hill in the road—its positioning looks odd, it appears to be sideways blocking traffic. I squint to be sure I'm seeing what I think I'm seeing.

As I reach the bottom of the highway and begin the ascent up the hill to get a better look, I notice four men in the back. I think I see them holding... guns. My heart races. My breath quickens.

Surely it must be another National Guard inspection stop, I tell myself, slowing slightly but continuing along the highway. There are no other cars in sight, just me and the truck. I decide to keep my steady pace and drive up the hill.

The truck turns ninety degrees to the left, now sitting half on the highway and half on the shoulder, straddling the white line. As I approach, I see that the men aren't National Guardsmen. They're in dark civilian clothes, their faces covered with bands of red cloth.

Oh gawd, oh gawd, oh gawd. Do I turn around?

They've obviously seen me approaching. I'm far too close now for them not to notice if I suddenly and illegally change direction in the middle of the highway. For a moment, everything in me screams, *Turn around!* But I make a split-second decision to stay on course, lock the doors, and keep my eyes dead ahead.

As I near the truck, the men simultaneously shift their gaze toward my approaching car.

Thirty feet.

Twenty feet.

I can't help it—I glance up and lock eyes with a few of them. I force a smile.

Ten feet.

They size me up for a moment, assault weapons in hand. I pass their truck. Then twenty feet past. I sneak a peek in the rearview mirror, holding my breath. *Holy hell, are they following me?*

But no. They seem to be looking around, gesturing to each other frantically, pointing at something in the other direction.

I keep peeking back—forty feet, fifty feet, sixty feet, a hundred feet—my fingers white-knuckling the wheel.

Phew. They aren't following me.

What the hell was that all about? And why did it have to happen twenty minutes after I found myself alone?

I breathe a deep sigh of relief but remain on high alert for the rest of the drive back to La Paz. *Girl, you're not in Kansas anymore.*

The thing is, just like all the safety warnings I'd read in group chats before making this trek, there are always stories on either side—about certain drives, certain cities, certain levels of risk. Some people find Chicago or Los Angeles incredibly safe, while others experience gang violence or end up in areas where they'd rather be *anywhere* else.

Any city in the world can be safe or unsafe, depending on where you find yourself and when. At this point, I definitely understand that Baja is a bit more wild west than anywhere in the States. But oddly enough, I don't feel unsafe. I'm simply in a country that hasn't yet reached the level of development seen in more industrialized nations, and I've traveled to such places many times before.

It's just time to be a bit more vigilant.

I return to La Paz and begin settling into my new country, city, and home. I'm staying in an inexpensive Airbnb for a week until I can look at a few housing options in person and secure something for my six-month assignment. I'm not looking for anything fancy, I don't plan on spending much time in my place besides staring at the back of my eyelids at night.

I find a great little spot from a sign in a café, run by a Mexican woman who owns several short-term apartment rentals in town. I'm going a bit frugal on lodging—not because I can't afford more, but because I'm trying to recoup the cash savings I lost in the divorce payout.

I move from my Airbnb into my new apartment, which has a simple galley kitchen with a two-burner stove, small sink, no dishwasher, and a smaller-than-typical top-freezer fridge anchoring the end of the white tiled counter. Some colorful Mexican tiles for the backsplash add a bit of zest to the open kitchen and living room. A high-top table with two tall bar-height chairs doubles as a workspace, dining table, and kitchen island. Down the hall, there's a simple bedroom with no door, a queen bed, a metal structure for hanging clothes, and a bathroom right next to it. There's not much of a living room to speak of—just a cheap red sofa from the likes of a Mexican Ikea. At around 500 square feet, it's cute, simple, and all I need for the next six months.

I wander the city on foot from dawn until dusk on my first day, exploring the meandering downtown streets. There are cute cafés, small shops, and tasty restaurants. I stumble across a little farmers market with about twelve room-sized tents selling local goods, T-shirts, honey, and fresh tamales. I grab a coffee and an absolutely delicious breakfast burrito—all for just a couple of dollars.

The gorgeous street art and hand-painted murals around town are incredibly colorful, and I take countless photos, stopping around every corner to admire another piece of free art.

Most buildings are no more than two stories tall. There are a handful of hotels, but even those only rise four or five stories above the narrow streets below. For commerce and clothes shopping, it's mostly small stores, family-owned tiendas. There's a large shopping center at the very edge of town with some surprising staples from the States—Starbucks, Little Caesars, McDonald's, Hardee's, Walmart, Home Depot, a large theater with stadium seating, and a Liverpool, which is basically the Mexican version of Macy's.

This square-mile shopping center is the only major commercial hub in a city with a population of around 250,000, which seems large. But with no towering skyscrapers and with a massively spread-out city footprint of 7,800 square miles, it feels rather small.

It seems La Paz is often overlooked by travelers drawn to the flashier nearby Los Cabos resorts, even though it boasts a wonderful malecón walking path along the waterfront and world-class beaches. Situated on the coast of the Gulf of California, or the Sea of Cortez, at the southern end of the long peninsula, the city has countless delicious street cart taco vendors and grocery stores nestled within their respective neighborhoods.

I'm glad to have my vehicle, as La Paz is so spread out—it makes wandering and exploring far easier. I discover some incredible beaches north of town, with crystal-clear turquoise waters and soft, pristine sand, but they're about a twenty-minute drive away. The water by the malecón, sadly, is a bit polluted from the marina and city runoff, so while I occasionally see someone swimming there, most locals and expats alike don't advise it.

I feel a bit giddy on this first day alone, embarking on my six-month adventure abroad. Already, the thought crosses my mind—*maybe I can stay longer*. If I do an amazing job, perhaps I can extend my stay. But I try to just think of it as a wonderful half-year trial of living abroad, with a safety tether to the United States.

I give myself the day off, only answering a few calls and emails to keep the ball rolling with work. I have my own goals and objectives for this opportunistic, invented role, but honestly, the handful of people above me at the company are so focused on IPO—on proving their worth and meeting all the KPIs toward that endeavor—that my success is largely self-guided, with no one bearing down on me.

At the time, I was still so deeply corporate-driven when it came to defining my value that, rather unbelievably, I wasn't even grateful for that freedom. Instead, I was annoyed that no one found my exciting new position important and pissed that I'd ended up as a pawn between two C-suite executives vying for control over the role and, more importantly, the company's international division. I was left questioning my relevance, worried I wasn't adding value.

Seriously. *I know.*

That societal achievement programming? That shit runs deep.

After dutifully answering my emails, I decide to wander the city late into the evening. As dusk falls, I hear a beautiful voice floating through the air, accompanied by an incredible electric guitar player and saxophonist. The sound drifts into my narrow, palm-shaded street, and I follow it to the frame of an old wooden doorway, golden light spilling onto the sidewalk crisply like a carpet inviting me in.

I step inside and see a small stage tucked into a corner, three musicians framed against a colorfully painted brick wall bathed in moody burgundy light. A few cactuses stand nearby, like extra bandmates. I find a little table close to the stage, order a glass of red wine, and simply sit there, entranced, savoring every moment. It's dark and cozy, and though I don't mind sitting alone, it's not something I'm used to or entirely comfortable doing.

The wine buzz keeps me company.

As I leave, I spot a poster informing me that the city's small orchestra will be playing the next night. Fueled by my cabernet haze, I decide to push myself to get out and about—I promise I'll take myself out on the town in a nice dress for a fancy romantic dinner and the orchestra tomorrow night.

It's worth mentioning that I'm definitely not a dress wearer. I only toss one on for the rare high-end event or occasional wedding, and that's really it. Right before I left for Baja, in my solo summer of attempting to come into my own, I made a point to get out of my comfort zone and challenge myself to wear a dress to work just once. Normally, I wore dark dress pants or jeans (thank gawd for West Coast business casual), sassy heels, a dressier shirt, glasses, and my hair curled or in a neat, low ponytail. I was prim and proper, usually sporting the most conservative pieces from J. Crew, Banana Republic, or Ann Taylor Loft—simple, basic, nothing too fancy.

To thrive in the corporate world, I found I had to be decisive, somewhat aggressive, and tuck away my feminine, expressive energy. I'd also had my fair share of male leadership lingering their eyes too long or making subtle passes, as sadly, many women have in the corporate world. The day I wore the dress to the office, I felt exposed, vulnerable, uncomfortable. Everyone in my department said, "Whoa, look at you! A dress?! Well, you look great." I swear they could feel me shifting uncomfortably. I just didn't feel confident expressing my femininity at work—plus, I'd been a tomboy and athlete all my life.

Hell, in fifth grade, I played on the boys' basketball team because there wasn't a girls' team, and as I was starting to develop, I felt so deeply self-conscious that I duct-taped my boobs down to be as flat as possible. I couldn't have a conversation with my mother about what was happening to my body, we didn't speak of such intimate things as mother and daughter, so duct tape was my superb solution when I had no access to a training bra. Duct tape: wonderful for so many things.

So here I am in La Paz, just a few days into being on my own in a new city and country. I put on that lovely dress I had worn to the office, splash on some makeup, curl my hair, and look at myself in the mirror. I actually feel somewhat confident. I head out into the night, strolling toward a wonderful restaurant just a few blocks away that I had spotted the night before.

At the host stand by the sidewalk, a gorgeous Mexican woman and man look straight out of *GQ*. I smile at them, walking past confidently, but when I reach the end of the block, I stop. I cross the street to the other side so I can get a peek inside from a safe distance, shielding myself behind the camouflage of the sidewalk trees.

I peek inside and see candlelit tables, white linen tablecloths, and groups of couples, families, and friends.

Um, no. This is a terrible idea.

I debate just going to a cute bar I'd passed on the way here, where I could belly up to the counter in a sea of comfy single bar stools. I hem and haw for about ten minutes, circling the block again, looking for other options that feel more solo-friendly.

Jesus, girl, you put the dress on, you look great, you don't even know a single soul in this town yet! Are you going to live or not?! Get your sweet ass in there!

Deep breath.

"Fine," I say out loud to myself as I walk across the street and up to the gorgeous host stand attendants.

"Buenas noches, ¿tiene una reservación?" *Good evening, do you have a reservation?* She doesn't smile and is fairly cold and to the point.

I should have figured that on a Saturday night I'd need a reservation. I smile apologetically and respond in Spanish, "Lo siento, no, tiene una mesa disponible?" *Sorry no, do you have a table available?*

She looks at me a bit terse. "Mesa para cuantas personas?" *Table for how many?*

"Una." *One.* I smile back.

"Solamente una?" *Just one?*

"Si, sola una." *Yes, just one.*

She glances at her host mate with what I'm positive is a look of annoyance. He, on the other hand, meets my eyes with warmth, offering a gentle smile. He says something to her quickly, words I can't quite discern, then holds up one finger to indicate needing a moment before heading off to the dining room to check for availability.

Behind me, a cute couple waits in line, their hands intertwined. I glance back just in time to see him plant a soft kiss on her forehead.

Hollllld Becca. Hollllld.

I smile and stand fidgeting, waiting to be seated. The lack of a companion is still so new to me—it's like missing an appendage. It's bizarre. I can walk into any corporate meeting with my team, executive leadership, or venture capitalists and present, collaborate, or negotiate with complete confidence. In the corporate world, I'd be striding down the halls quickly and powerfully in my high heels, swinging into conference rooms eager to take up space, to be the focal point, to make decisive decisions. That was my element.

But taking myself out on the town in a dress, my hair elegantly curled? That has my legs a little wobbly.

A small bar next door spills the lyrics of Alicia Keys' *Girl on Fire* into the night air. I zone out for a moment as she belts out her anthem of fierce, resilient womanhood, grounded yet unstoppable, rising above the chaos of the world with sheer inner strength. I try to tap into that energy.

"Señorita, tu mesa está lista." *Miss, your table is ready.*

Super. Such an eerily fitting song to escort me inside. I smile broadly, pull my shoulders back, and confidently follow the kind, rather handsome host to my table.

As I step through the elegant white stone archway at the end of the long candlelit hallway leading to the dining room of the gorgeous

Mediterranean restaurant, I take in the scene—the tables filled with people gathered with their loved ones, the entire space buzzing with chatter, laughter, and the warmth of shared company.

For a split second, I feel deeply and terribly alone.

Nope. Not now. I shake the feeling off.

I'm led around the left side of the expansive open dining room, bathed in warm, inviting light. The red terracotta-tiled floor glows under the soft lantern fixtures, their golden light casting a welcoming hue. Gigantic palm-leaf paddle fans swirl the warm Baja evening air overhead, while white drapes, hung from floor to ceiling, add depth and softness to the space. Swaths of flowing white fabric stretch across the sky, acting as a makeshift ceiling in this otherwise open-air restaurant, helping to ground the sounds of conversation and laughter. Greenery spills from every corner, adding a lush vibrancy to the scene.

In the corner, a small acoustic band plays, just a clarinetist and a pianist in dapper attire.

I want to turn to someone next to me and squeal about how absolutely *lovely* this place is.

Instead, I say it to myself silently.

Eek, I love it!

I love my dinner date's enthusiasm.

I'm seated at a table set for four, complete with plates and glasses arranged for a multiple-course culinary adventure. My host pulls out my chair, gets me settled, and promptly returns to the front of the restaurant.

Moments later, my waiter appears—dressed in a crisp white shirt, black vest, and neatly pressed black pants—carrying fresh water and a small amuse-bouche: a locally grown date with mint and a sprinkle of seasoning from the chef.

"Buenas noches, señorita, estamos esperando a otros?" *Good evening, miss. Are we waiting on others?* He smiles warmly, his Spanish slow and deliberate so I can follow.

Can't a lady just take her damn self out?!

I smile back, no turning back now. In what I feel is pretty solid Spanish, sans the gringo accent, I respond, "No, solamente yo." *No, just me.*

I glance around the nearly full restaurant—every other table is filled with couples, families, and groups of friends. Not a single other person is dining alone.

The waiter gives a subtle nod to someone on the dining floor, and since my table was originally set for four, two waiters sweep in and begin clearing the extra settings. Wine glasses, water glasses, dinner plates, salad plates, silverware, and napkins—all removed with an exaggerated clinking and clanking, as if signaling to the entire restaurant:

"Heyyyy everybody, this lady is dining completely on her own on a Saturday night!"

I sit there, momentarily mortified, staring at the vast emptiness of my oversized table. And then, I just start laughing. The whole scene is comical, really—straight out of a *Seinfeld* episode with the excessive noise and the absurd amount of time it takes to make the table fit for one.

I lift my wine glass into the air, grinning as I point at it enthusiastically. My waiter smiles broadly and swiftly hands me the wine list.

Come on, get it, girl, I say to myself, pushing past the initial discomfort and settling into the space—and my own company. I open the beautifully bound menu.

"I'm totally fine with whatever you order," I offer kindly to myself.

"Amazing," I offer back. This is going to be a fantastic date.

I'm delighted to realize I am having one of the most delicious meals of my life—filled with music, too much wine, and incredible food in this unbelievably magical spot.

A birthday celebration unfolds at the table next to me, and I smile, clap, and cheer along as the whole restaurant sings *Las Mañanitas*, the traditional Mexican birthday song. A small Roman torch candle, so common in Mexico, enthusiastically dances atop the cake as it makes its way across the restaurant to the birthday girl. When it finally lands in front of her, it sparkles passionately, its flame rising well above her head. I make a mental note to learn the song, as I only know snippets.

I finish my meal with a lovely aperitif and gelato before promptly escorting myself to the orchestra just a few blocks away, the stars shining down happily to guide my way.

The night air is a divine 74 degrees, with a hint of sea salt sprinkled in. I stroll into the quaint auditorium, which appears to be a small church near the center of town, with folding chairs set up haphazardly. Okay, *orchestra* may have been a bit of a stretch, but I so enjoy the evening of wonderful music.

I'm grinning ridiculously, partly due to my delightful wine buzz but also because I'm so proud of myself. I didn't surrender to the discomfort and head home. I knew in that moment I could choose to feel confident, or I could let my mind win and my emotions spiral. The only one telling me I was lacking anything was *me*.

At that moment, I couldn't completely see myself outside of my own mind's mean chatter. I couldn't yet see just how far I'd already come. I couldn't fully grasp the woman confidently living on her own in a new country, on her own terms, carving out a position she had created entirely from scratch.

Still, I did manage to let go of expectations for my first romantic night out in Mexico and simply enjoy my own company. *Baby steps on the bus.*

Wouldn't you know it—early the next day, I find myself running to the bathroom.

Again.

And again.

And again.

And again.

And again.

I'm losing all those valuable daily fluids, from both ends. And this goes on for about twenty-four hours. I feel absolutely horrible.

I sink into a whirlpool of despair, mentally spiraling downward for days. I am alone in a foreign country, with not a single soul who knows me within two thousand miles, except my Airbnb host. Physically and mentally exhausted, I begin to sob.

I spend about three days like this until I grow so weak I can barely make it ten feet to the bathroom. I start to get a little worried. Then, I start to panic.

Because of my aforementioned Christian Science upbringing, I think my worries about being sick are far worse than most people's.

To this day, when I get sick, I still experience a decent amount of anxiety and fear.

You see, the handful of times my brother and I got sick as kids, we felt like we were failing at being good Christian Scientists. If we got sick, it meant we were letting our parents down. We felt we weren't praying the right way. Sickness was *our* fault because we weren't properly reflecting our true nature as "God's perfect children." At least, that's what the church said.

Looking back, it was rough, to be honest.

I had the realization at six years old that something was really off with the religion, but my caregivers were the ones guiding me, so I buried my fears. I didn't speak of them again. I simply played the part of the enthusiastic learner.

But my brother wasn't so lucky, he developed some pretty severe anxiety and OCD in his teens and twenties from our upbringing that took quite a while to overcome.

I truly believe everyone should have the right to practice whatever religion or spiritual beliefs they choose, but when those beliefs affect a child's *physical health*, it gets a little dicey—blurring the line between parental rights and a child's safety in ways that are difficult to ignore.

So here I sit at thirty-nine—alone, sick in a foreign country, my strength weakening rapidly. I'm still struggling with fearful thoughts creeping in. My mind messes with me. *What's wrong with me? What could it be?* I go down the WebMD tunnel of terror.

***

I sit in my pile of sweat and discomfort, thinking back on these memories, fears soaking me too, and by day three, I'm barely able to get out of bed. I message my Airbnb host, asking about a good hospital nearby for expats. She is so kind, she messages back that she'll be there in ten minutes to take me herself.

I'm not good at accepting help or being seen sick, so I push back. She insists.

Before I know it, I'm swooped up and taken to the hospital just a short drive away. I'm so grateful for her local knowledge and kindness. She speaks rapid Spanish to the front desk, and I'm too tired to follow along.

I'm in to see a doctor within twenty minutes. He speaks to her, and she translates for me: it's a mix of traveler's diarrhea and a bacterial infection—common for a *"new arrival"* as my system adjusts to the local bacteria. I get stomach nausea medicine, Pedialyte, and broad-spectrum antibiotics. He instructs me to follow a very bland diet for the next three days and sends me on my way.

We stop at the front desk to pay, and I panic. My insurance doesn't cover me here.

They inform me that my doctor visit, plus all my medication, is $1,276. I blink several times. I tilt my head.

The front desk woman stares back, smiles, and repeats herself: "Sí. Mil doscientos setenta y seis. O, cincuenta y ocho dólares."

I have a flashback to Spain and the Camino de Santiago. It sinks into my weary mind—of course, she was saying pesos. The entire visit is *sixty-three dollars.*

I could cry. From exhaustion, from joy, from the sheer relief that there is medical care in this world that doesn't aim to bankrupt you or make you *more* ill.

I feel truly blessed in this moment as I'm driven back to my little studio by my kind Airbnb host. She offers to check in on me tomorrow, and I smile, exhausted and hunched over.

"Thank you so very much," I say. "I'm so grateful for your help."

I barely make it inside, take my medicine, and fall straight into bed.

I recover over the next few days and begin settling into a rhythm of work and city exploration around La Paz.

I meet with potential companies around town to acquire for my company, aiming to rapidly expand our presence in Mexico while also helping to grow and organize international marketing efforts. There's a power play happening with my split bosses, and I find it difficult to get backing and clear direction out to the remote teams. My role is unclear, and the collaboration is a mess.

I don't force it. I focus on the local market acquisitions instead. I'm lucky to be able to travel to the various cities around La Paz and

Baja California Sur, exploring business opportunities while playing tourist along the way—staying in great hotels, eating delicious food, and wandering the streets. *Pinch me.*

In the afternoons and evenings, I hit the beautiful beaches around La Paz, dipping into the warm, clear waters—repeatedly baptizing myself into my new tropical life.

I go swimming alongside the insanely majestic whale sharks that come to the area each season, their size and energy taking my breath away. Eventually, I learn that whale sharks are neither whales nor sharks, but rather the world's largest fish—growing up to eighteen meters long. They're known as *gentle giants*, slowly flowing with the rhythm of the sea, guzzling plankton as they glide.

I stuff my face frequently with ceviche and Pacificos.

I think back to the weeks before, to my illness.

What do you want, Becca? The pain of growth or the pain of staying where you are?

What if everything I've gone through is preparing me for what I've always silently asked for?

What if.

Chapter Ten

Alexa, are you there?

I finally meet a few of my neighbors in my cute little apartment building. One woman in particular, Tricia, lives upstairs and is on a similar journey of solo self-discovery in Mexico. She's from the Pacific Northwest too. We hit it off right away and spend quite a few nights on the apartment rooftop, soaking in the sunsets, sipping Pacificos, and chatting about life, love, and being an expat.

She shares all her Tinder escapades, and I decide—it's time.

One evening, we whip up a Tinder profile, and I hit publish. I dub Tricia my *México Paige* since both have been my online dating cheerleaders. I tell myself I may not be ready for a commitment, but I'm *so* ready for some hook-ups.

Anyone at the end of a marriage knows sex is basically non-existent—or hell, at any stage of marriage. I think the Former and I had sex *once* in our last year together, and of course, we were rather inebriated. The rest of our affection was sporadic and had waned considerably in those final few years. We had such lackluster sexual chemistry, and now, as I approach forty, my sex drive is through the roof.

At this stage of my journey, I should know that before I try finding the right person to be in a relationship with, I first have to *be* the right person for myself.

I'm not even close.

I'm not even sure who I am or what I really desire out of this one precious life.

It's a week before Thanksgiving, and I match pretty quickly with a handsome Mexican man named Mauricio. As a Midwestern white girl, I've had a distinct lack of diversity in my dating life, so these beautiful Latino men are a splendid change for me.

We chit-chat a bit, but his vibe is so welcoming that we quickly agree to meet in a neighboring small town on the Pacific side of the peninsula over the weekend since I have a work meeting there.

Two days later, I'm sitting in front of him, having my first date in fifteen years.

We met at a small bar in this quaint town where the tables are mostly lawn chairs and plastic tables. I order a beer.

"I don't usually drink, but what the heck." He orders a beer too, in his rather excellent English.

I smile and contemplate how in the world I would couple with a non-drinker—drinking is such a part of the Midwest culture I grew up in and a key activity with most of my circle of friends.

"How was your day?" I smile, leaning in, genuinely eager to learn more about him.

We hit it off, chatting about navigating Tinder for the first time, how we're both recently divorced, and how we're trying to find our rhythm again in life with our newfound freedom.

"I had a nice, relaxing morning to myself—rode my bike to play tennis by the ocean, worked for a couple of hours, then came to improv class, had a little happy session, and now I'm chilling with you. Later, I'm going to listen to some live music if you want to join. My life is turning into this balanced awesomeness!" He smiles broadly and earnestly, full of enthusiasm and joy.

He's got longer hair tied into a small bun at the nape of his neck, a lovely short beard, surfboard shorts, and a simple cotton t-shirt. A hemp necklace hangs loosely around his neck.

"What's a—uh...happy session?" I ask, tilting my head, smiling and laughing. Thinking to myself, *please* don't be talking about jerking off.

"It's a tobacco sniff you blow up your nostrils—it's intense, invigorating, and grounding all at once. It's called *rapé*, super amazing stuff for opening your crown chakra to the wisdom of the universe."

Something in me sinks, and the judgment gauntlet slams down firmly. Blowing tobacco up your nose in the middle of the day? Crown chakra? Yeah, no.

"Dang. I've never heard of that. It definitely sounds...interesting, I suppose." Nothing in me remotely wants to try this. I'm a bit too corporate, and he's a bit too hippie dude for me, but I sense the makings of a friendship. I enjoy his positivity, if nothing else.

We have a decent rest of the night, chatting about life, yoga, partnership, balance, materialism, living in Mexico—all the things.

"Hey, what are those circular scars on your arms?" I ask, noticing four small, evenly spaced scars in a neat, intentional row on his upper arm.

He smiles broadly. "This is the healing medicine of *Kambô*."

"Kambô?" I tilt my head again, like a curious pup.

"Kambô is a species of frog in the Amazon. A bit of their poisonous secretion is scraped off their backs—it's used in a healing ritual, mainly in South America. It's named after the secretions of the giant monkey frog, and it's used as a traditional medicine in purging or cleansing rituals. It treats many illnesses, including depression and anxiety. I've used it countless times to heal myself and others. I can send you some documentation."

I stare back.

Sure, I had that one summer of coke as a waitress in college, and I dabbled in a bit of mushrooms and ecstasy while partying in my early twenties, but this? This is a bit too woo woo for me.

"Well, that sounds like quite the magical frog. Do you kiss it as well?" I ask, chuckling at my bad joke.

He smiles warmly and laughs wholeheartedly."You know, it's getting late, and I need to drive back to La Paz. I'd love to meet up again soon and hear more about it."

We agree to split the bill and step out into the beautiful, starry desert night. There's zero romantic vibe happening, so we give each other a big hug and talk about staying in touch, even though our cities are an hour apart.

"Have a wonderful drive and restorative sleep!" he shouts as I hop into my car.

I love his uniqueness and think to myself that I could use a splash of his zen energy.

I arrive back home, and as I swing open my front door, I immediately notice that my Amazon Spot, which usually sits on my kitchen table, is missing. My heart pounds in my chest. I scan the room for signs of forced entry or, worse, someone still inside. I cautiously poke my head around the corner into my bedroom, checking if anyone is in the bathroom. Thankfully, there's no one.

I message my host immediately, and she arrives within minutes since she lives just a few blocks away. We look around to see if anything else is missing. My suitcase has been rummaged through a bit, and it appears my AirPods are also gone. The door to the courtyard is ajar, and we realize that the small kitchen window overlooking it didn't have a working lock—someone must have crawled in.

I'm exhausted, frustrated, and uneasy. She kindly offers to pay for the Amazon Spot, but I wave it off, too tired to even process it.

"I just need to sleep," I sigh.

She nods understandingly, and I usher her out before jamming a wood clothes hanger into the window track to ensure it can't be slid open. I crawl into bed, barely sleeping at all, convinced I hear rustling in the night.

I step outside groggily in the morning, heading to my truck to grab a coffee, when I see Tricia coming down the stairs from her apartment. She takes one look at me—disheveled and bleary-eyed—and asks, "What's up? You okay?"

"Ugh, no." I groan. "Someone snuck into my place last night and stole my AirPods and Amazon Spot. Jeanette said this happens in the city from time to time. They tend to swipe things they can easily sell, like electronics."

She stares back at me blankly. "Wait—you were gone yesterday?"

"Yeah. I've been gone all week in southern Baja for work. I just got back last night. Why?"

"Well... I thought you were home. I saw a short, skinny woman with long dark hair come out of your apartment last week."

"Whaaaaat? Out of the front door? That would require my key." I stare back dumbfounded. "I figured she was your cleaning lady or a guest or something. But... there seems to be something weird going on with access because two nights ago, I woke up in the middle of the night to find a silhouette of a man standing in my bedroom doorway. I freaked out, yelled, and he took off."

"I'm sorry, wait—inside your place?! Did you tell Jeanette? How did he get in? This means people we aren't aware of have keys to our homes! How are you still here? Why are you not freaking out?!"

She looks a little sheepish and a lot embarrassed. "Yeah, I know. But I've been here a while, and it's only happened once. Plus, I don't really have anywhere else to go. I mentioned it to Jeanette, but she said no one else has the keys."

"Bullshit. This is *fucking* bullshit. This apartment is full of Airbnbs, and we use old-school keys. I bet they rarely change the locks, and someone has made copies. There could be *multiple* people with copies. I was just robbed, and now I have people strolling out of my place in the middle of the day while I'm away working? *Fuck this.*"

I don't even bother heading for the coffee I so desperately need. Instead, I spin around, march back into my apartment, flick on the lights, grab my suitcase and travel bags, and start shoving all my shit into them.

"Wait, what are you doing? Are you leaving?" Her timid voice wavers.

"Hell yes, I'm leaving! Really? We're *totally* not safe here." I keep packing, flinging everything into my few bags.

"Just like that?" she asks slowly, almost sadly, in disbelief.

"Just like that."

In a matter of two hours, I have everything packed up and loaded into the back of my 4Runner. Traveling light has its advantages.

I message Jeanette: *I'm sorry, but I don't feel secure in the apartment, and I'm leaving. When can you meet me? I would like a refund for my unused rent, five days, and reimbursement for my Amazon Spot and AirPods, as the window and door weren't secure. Security is a basic amenity that should be provided.*

She responds that they'll come to fix the window and lock tomorrow but doesn't apologize. I'm finding this is a thing in Mexico—*sorry* isn't commonly said. People are usually late by 15 to 30 minutes on the regular and rarely apologize when they don't do their job or provide a service as expected. It's an odd cultural thing. The more upset you become, the less they show concern or apologize.

I wait for Jeanette in the dining area. She shows up an hour later.

"Look," I say, "the whole agreement with rent is to provide safety and security for tenants, and the building's security and keys were compromised."

She stares me down, unblinking, calm and expressionless. "I have been speaking with my partner about this issue, and she said you can leave today, and we will refund the five days' rent. But I have been told you would need to file a report with the police station in order for us to be able to determine who is responsible for the electronic losses."

The kind woman who took me to the clinic has vanished.

I stare at her, fuming. "Seriously? You already offered to pay for it, and the security of my place is *your* responsibility!"

"I don't know who has the keys, and I didn't know the window had no lock." Stone. Cold.

I stare back. Fine. I'm over it. I just want to leave. "Give me the rent money." I put out my hand, palm up, staring back firmly.

She hands me some cash, and I head to my car. Tricia is standing behind her in the building doorway. I will truly miss our sunset chats on the rooftop, talking about our adventures in adjusting to solo female traveler Baja life. Before I leave, I walk back over and give her a big hug.

"When I find a good spot, I'll send you a message. I wouldn't stay here. This isn't safe."

I glance back at Jeanette, who's moved off to the side, still watching—her lips curling into a small, wry smile. Somehow, she seems pleased with the situation.

I'm *fuming*.

I head for my truck and drive off without a place to go. I message a few of the other expats I've met around town, as well as the expat Facebook group, and within a few hours, I've thankfully found a new place a bit further off the main drag.

The new place definitely looks rough. There are wires running all over the outside of the building, and bars on the windows and door. *Welp, I guess it's definitely more secure.* I've got that going for me, which is nice. There's another expat living upstairs who's been here for eight years, she says it's very quiet and safe. The owner is motherly, kind, and invites me to dinner at her home that evening.I ask if there are any other spots available, and she says maybe in a week or two.

I message Tricia to please be careful, to put a chair under her door-knob, and to reach out to the same network if she decides to leave.

I'm grateful to have trusted my instincts, gotten out of there quickly, and landed in a new spot. I hope she can do the same, and soon.

It's two weeks until Thanksgiving.

Luke said he was going to spend the holiday with our mutual friends south of Seattle and that, of course, I was invited too. Our friends with the cabin outside of Seattle said to come over afterward for a long weekend of rest and relaxation in the mountains.

I should have taken space.

I shouldn't have escaped the solitude that life was trying to offer me just two months into our divorce being official, but I couldn't spend the holiday alone.With all the travel, I wasn't admitting to myself that I was using survival buoys to keep from fully dipping into solo waters, obviously not ready to submerge.

I didn't yet understand that staying friends is okay, but to heal, you have to step away from what broke you—to get some grounding within yourself first.

I ignore my intuition, wrap up work before the holiday, and fly up to join the Former and our friends for a long holiday weekend in the Pacific Northwest.

It's safe. It's secure. It's some *very old* patterns I wasn't willing—or capable—of letting go of just yet.

Their house is packed full, so we end up sharing a room for the Thanksgiving holiday. Oddly, again, it's not weird. It's like we were never even married. The decade and a half of walking a common life path together is still there, but now our connection is purely friendship.

Everyone asks how we are, and how we're possibly okay sharing a room and a bed.

We actually are. We're getting along beautifully. Everyone is in awe that we're making this transition with such care and kindness. I wasn't sure what I expected, but I'm so glad that we are.

We finish the wonderful, long holiday weekend back at our dear friends' cabin in the mountains, the same one where we spent the Fourth of July—the rustic red, storybook-quaint cabin that sits right on the riverside. It oozes zen with the sound of the rushing river, mist hanging over the pine trees, and the mountains off in the distance at the end of the riverbend. We simply veg out—drink way too much coffee, watch movies, play games, build a miniature ceramic Christmas village, drink too many Old Fashioned Sweets, hit a lot of weed, rinse and repeat. It's wonderful to experience this snowy getaway with old, familiar friends. But by the end of the week, I'm also *annoyed* with myself.

I'm living in the comfort of my past, spending the holiday here with Luke, when I'm craving creating my own cozy space for myself south of the border.

I promise myself that when I get back to sunny Baja, I'll lean in *fully* and start carving my own path.

Chapter Eleven

Oh, Tinder tales.

After my self-imposed yo-yo of escapist travels, I'm back in Baja for a few weeks and I notice my new place is quiet and very secure, but a bit isolating. Without the common area and courtyard of my previous place, I don't see too many people coming and going throughout the day. Fortunately, I get regular interaction in town at my favorite café, where I work most days.

I finally settle into a rhythm for a few weeks—working at my café each day, walking the malecón and city streets in the evenings—but then I need to skip town yet again. This time, it's to gain some work stability, spending a long weekend over in Cancún to meet the Mexico International Team. My goal is to explain my role and purpose, gain alignment, and better support them with marketing for their respective international teams.

I find there's quite a bit of resistance from a machismo sales manager who insists Baja is *his* territory. I tell him to chat with his boss and write it off as big ego syndrome. I'm also fighting hard not to let the lack of corporate support, guidance, role clarification, or funding rain on my expat opportunity parade.

Everyone else on the trip is warm, wonderful, and grateful for the support in growing their international efforts. Despite all the lack of clarity and backing from corporate, I *still* just want to help them all succeed.

As I make my way back home to Mexico's west coast, I start chatting with a new potential love interest on Tinder who seems to share a ton of similar interests with me. He's a creative in the film industry, a surfer, snowboarder, and adventure junkie who actually has his financial shit together. His name is Brody and he's got a really cute smile with dimples, built but not *too* built. Seems promising.

We chat back and forth, he comes to Baja frequently since he's building a home there but still lives in Cali. He's coming down for the Christmas holiday, and we decide to meet up on the Pacific side of Baja in a little surf town just before Christmas. He's staying at a cute seaside surf hotel and suggests I pop over for a day or two.

I text him: *That's a lotta time together for a first hang... what's our safe word if we find each other really annoying?*

He messages back: *idk, adios. Lol. hey, don't want u to feel any weird pressure. Should we just start w surf lessons tomorrow*

Okay, maybe not the finest texter, but I love that he's calling a spade a spade on the pressure front. He says there's a spare bedroom and I'm welcome to use it. Screw it. *Por qué no?* as we say in Mexico. Why not?

I plan to potentially stay the night—vibes pending.

I roll up and see him sitting seaside at a little white plastic patio table with a few guys, toes in the sand. *Oh. I thought it was going to be just us, but I guess not.*

"Hola, I'm Becca. Nice to meet you." I walk up confidently with an enthusiastic wave. Corporate life has at least given me the ability to hold my own as the only woman at a table of men, plus their energy is extremely surfer chill. I totally feel safe.

We size each other up—because a photo can only tell a tiny part of the story. Nothing replaces in-person energy. I can immediately tell we're both as attracted to each other as our profiles promised. We hug, our arms naturally lingering. He introduces me to his brother-in-law and some other friends, all of whom seem kind and friendly. We sip beers, chit-chat, and have a really good evening.

I tell myself: *Young lady, do not get drunk and sleep with him. Do not get drunk and sleep with him. Do not.*

I'm proud to say that after the fourth or fifth beer, when it gets late and he asks if I want to stay with him or take the spare room, I manage to hold my ground. As he asks, our eyes lock—there's definite invitation behind his, but also a shadow of cocky puffery twinkling behind them, dancing with benevolence.

"I'll snag the spare room, thank you." I follow them back to the seaside bungalow. At the top of the stairs, our eyes lock again, hesitating before we head to the opposite ends of the hall.

"Good night, sleep tight." I smile coyly, turn, and head across the hall to pass out in my own cozy room, waves crashing a hundred feet away, the perfect relaxing sound machine coaxing me to sleep.

In the morning, it's definitely a smidge awkward—I haven't spent the night in the same place with a man I was potentially interested in hooking up within fifteen years. But at the same time, it oddly isn't. He greets me warmly with a hug, makes us coffee and some tasty breakfast burritos, and we plan my first real surf lesson. Well, *technically* my second.

I did have one lesson on Waikiki Beach in Hawaii during my five-year wedding anniversary trip, but that hardly counts. I was on a gigantic 10-foot-long blue board, and my surf instructor did all the work—I barely paddled. This time, I'm actually going to try.

Let me be clear: *In my mind, I've always been a surfer.*

This is the woman who began religiously subscribing to *Surfer Magazine* her freshman year of college—in the dead of winter, in landlocked Wisconsin—roaming the dormitory halls wearing Roxy gear as an eager yet clearly clueless poser. You see, I had never touched a surfboard in my life, but I was obsessed with the beauty and energy of the sport—the stunning turquoise barrels I'd seen humans gliding beneath in countless videos and glossy magazine spreads.

Other than that one fake Hawaii lesson, I'd never really given it a go.

Let's just say I was insanely eager, but today, the waves are a little strong.

He's trying to help me, but he's a little too coachy, a little too controlling—not really letting me flow with the energy of the ocean and trust my own body's capabilities. Oh, the irony! It's also a little unnerving having him stare straight up my crotch as I paddle in my bikini.

On the fourth wave, he yells for me to paddle as hard as I can and pushes me into it. It all happens in an instant—I get flipped rapidly, thrown to the bottom of the ocean, twisting and turning in the washing machine of darkness. I barely get to the top before another wave hits. Then another.

Panic starts to creep in.

I swam competitively from ages 10 to 18, then rowed for a year in college, winning a Big Ten Championship my first year. After that, I spent four years as a starter on my collegiate water polo team, playing almost every single match. That involved sprinting back and forth in twelve feet of water while getting punched, kicked, and nearly drowned by opponents' grappling hands.

Despite all of that water comfort I possess, at *this* moment—I need to get the hell out of the water.

The rip tide is strong, and I get pulled and pummeled by countless waves before I finally manage to crawl out and flop onto my back on the beach, utterly exhausted and breathless

This surfing shit is *legit*.

I'm hooked.

He's kind when he comes out of the water, but my tomboy competitive edge is definitely kicking in, no damsel in distress for this gal. I'm annoyed and disappointed in myself, but I attempt to play it cool, plastering a huge smile across my face.

"Damn, that was a hell of a rush! Are you hungry?"

We call the surf lesson good and spend the rest of the day eating tacos, devouring sushi, catching the sunset...along with far too many margaritas.

Late that evening I find myself in the dark stairwell of the seaside palapa hotel suite, saying goodnight to him, and then, promptly shoving my tongue down his throat.

And then it's *on*.

He's pushing me into my room—clothes flying, limbs grabbing, bodies grinding, thunderous groans and then...silence.

I wake up in the morning and look over, very aware of where I am. He's still next to me in the sea of sheets. Waves crash melodically outside, and the dried palm leaf ceiling above me has small, random holes where the sunlight spills through, creating a disco-ball effect, sprinkling rays of daylight throughout the room.

I'm a smidge hungover. Okay, a *lot* hungover.

He wakes up, looks over at me with a smile and a devilish grin.

"That was fun," he says, reaching for me, pulling me in for a warm kiss.

I smile back shyly.

"We did pretty damn decently."

Which translates to: it went about as well as blackout, drunken, first-meeting sex can go.

"Want a toke?" He lights a joint, taking a deep drag then handing it to me, and we puff away, staring at the texture of the palapa ceiling like a work of art, listening to the waves. We chill in bed for a while. I *really* don't want to get up and do the whole broad daylight checking out my naked body thing.

I stretch coyly, sitting up and wrapping the sheets around my chest, peeking around for where my clothes are strewn about the bedroom. I look down at the crisp white sheets.

Oh dear lord baby Jesus. Blood. *Everywhere.*

We are talking a full-blown menagerie of varying shades of red, splattered across the sheets *à la* a priceless Jackson Pollock painting—yet infinitely less aesthetically pleasing.

"Oh gawd." I stare blankly, mouth agape.

"What?" He finishes the joint and slowly sits up next to me. "Ohhhh shit." He stares at the bed. Then back at me. Eyes wide.

He sees the look of horror on my face and thankfully starts to laugh. "It's all good, no worries. This is why we have housekeeping."

I smile sheepishly, grateful for the ease added to the moment.

We pop out of bed, momentarily forgetting our nakedness, strip the sheets, and pile them in the corner. I scribble a little note that says: Lo siento!! (*Sorry!!*) and place a 500-peso bill on top. They'll probably just toss them straight into the garbage, but I feel terrible leaving them like that.

We get dressed and head downstairs, where his brother-in-law greets us with a knowing grin. We grin back—full-blown *yeah, we banged* energy. His eyes go wide, a sly smile forming as he tilts his head in a silent *Uh-huh... yeah, I heard ya.*

We all head to enjoy breakfast by the sea.

"What a *fucking cunt!*"

I jerk my head up from my menu, eyes bulging out of my head.

The surfer dude is staring at his phone, *fuming*. My ears start ringing as I try to process what I just heard.

"This bitch... damaged my short-term rental... ignored the sign... what a cunt!"

The word slices into my ears again.

He's *going off*, totally melting down. I flag down the waiter—I desperately need a coffee.

I get that the situation is frustrating, but that word is my least favorite in the English language.

Then, suddenly—the *N-word* has joined us for breakfast.

I freeze. Jaw. Hitting. The. Sandy. Floor.

All the brunch boundaries? *Crossed.*

"Um... why are you using that word?" My tone is all curiosity laced with heavy reproach.

He picks up on my disgust. "Ohhhh, yeah, no—my daughter's best friend is Black. I have a ton of Black friends. We've talked about it. It's cool."

Ummmm. No.

I do not have the hungover mental capacity to unpack the full scope of *everything wrong* with this justification. I should have thrown down some cash, called it good, and left.

But—well. The sex was fantastic.

We finish the day hanging out, but his face is mostly buried in his phone, and I'm still mentally replaying his terrible vocabulary choices.

I am so desperate for physical connection that I brush it off.

I *know*, I *know*, I *know*.

Not proud of myself either. Would you believe I stayed the night again—and banged him *again*—before taking off the next morning?

Well, I did.

No judgment, remember? I get it. It's *really* hard not to.

The next morning we share a quick hug, and he says he'll message me. I just smile, nod, and wave as I hop into my truck, not bothering to get into it.

On my drive home, my mind conveniently deletes most of the things that made my stomach churn about him. Maybe his anger got the better of him, and it really *was* a terrible rental guest situation. Maybe that's why he was glued to his phone the whole time, largely ignoring me on our first date.

I said I wasn't looking for commitment, that I just wanted some flings—but deep down, I think I just want to feel *really* desired by someone.

I am caught up in the fear of not being chosen. Of not being good enough.

So, I lean in further. I temporarily soothe myself with a nice, familiar, good old-fashioned chase. Perhaps I am confusing dysfunction and a bit of chaos with love and chemistry. Perhaps I'm ignoring the very things right in front of me that are causing anxiety in my relationships.

Wonder where I could have learned that?

***

I'm back in La Paz just a day before I'm set to fly home to Wisconsin for Christmas. At this point, my dad is almost completely bedridden and getting considerably weaker. Although he desperately wants to stay true to his Christian Science beliefs and make my mother happy, he has finally succumbed to taking prednisone and blood pressure medication. He's even gone to a few doctor visits after an emergency urinary tract infection, one he waited far too long to get care for, nearly sent him septic and landed him in the ER.

He was so terribly frail when he asked me on a recent call if I would be coming home.

This daddy's girl wasn't sure how much time he had left, and every day, I found myself thinking: *What if today is the last day we speak?*

***

I fly home to spend Christmas with my family—the first Christmas as a divorcée. This is my first Christmas without Luke, who's still on the West Coast, spending the holiday there. The first Christmas without my Former's family. Without the cute nieces and nephews I've watched grow up. It's a lot to process, and so I largely don't.

My dad wants to order his absolute favorite pizza in the whole world, Paisan's. It's the single restaurant that has been the cornerstone of our family holidays and birthdays. I loved it so much I waitressed there all through college, paying my tuition and eating it at a discount. Of course, Mom and Dad would come in every few weeks for a shift to see me, and to devour their perfect Italian thin-crust pizza.

We all gather in the dining room. My dad struggles for ten minutes to make it up the stairs between labored breaths. I step in to help ensure he makes those final steps to the table.

My mom, dad, brother, and I sit together, grateful that he is able-bodied enough to join us. He smiles and eats with such appreciation and joy, but I can see the sadness in his eyes underneath. That desperation—knowing his body is failing him but his spirit is still so bright, strong, and vibrant, still fighting to be alive.That sadness that prayer has not turned things around.The despair that he can't show the children he loves so deeply, or his wife, that his spiritual state is strong enough to heal himself.

I keep a huge smile on my face through dinner, keeping things light and enthusiastic, but there is so much worry, fear, and sadness buried deep inside me. I am *terrified* watching his physical decline. No one prepares you for watching your parents age, yet alone rapidly deteriorating. Pair that with the weight of this first holiday on my own, and I don't dare let more than a peep of that collective sadness in.

It's like putting a pinhole in the Hoover Dam—letting a tiny stream jettison into the air—knowing, *Yep, that's about enough release for now.*

It's all a lot to process. A mountain of unknown mental trauma built up.

My brain helps me out with a lot of dissociation, detaching myself from the reality staring me down.

***

The day after Christmas, I find a post-it note in the office in my mother's handwriting:

"Becca + Luke are just in a mental place." It's sitting on top of a *Christian Science Monitor*.

Meaning—she was doing prayer work to "know the truth," to affirm that we'd heal the *mental place* she believed was at the root of our relationship issues. That we were just stuck in mortal mind and ego, and if we could return to Love (capital L), we'd find our way back to each other. It was a total Christian Science spin—glossing over reality with spiritual positivity.

Breathe, Becca. Breathe.

I feel so guilty, but I just can't be here. I just *can't* handle all of this.

I mention that I feel awful for heading back south so soon after the holiday, given my dad's weak state. My dad knows how hard this is for me.

"What are you going to do here? Watch me lie in bed?" He smiles at me from under the covers, his voice still somehow warm despite the weakness. "Go, sweetie. Adventure for us both."

I smile, hug him tightly, and fight back a tsunami of tears.

I'm back on a plane, heading south to Baja just a couple of days before New Year's.

I need *a lot* of numbing after the holiday, so I take myself out on the town in La Paz for New Year's Eve, solo, for a heaping pile of chile rellenos and an excessive amount of Mexican white wine.

The northern Baja peninsula, just south of Tijuana, cultivates some incredible Mexican wines that, in my humble opinion, give Cali a solid run for its money. Who knew?

I spend New Year's Day on my own, craving sea time. I drive back to the little Pacific-side surf town where I previously made a disaster of the perfectly crisp white sheets with Tinder Tourette's Boy.

I stare at the ocean—so gorgeously calming and serene. I stare at the colorful rack of surfboards at the seaside surf shop—so ridiculously beautiful and enticing. Something inside me tugs at my core. I ignore it.

I stop in town for some cheap shrimp tacos at the spot that is quickly becoming my favorite. It's just a small tin shack with a deep fryer and a hot plate for warming tortillas, plus some plastic spoons and Tupperware buckets filled with salsa, sauces, cilantro, diced coleslaw, and guacamole sauce. A satisfying dollar per taco.

I stuff three into my face happily, served by the joyful, plump Mexican grandma who offers me fresh agua de jamaica, *hibiscus-infused water*, to wash them down.

Two older gentlemen are cheerfully chatting next to me, and we strike up a conversation. They are charming, intelligent, and witty—one speaking in a delightfully fun British accent, the other in Russian.

They invite me to their little full-moon party that evening.

Fuck it. Por qué no? *Why not?* It's my Mexico new life motto.

Following their hand-drawn napkin map of the oddly angled, meandering dirt roads, I manage to arrive at their little seaside casa compound just as the sun is starting to set. After a few wrong turns, of course.

I'm cheerfully welcomed inside the gate and handed a margarita. Fresh fish and shrimp sizzle on the outdoor grill, filling the air with delightful, enticing deliciousness. People are buzzing around—chatting, laughing, cheering. It's a mix of old souls who've known each other for decades and a few new friends like myself.

There's the typical friendly chit-chat:

"How did you come to be in Mexico?"

"Where are you from?"

"Where are you going?"

These are some of my favorite conversations, and in this hodgepodge of people, you *never* know what you're going to get.

I'm running from myself.

I'm running to find myself.

I'm running from my past.

I'm running to retirement.

I'm running from the law.

I'm running to a new life.

I'm running from my ex.

Stories all about *searching*.

Following signs. Trying to do better. Failing. Trying again. And again. And again. And again.

I'm in good company.

I find myself on the rooftop with just the Brit, speaking of the beauty and serenity of Baja when the full moon begins to rise over the jagged black silhouette of the Sierra de la Laguna Mountains.

I gasp. The moon is *massive*, so absolutely stunning and magnificent it takes my breath away. The clouds gather around it in a scattered veil of support. We simply stare in silent awe and admiration. The Russian—who, it turns out, has been the Brit's best mate for decades—hops up onto the roof joyfully and exclaims, "The sea is dancing with the moon!"

We turn towards the sea in the opposite direction and see the moonlight sparkling brilliantly across its surface. We soak it in, commenting on the importance of seizing the moment.

In perfect unison, we all turn to look at each other and yell, "Let's go for a swim!"

Fueled by margaritas, a bit of weed, and pure full-moon energy buzzing through our veins, we sprint past the party toward the crashing ocean a few hundred feet away.

A few guests jokingly yell after us, "What's on fire?!"

I turn back over my shoulder mid-stride, "Us!"

We run straight into the sea, stripping naked without a second thought.

We laugh and splash with no judgment of each other's bodies. No gawking. Just pure, childlike enjoyment. I float on my back and stare up at the *stunning* full moon.

My naked body is enveloped in the warm liquid black, the golden moonlight dancing on the surface like a coating of oil dancing on top. My body is tenderly cradled by the salt water, gently rocking me to the rhythm of its nurturing, soothing, unfathomably vast sea body.

The expansive energy seeps into my skin, my bones.

Maybe it's the margaritas. Maybe it's the weed.

But something *shifts*.

I can feel the vice grip I've had on controlling my life's trajectory starting to loosen. I am beginning the journey of coming into my own. I just flatlined—and the sea surged through the core of my heart like a defibrillator, sparking my pulse back to life.

The sea spills into my ears, whispering...

You know, you don't have to be that person anymore.

I feel so silently loved. So nourished without expectation. So deeply understood. The calm quiet surrounding me suddenly makes an idea that was simmering beneath the surface abundantly clear.

In my bliss, I make a mental note to message my landlord in the morning.

Because what I've been doing so far in Baja? It's been a *lot* of distracted numbing with busyness and alcohol.

But trying to outrun emotions is about as easy as trying to lose your shadow in the afternoon sun. I thought I was bobbing and weaving pretty effectively, yet the entire time, there it is. Lurking. Waiting. Right behind me. Waiting for me to turn around and face the dark, deeply buried emotions that needed tending to.

***

I sleep in my truck—not just to avoid driving back to La Paz after drinking, but also because I've been told nighttime is when the cows, goats, and horses like to mosey onto the highway.

I do love a good Irish goodbye, but we all managed to exchange numbers the night before. In the morning, the casa still appears quiet, so I leave without saying farewell.

As I start the engine, I'm flooded with the memory of that burning urge—under the full moon's light—to act without delay. I grab my phone and fire off a message to my landlord. I thank her for the great new space but let her know I need to be out by the end of the month. It's the second of January, and my lease is month-to-month. She says she's sad to see me go but understands. And just like that, it's done.

I don't know exactly where I'm moving, but I think, *Girl, you've been wanting to be a surfer your whole life. Why don't you go live by the sea and actually do it?*

You're turning forty this year. What the hell are you waiting for?

Until recently, I had completely forgotten that my younger self desperately wanted to learn to surf. I buried her desire under the corporate climb.

Damnit—it's fucking time.

I work for a few weeks before heading back to my corporate office in Portland for their ten-year anniversary party and to check in with my boss and coworkers. I was feeling vulnerable down in Mexico and wanted some face time to remind everyone I was still kickin', and making progress. And I was. I had several solid opportunities for acquisitions and was gaining traction with the international marketing teams.

But as I stroll into the building, something has shifted. The luster is gone. There's something lifeless about the vibe inside that I hadn't fully noticed before. I look at everyone's faces, their body language—it all feels so much more forced, fake, robotic than it did just three and a half months earlier when I left.

Maybe they had shifted? But I knew it was *me*.

I had spent so much of my life learning to conform, to ignore my boundaries, to say yes to things I didn't want to do, to manipulate to get what I needed.

A chameleon.

I never demanded integrity because I had none.

And now, I could see how truly inauthentic my life had been.

It *is* nice to see my amazing co-workers during the visit, but I can't get out of the office fast enough. As I exit the building, the elevator stops on the ground floor. The doors glide open and Robert steps into the elevator, a ghost from my past drifting right in front of my eyes. We lock eyes for a moment, saying an awkward hello. The memory of my past self makes me shudder. I wonder if he's thinking about our disaster of a Vegas encounter. I hustle out of the building and don't look back.

And would you believe me if I told you that, while I was in Portland, I got a few rather romantic texts from Brody—so I decided to add a last-minute stop outside of San Francisco?

Well, kids... I'm sorry to say, I did.

He was a *lifeline*.

At breakfast the next morning, after hooking up the night before, I watch as he stares at his phone, barely looking up at me. He says he has a few hours of work to tackle so I offer to leave him to it, spending some time checking out his town. I end up waiting around all day, assuming he'll reach out when he's free. He never does.

Finally, as dusk falls, I cave and text: *So, meet back at your place?*

He replies: *Oh, hey, ya! We're home.*

Ah. Okay. Good thing I've been killing time for five hours. Nobody is busier than a person not truly interested in you on a three-day visit.

Honestly, in retrospect, I just wanted a warm body. And that's all I was getting. I was chasing someone unavailable, and I turned his distance into a commentary on *my worth*. Some part of me just wanted to be loved so badly. I mistook his pullback as a challenge, something I had to overcome. Something I had to earn. As if proving myself would make him choose me.

Dear Lord.

I realize this isn't so different from how I bonded with my mother. Winning swim meets, bringing home ribbons and trophies, that's what got her excited. That's when she seemed proud. That's when she lit up. I had learned that winning was how I proved myself.

I carried that into the corporate world—always trying to earn the ribbons and trophies to prove my worth.

And now? I was doing the exact same thing with him.

I left a few days later, but I'm embarrassed to say I kept texting him. Kept chasing. Kept sending love his way. Returned only with his self-obsessed vibe.

He would message, say he was coming to visit, then go dark.

What I didn't understand then was that chasing unavailable people is a sneaky way for the ego to avoid intimacy. Chasing unavailable people is self-abandonment.

People can only meet us where they've met themselves, and we're only capable of giving to others what we've given to ourselves. And I wasn't capable of nurturing myself yet. I was romanticizing someone who was unavailable—because, deep down, that pointed to my own unmet needs. My own wounds.

And my emotional wounds? They were festering.

Damn near in need of partial amputation at this point. Yet I wasn't seeking medical attention.

I was still in basic survival mode—clinging to physical company and sex without *true* intimacy.

Which is about as pointless as relying on chewing gum for nourishment.

Lots of action. Not a lot of sustenance.

I blame my discontentedness on his emotional unavailability, yet I had barely allow an inch of space to process my own emotions. No person or relationship can offer you a sense of wholeness and completeness. That has to come from within, and I am so disconnected from my own nurturing energy that I desperately need to give myself.

I am still seeking this outside of myself. We engage in fixing or saving others even if all the red flags are there, because those red flags feel like home. I was hopping date to date to distract myself but wasn't taking the time to heal from my wounds from my divorce.

In my mind, I was so happy it had finally ended, and we were great friends...so what wounds are there to heal?

Wrong. Ohhhh. So. Wrong.

Denial isn't just a river in Egypt, as Dad would say.

Chapter Twelve

A Spider's Web

I land back in Baja with a few weeks to go until my move to the coastline. I purchase my first surfboard—an eight-foot foamie Wavestorm—and feel ridiculously pleased with myself. Next thing I know, I'm packing up *yet again* for my move to my little teeny-tiny dirt road town by the sea, my foamie board adorned with its chillax rasta colors strapped to the top of my truck.

Damn, it feels good to be a gangster.

I arrive in my adorable, quiet village and wake up to the Sierra de la Laguna mountain foothills rolling across the horizon just outside my patio door. I'm surrounded by cheerful bright yellow concrete walls made to look like adobe and an aged cactus patio railing that looks a lot like sun-bleached teak with Swiss cheese holes. I'm living above the only tiny market in the village, and I wake to no traffic, no people, *no nada*.

Just desert beauty. Barking dogs. The occasional rooster crow. The sight and subtle rumble of the sea a couple hundred yards to the right.

And do you know what I did on my very first day?

You guessed it—I still wasn't done avoiding healing myself *just* yet.

I hop into another Tinder date instead.

I agree to meet my date for a surf after a few days of texting, he caught my attention with his enthusiasm and the fact that he was an amazing communicator. Always responsive. Actually asked good questions. Seems promising.

Enter Armando.

Tall. Athletic. Bald. A Mexican surfer with deep emerald-green eyes and a smile that coyly pulls you in.We meet on the beach for a surf, and there is immediate sexual chemistry. He's got fabulous, self-confident energy. We hang, chat, and surf.

Unlike Brody, he's an extremely patient teacher, and I'm delighted to snag a few good waves. Afterward, we lazily lie in the sun, the warm sand enveloping our worn-out bodies.We're both starving, so we make a plan to grab some food in town, 15 minutes away.

He follows me back to my place on his off-road, sexy BMW motorcycle, covered in his weathered black biker gear.He pulls up, peels off his helmet in his dusty gear, sweaty, sexy, head glistening.

A bit of a Mexican Mad Max.

Uh-oh.

"Hey, do you want to come in and siesta before lunch?" I smile down at him from my doorway above the little market.

He smiles slyly. No words needed.

I want to have boundaries. I *want* to wait.

But more than anything, I just want to numb myself with physical connection.

We twirl into my room, kissing while clothes come off like batter flinging from a mixer, splattering around my little apartment. I find myself upside down, with a lovely view of the mountains outside my window, pressure and pleasure coming from interior spots I *didn't even know I had.*

I'm moaning at the volume of a five-alarm fire warning system and distantly hope the sweet older gentleman who runs the market below doesn't think I'm being attacked. These concrete walls reverberate like a confessional in a monastery, every sound bouncing back with full moral clarity.

He adds *more* pressure, then—

"Oh my Goooooooooooood!"

The pleasure and warm, slow-flowing release from the depths of my being is absolutely divine—an energy unknowingly damned, *desperate* to be freed.

I lay there laughing out of pure delight, my body buzzing beautifully. Ever so slowly, I peel my head up off the side of the mattress to look right side up again, then glance down at him, meeting his gaze—eyes sparkling with pure delight and satisfaction.

Then I realize the bed feels rather... damp.

"Um, oh gawd. Did I, um... I didn't..." My eyes go wide, my head tilts to the side, forehead furrowed. "Did I... I didn't...?"

He smiles back.

"Nooooooo," he sings playfully. "This is the cascade from your beautiful vessel that creates humanity. You seem to have not been... properly tended to in quite a while."

My face flushes ridiculously red.

What man says things like that?

"I had no clue I was... capable of such a release."

I look up at him, grinning like the Cheshire Cat, and we both burst out laughing.

I toss my head back off the edge of the mattress, staring outside, delighted with the new perspective. I'd had such limited sexual adventures since my early twenties. Luke and I had a very *meh* sex life for us both—he wanted to dominate, and I wanted our romps to be passionate and heartfelt.

I am definitely not completely comfortable in my own naked skin at this moment. I need emotional connection before diving into bed again with someone, but I'm faking it—nicely. To him. And to myself. I allow myself to be temporarily blind to my own insecurities and my need for deep human connection at this stage in my life, covering it with the band-aid of fleeting physical pleasure.

I mean... but the *pleeeaaasuuure*.

As far as distractions go, it's a *divine* choice.

My phone buzzes. As I watch him head to the bathroom, I take a peek.

My dad has been hospitalized. An ambulance had to come, and he was rushed to the ER.

For my dad to accept that level of medical care, I know it has to be bad.

Armando comes back to find my face welling up, tears beginning to spill.

I *try* to hold them in. There is an immediate, palpable awkwardness.

I manage to squeak out something about my dad not doing well. He slowly gathers his things, says sorry that this is happening to my dad, and quickly exits.

This should have been the massive red flag.

I collapse onto my bed and cry. All I want in this moment is to be hugged and comforted. I feel like a complete idiot for diving right into bed with him. Who leaves like that after *just* being inside someone?

Someone who is fun, very communicative, and adventurous—but emotionally unavailable, that's who. Otherwise known as, at this juncture in my healing, my perfect match.

He texts a while later: *I know you have things on your mind, and I don't want to interfere. If you want to talk, let me know. If you want to get distracted and continue with the plan, we can pick it up where we left off. Thanks so far for everything, and I hope things are as good as they can be with your family. Health is a big issue.*

I text back: *Thank you. It's been rough with the family. I was having a down moment processing some news about my dad's health. I'm driving to coffee in a few moments. I'm still continuing with the plan for the day. You're welcome to join me, or we can connect another time when it feels less awkward for you.*

I didn't really want to go anywhere that afternoon, but I desired company in this moment of fear and loneliness, so I pretended I wasn't terribly scared by the news of my dad's health and invited him anyway.

We meet at a cute coffee shop in town an hour later. It's definitely awkward. He wants to talk about pleasantries and avoids anything that could stir up emotions. He spends a good portion of our time together with his face in his phone. I just want some company, so I take it. I can feel my face flush, my heartbeat quicken, a knot in my stomach. I ignore the gut feeling.

We hang out the rest of the day, and I push the terrifying news about my father being admitted to the ER out of my mind. We have a decent enough time, and then in the evening, he heads south back to Cabo San Lucas where he lives. Later that night, he texts me tips on how to make smoothies and other fun yet odd nutritional facts. There are no texts inquiring about how my dad might be doing. Earlier that day, he made a comment about the diversity of spiders, snakes, and other creatures in Baja.

I text him a photo of a large black spider I find in my place that evening and tell him I'll have to face my immobilizing fear of spiders before I can sleep.

He texts back: *I think your journey may be taking you where the lessons are.*

That statement will prove to be so ironically true, especially coming from him.

Chapter Thirteen

Spin time hits.

My cozy place above the market emanates solitude, with nothing in sight each morning but the mountains and the desert landscape. It's the first time in my adult life I've lived full-time away from the buzz of city life. Instead of the hum of cars, the hum of nature inspires me to finally begin meditating. I'd heard from countless people how helpful it is for centering one's mind, and with the news that my dad was in the ER—albeit stable now—I was overwhelmed with anxiety over his constant health battles. I was willing to give it a go. I start using a meditation app and begin meditating for twenty minutes each morning after breakfast.

Why am I thinking constantly throughout each session? I thought the point was to silence the mind. I Google whether this is normal and I'm reassured that many people have the misconception that we shouldn't have thoughts during meditation. A few masters on the topic share that it's simply the nature of the mind to think, and that you can't stop thinking by thinking about it.

I read that the idea of meditating is simply the act of practicing kindness toward yourself when thoughts arise—not getting frustrated, but allowing yourself to witness the thoughts, let them go, and then attempt to calm the mind again. The purpose is to be aware of the thoughts, to see them with curiosity but not engage. It allows you to begin witnessing your mind, your thoughts, and to start developing awareness.

To witness means simply noticing what is, without reacting, labeling, or trying to change it. *Ah, so the thoughts have a purpose!* I stop being so judgy with myself and allow the process to be what it is.

I also notice that when I begin a guided meditation, I can't do the body scan—I can't actually feel my body or what is happening in it. It's an odd sensation that's hard to describe. I know this disconnect between mind and body is likely not a good sign, but I don't know how to fix it so I decide to keep plugging away at it, trying a little each day.

Reading has become a favorite way to spend my desert days, so when Armando mentions a favorite book of his, *A New Earth* by Eckhart Tolle, I download it on my Kindle and dive in. My dad loves to write, the entire back wall of our family room growing up was nothing but books, so naturally, I love reading. As a kid, I'd be told it was time for bed but would sit under my covers with a flashlight and my stuffies, reading into the wee hours. This probably also explains why I needed glasses by seventh grade.

Despite the wonky Christian Science upbringing that pushed me away from religion—and most conversations involving God in my adult life—the word *God* still carries a lot of guilt, shame, and anger from my childhood. But I find I still have a strong spiritual curiosity in me. In fact, that was part of the reason I started to feel misaligned with Luke. He is an atheist, and although I'm not religious, I had always enjoyed the work of the Dalai Lama—*The Art of Happiness* was a favorite—along with other light spiritual and ethereal existence books like *The Alchemist, The Celestine Prophecy, The Untethered Soul, The Seven Laws of Spiritual Success*, and even the subtle nods in *Eat, Pray, Love*. They had always inspired my curiosity about searching for *more*, but in the last decade or so, I did very little to pursue that curiosity. Now, I'm so happy to have the time and space to begin again, learning what a higher source means to me on my own terms.

As I settle into my new place, an absolute torrential downpour begins, which is highly uncommon for Baja in February. The region only sees a dozen or two rainy days each year, usually during hurricane season. The sound of the rain is deafening, and I notice water starting to leak through the ceiling. Then a few drips run down the wall. Then the ceiling gets soaked, and the lovely new white plaster begins to crumble, falling in clumps onto the floor. Within three hours, 80% of my new place is wet, with about an inch of water covering the floor.

I start gathering my suitcase and bags, stacking them in the last dry corner. By the evening, the rain finally lightens, clearing to blue skies and sunshine. The desert ground and landscape soak up the much-needed moisture like a sponge. A few hours later, looking outside, it's as if no rain occurred at all—but inside my new place, it's close to uninhabitable.

I get my landlord from downstairs, and he looks around, shrugs, and says, "Abre la ventana." *Open the window.*

The American in me gets rather angry, demanding a refund—this isn't inhabitable, the structure is failing! I wave my arms about, pointing, my eyes practically bulging out of my head. He stares at me, tilting his head. No response.

I firmly state, "I am going to look for a new place."

He simply says in his calm, broken English, "Okay. You stay here until find new place for you." Like this situation isn't even remotely a big deal.

"Of course I can stay here, I've paid for a month's rent!" I stomp off. *Why can't I just get bloody settled somewhere?*

I don't allow myself time to wallow. Instead, I open the front door and windows. I ask the landlord for a fan, of which there is none, and vow to find a new place tomorrow after I've caught up on work and had my coffee.

I mention the flooding to Armando, who feels the fan is a solid option. *Sigh.* In some instances, Americans simply demand things get resolved a smidge faster. He quickly realizes that path isn't going to cut it and sends me a few promising places to rent. We continue texting flirtatiously about life, ideas, spirituality, and interesting recipes, distracting me from all the burdens weighing on me. We make plans for the weekend—for more playful sex and surf. I find I'm really looking forward to seeing him. All the feelings of not being seen or cared for when he was here last melt away into the endless sea of future desires.

Two days after my apartment floods, and a day before we're set to hang out again, I begin to feel awful. A sore throat, fever, chills, and a terrible wheeze settle in my lungs. A brutal cough forms. I text Armando to cancel. He replies: *No worries. Get better soon.*

And then, I find myself feeling so awful that it makes the La Paz sickness look like a cakewalk.

By day two, I'm standing in the kitchen, barely able to take in air. I'm wheezing badly. Then the cough hits, and I cough and cough and cough and cough and cough—so hard I turn and throw up into the kitchen sink. It actually feels like I might cough up a lung. I can't catch my breath. I don't know what's happening, and it occurs to me that I need to go to a hospital.

I sit down, trying to regain my breath, and eventually convince myself it's just my old Christian Science illness-anxiety. Everything is okay.

Then it hits me—oh my *gawd*—all that rain. Obviously, this has happened here before. I push my finger into the still-damp stucco ceiling, and it sinks in a half inch. *Oh shit.* There must be mold in here. I'm terribly allergic.

Night is falling, I'm exhausted, I can't breathe. Panic sets in. I grab a pillow and blanket, head out to my truck, and try to sleep there. I suddenly realize I have nowhere else to go and no one close by to call. I decide I'll throw money at this problem and get a room at that cute seaside hotel I saw first thing in the morning.

I feel as though I'm dying but I find I'm less terrified than when sickness struck me in La Paz. It's like that illness trained me for this one. I barely sleep, focusing instead on my meditation practice and I *try* to see the positives in this situation. Otherwise, I'll dig myself into a mental black hole that'll be hard to crawl out of. I picture a nice, dry hotel room right above the sea tomorrow night and tell myself, *You're okay, you're fine, you're safe. You'll feel better in just a day or two more.*

I wake at dawn feeling like a disaster. Luckily, the market is right below my place. I mange to make my way down to grab an Electrolit and some crackers. Then I head back up to my place, load everything into my truck in four utterly exhausting trips, and move—yet again. This time just a minute up the dusty dirt road to the simple seaside hotel.

I pull up to my new place, put the truck in park, and see a text from a co-worker. It's a video from our company-wide update call. I press play and watch, stunned, as our CEO's voice wavers then cracks. The Steve Jobs-wannabe, who rarely shows an ounce of emotion, is fighting back tears. He says it's time to step down.

Despite all the fights, the repeated department dis-mantlements and re-mantlements, the lack of direction, the lack of thanks for my work or my team's work, I *do* feel for the guy. And, in this moment, I feel grateful to him. He exported me to Mexico, giving me the distance from the insanity I need dearly in life right now.

I finish the video and quickly put it out of my mind, happily leaving the chaos of corporate life in the rearview mirror. I barely make it up the stairs to my new place, unload nothing from my truck, collapse into bed, and sleep for the next two days, never leaving my room.

I drift in and out of consciousness: sleeping, trying to get liquids down, coughing to the point of exhaustion, and repeating. I push the CEO and the company completely from my brain. After four long days, I begin to feel a little better, but the painfully persistent cough lingers for a full ten days. *Huh. It must not have been a mold issue after all.* It certainly didn't feel like the flu, no typical runny nose, just my chest completely wrecked.

Little did I know that as I settled into my new place, trying to secure some semblance of rhythm, regularity, and security, that my world—and everyone's world—would be turned upside down by a global pandemic. And soon, I would know *exactly* what my symptoms were.

Unaware of the avalanche of chaos barreling toward me, I continue working and sexting with my love interest now that I'm feeling better. We make plans to hang out in the coming days, but I let him know my cycle is coming up.

I text him: *Full disclosure in your decision-making, I'm very much on my cycle through Monday... but I'm so craving chats on life, hand-holding, massages, dancing, snuggles, but only that at this time. If that isn't of interest, no worries at all.*

He replies: *Are you implying that my decision-making would be influenced by that? Full disclosure, I desire you! I enjoyed being with you! Doing everything we did. And sex is or would be a good part, but not the only one* and not the most important for sure! And I have found that pleasure, even sexual pleasure, is much more than okay. I like that we have very honest communication.

I reply: *I enjoy the honesty as well.*

Then, I decide it's boundary time and send him a small novel:

No implication, however, I was uncertain if our first visit set a precedent, so I wanted to be open and honest so you could best decide how you spend your free time this weekend. Full disclosure, I enjoyed being with you too! On the beach, I felt an immediate ease and connection with you. I do wish we hadn't done the dirty because I'm learning that diving into that right out of the gate isn't as fulfilling for me versus waiting...or at least waiting until it feels natural. For us, it felt a little forced. I'm definitely guilty for instigating. So I love that you also feel that isn't the most important thing. Right now, I'm really craving pleasure and physical touch besides that.

Yes, girl, boundaries. *Good.*

His response: *Good!*

Great. Boundaries established.

We continue to text and flirt and play. I send him a video of me dancing playfully to some reggae music while painting an abstract Baja scene. I'm not terribly good at it but it brings me such joy to mix and play with the colors like I did as a child.

I message him: *Peek at my vid.*

Him: *Not ready to finish my concentration yet. I am thinking of you as I get ready to splatter everywhere! But the name of my game now is ride the edge. Edge but don't finish.... restart as many times as you want but DON'T finish.*

I join in: *I was just thinking of you as I stroked my paint brush back and forth, up and down...*

Him: *I am going to use a clean brush on you next time we meet!*

Note to self, find an art store, stat. We both finish our flirtation, we finish ourselves together, connected by our screens. Receiving texts from a man that are sexual but not vulgar, open yet not compromising, playful and experimental is so new and exhilarating to me.

He says he'll message me tomorrow with our plan for the day. I don't hear a word. Still, I resist reaching out because he said he would message me. So instead, I check my phone every thirty seconds, like a lab rat hitting a lever for a hit of dopamine. Only in my experiment, the reward never comes, just the slow-drip heart flutters of hope. My wires are crossed. I've somehow confused longing with love, anticipation with connection, pleasure with pain.

I can't stand waiting one more second so I finally message late in the day: *What's up?*

He says: *Oh I was going to drive tonight but it didn't seem like a good idea to me, so maybe tomorrow?* I showed nothing but eagerness about seeing him this evening.

I call that out: *Ah, I was definitely game, but thought from your last message you would message me today to make the plan?*

Him: *What makes sense for you now?*

Me: *Come on up!*

He arrives late at 8 p.m., his motorcycle announcing his arrival with a billowing dust cloud drifting past the silhouettes of cactuses up into the star-sprinkled desert sky. I'm eager for the company. This time, I hold my boundary, no sex—just a dinner of flank steak quesadillas paired with red wine, easy conversation, and a friendly sleepover.

In the morning, I get a call from Mom letting me know Dad is out of the hospital and back home. My mom sounds exhausted. Typically, she leans into anything I share with a negative outlook, which led me to share less and less about my life over the years. But after I moved across the country, we slowly started to heal our relationship, opening up to each other a little more. She even wrote me a lovely letter expressing her admiration of my kind heart, and gratitude for the joy I have brought to her life, closing with "So you see I do have emotions but they are a little further from the surface than a lot of people I guess." It meant the world to me. That's when I started forcing our phone conversations to end with "I love you." I heard other kids say it to their parents growing up and was always jealous. It felt awkward at first, but nearly two decades later, it's second nature. I've always known my parents loved me, they wrote it in countless cards, but there's something about *hearing* it. No wonder my love language is words of affirmation.

"Thanks for calling, Mom. I'm so glad to hear he's okay and back home. I love you."

"Me too. I love you too." She sounds so far away.

I hang up and pocket my phone. I glance at Armando, and he quickly avoids eye contact. I'm sensing a pattern—he seems to avoid anything that stirs up emotions, especially when it comes to family. Without sex connecting us this visit, there's a noticeable distance, a coldness, a lack of presence. I realize he's able to be expressive over text, but in person, there's a massive emotional wall around his heart.

Over a simple breakfast of eggs and toast, I decide to dig a little deeper. Eventually, I manage to get him to open up just a little, about his own family. I learn about a recent former long-term partner and a daughter in mainland Mexico he hasn't seen in quite some time. Suddenly, things begin to make sense.

***

The following week I'm in Cabo San Lucas for work. We meet in a wonderful all-inclusive hotel. Me, corporate, all done up in a dress, hair curled. Him, fresh off his motorcycle, sweaty, rugged, in a casual t-shirt and jeans.

Him: *You're going to have to come to the lobby. The guys are nice, but don't like me.*

Me: *Well that's no fun. Sorry. Heading over.*

Turns out the hotel staff found him to be a bit too rugged for the establishment. Screw that!

We go out for a nice dinner, holding hands as we walk, engaged in wonderful, intelligent, meaningful conversation. He is charismatic and chatty but doesn't totally hear me. I notice he's eager to speak before I finish—he listens, but only on a surface level. His stories are full of enthusiasm, yet he just can't connect with me on a deeper level.

It reminds me of my father at times. I love my dad so ridiculously deeply, and I know he adores me. I know this to my core. But despite our countless outdoor adventures growing up, our weekly emails, frequent calls, thoughtful cards and shared stories, he doesn't *know* me deeply. I spend a lot of time listening to him share. He doesn't ask about my feelings or worries, and to be fair, I don't share them too frequently either—because we've never had that kind of emotional dialogue. We simply don't go beyond life's pleasantries and basic fatherly support. Maybe I should open up more to him. But for some reason, I want him to ask me to.

So you see, I want to be seen and understood to my core by a playful, charismatic man.

Armando is never going to provide that, except for the aloof playfulness.

What's a gal to do?

Return to the hotel room and absolutely *destroy* the second queen bed. Every position, every angle, every object, music blaring—pure pleasure pony express rolling on through. We don't kiss passionately or often. Nothing is slow or gentle. It's a lot of rapid dancing and exchanges, a helluva lot of fun but not deeply intimate.

We wake in the *other* bed, next to each other as usual, but never snuggle. He must head off to work. As he gets up, he looks over at the second bed.

"Oh nooooooou," he groans in our playful Americanized Spanish accent. Like Cabo, but *Ca-boou*.

I lift my head. "What's wrong?"

He points. Disaster. A full-blown, red-splattered mess.

"Oh shit. My cycle." Good lord, seriously? Not *again*.

"That's gonna need a dozen cycles in the washer and a dozen Hail Marys to get clean," he laughs. "Leave the cleaning crew five-hundred pesos." He walks over, plants a kiss on my cheek, and heads for the door. "Enjoy the day. Thanks for dessert last night—it was delicious."

With a wink and a seductive smile, he's gone.

I text him later that day: *How was your day, decent?*

Armando: *What??? A decent day? With a morning like that how can a day just be decent?*

Me: *Haha, agreed.*

Armando texts me later that day: *I quit my job today!*

Me: *You did?! Congrats how are you feeling?*

Armando: *When you wake up realizing lifes too short to not say FUCK IT, it's not working. Let's do something about it!!*

Me: *Love it!!! 100%!!*

Armando: *Love myself!*

Me: *Exactly!! Hell, that's why I'm in Baja. Get some space to figure out what's next, it involves the same. Loving me! Proud of you!*

Armando: *The great intentions and shining light on what good you see in me has been good. When you come back we'll see what you think of my cover letter and maybe an interview to test the waters.*

Me: *Absolutely. I'll likely need to run a skills test analysis as well. We can start with lingual strength and agility. Hope you're game.*

Armando: *Yes please!*

And so it goes. Playful texting, talks of good podcasts, playlists, the importance of gut health to overall health, finding life flow, funky healthy cacao recipes, the unhealthiness of corporate life. We talk and text but it continues to remain surface-level in terms of emotions. We've been texting and hanging out for nearly three months now. He always responds quickly, his texts are kind and considerate, he's always eager to hang, but in person he is reserved. He doesn't have his heart open and available, and that's all I desire in the whole world right now. As I head out on a little work trip and as I'm boarding the plane, my curiosity gets the best of me.

I text the epic novel women should never text (men typically work in three-sentence maximums), but I push my luck: *Hey so look, as I dive further into meditation and A New Earth, I'm trying to get better about my ego perceptions vs reality. So far we have had good fun, enjoyed each other's company, but you lean towards not getting personal with me, or really asking questions to get to know me better. Knowing you, this is intentional on your part, yes? No judgment. You seem to want to keep interactions very light with me, perhaps just friends with benefits because I'm not a good fit or you aren't looking for more at this time. Can you shed any light there for me?* I hit send, anxiously biting my nails.

Shockingly, fifteen minutes later, I get an equal novel back: *Ok. I don't ask questions to get to know people. I simply observe how they act upon situations, it's not about you it's about how I AM. Don't assume. In general I take things very light. I focus mostly on the present and a little on adjusting directions towards the future. I don't know the difference between friendship, friends with benefits, lovers, partners, couples or any categories. What I know is that if I spend time with you it is because I want to spend time with you and as I spend time with you I get to know you. What we do while we spend time is what I would have otherwise would have desired for myself (eating delicious things, going to places I haven't been to, doing things like surfing, etc) and if sex is one thing that we also enjoy even better!*

I am not looking for anything to fit because I am complete. I look for people to flow with me. I find you very interesting. That's why I look forward to spending time with you and sharing myself with you. I sense that your head is spinning too fast to try and make sense of your heart and gut. Many processes in many areas with many changes. I have found a good formula not to overthink things and enjoy them for what they are (not what they were or could be). Breathe when you feel anxious. Enjoy what's in your hands even if it is for just an instant.

I volley back: *You're a rare creature, Armando. One I haven't met in the wild before. I'm still learning how you are. I'm still wired to categorize things, to fit people into boxes. Fifteen years with one person will do that. But I'm changing. Mourning the old me. Becoming someone new. Free. I still plan too much instead of being present. I'm making progress. Slowly. You're right, my heart, head, and gut don't always sync, and when they don't, I spin. Ninety percent of the time I'm grounded. But the 10%? It can roar. I love fiercely. Especially when I've been physical with someone. It can cause unnecessary spin. I'm trying to break in my newly free heart, like a wild horse, trying to guide the power with grace, without losing the edge. Right now, I'm still circling the corral..spinning, passionate, powerful, afraid, alive. Thanks for listening. I'm such a damn emotionally raw animal, I'm tearing up in the airport. Appreciate your honesty and transparency.* Umm, who even *am* I right now?

Armando: *Do you keep a journal or diary? It is a great tool to start and end the day. Just a thought.*

Me: *Lol, I do. Every morning after meditation. My flight is about to take off. Thank you so much. Have a beautiful rest of the day!*

These are my scattered attempts for Corporate Becca to begin tapping into Baja Becca's emotions. I didn't yet know how to fall in love without losing myself. I didn't know how to be vulnerable, to allow my needs to be expressed and seen without fear.

As I return from my work trip to visit our Cancun division, I find myself running through the Mexico City airport to catch my flight. Countless TV screens sprawl with something called COVID-19, just beginning to hit the news—it's early March 2020. Announcements blare through the terminal about respiratory symptoms, and I think back to my illness a few weeks ago.

Holy shit. No wonder it felt different than the flu.

IT'S GONNA GET MESSY

I'm positive I had it at my flooded apartment—the awful wheezing, the feeling of nearly coughing up a lung. I have no idea yet how bad this is, but I *do* know that being in a massive airport is the worst place to be, so I use my scarf as a makeshift mouth cover. I've got to get back to Baja.

Luckily, my flight departs, and I land safely. I find myself moving yet again, this time into a little studio just around the corner from my temporary hotel space in my little dirt road town. But at least this place is secured for a full month.

I can't believe it, I'm supposed to return to my corporate office life in Portland on April 1st. The thought of it feels impossible. So, I chat with my boss. He says there's a possibility of extending my position in Mexico and to stay tuned. He also mentions, "Given all the recent global changes, not sure it makes sense for you to attend VRMA."

VRMA—the international vacation rental conference in Portugal. I already have my flight booked. My heart races a little.

Does this mean my position is in jeopardy?

He reassures me the company is reevaluating its travel policy due to the growing concerns over this coronavirus.

Four days later, he's fired.

I'm now reporting to the interim CEO, and I'm told a replacement will be announced in a few weeks. *Sit tight.* This makes boss number four in four months. No communication, no support, no direction, just an ever-growing unease.

I try to center myself, to focus on the perks of this remote job, but in this moment, it isn't easy.

So, I take this as a sign to work incredibly lightly and surf as much as I can. I hang out with Armando more—more cooking, more playing, more surfing. He sips things out of my belly button and other lovely crevices. We spend long weekends together sleeping, cooking, surfing, sexing, diving into a menagerie of life conversations.

I should clarify, my version of surfing at this time is simply *trying* (again and again) to stand up in the whitewash as the wave is nearly to shore. It's not easy.

One day, we're out at a coffee shop, and he gets *very* flirty with the barista. Leaning in, winking, obviously flirting—ignoring me completely as they speak in rapid Spanish for the better part of an hour. He doesn't even try to include me in the conversation.

Later, he looks at me and sees I'm upset. "What? We were talking about coffee."

It would appear I'm busy distracting myself from everything collapsing around me with yet another round of breaking my own heart.

He heads home to go to work that afternoon.

I text: *Hey, thanks for being patient with my moment of frustration this weekend. I had no cause to be possessive. I don't want a relationship.* (Lies Becca, lies). *I simply care about you and really enjoy spending time with you. I must still be undoing my 15 years of monogamy brain when I'm intimate with someone. It's damn hard conditioning to shake. Anyway, I had a great time. If we decide to spend time together in the future I'll be sure to not let those moments creep in. I need to remember I'm just a friend with benefits not your one and only.*

Armando: *Good! I am mostly cool with everything. I like our friendship.*

I am hurt and decide to bring up more things that have been bothering me.

Me: *Your deep commitment to self-love is admirable, but sometimes, it feels like there's not much space left for curiosity or openness about how others move through their own highs and lows. I often ask about what's going on in your life because I genuinely care. But you rarely ask in return. Why is that? From where I sit, it gives the impression that you're not all that interested in really knowing me.*

Armando: *I think that if you want to share something or tell me something you will and if you ask me something I'll answer and if I want to tell you something I will. If that happens or not I don't think it means anything other than it happens or not. I respect your way of caring and understand your inclination that I would show it in a similar way. I recommend you not try to use the same magnifying glass for anything nor judge things under the same light. Read actions over "rules" and words, find the truth behind the ways. Be open to people doing things differently without "meaning" what you think. Or maybe I am an asshole and a very selfish guy and it's good you are finding out now rather than later. I respect your views although they are new to me. I'm going to process that. Thanks for your honesty.*

Armando again: *The last part about me being an asshole or selfish well I truly believe I can potentially be but prefer to see myself in a more positive light.*

Me: *How you process things is likely quite factual and obvious to you, it is not to me as we are not one. I care about you very much, but my fierce loyalty comes with a give and take. I'm just not sure if there's room in your orbit for me in a way that says "welcome home" in my native language. I have a strong desire at this time in my life to be seen but more importantly heard. Native language being, my more emotive self.*

Armando: *Ok. Good that you show me how you are and share with me what you feel you need.*

Me: *Good. Consider my head checked. Looks like my company is locking down all travel on March 18th and I have a potential return date of April 1st, so I may have a job, but I will need to leave Baja.*

Armando: *Beccaaaa! I just read that Covid doesn't live in high temps so for your own good, I am going to keep you as fuckin' hot and cachonda caliente for as long as I can!*

I genuinely appreciate the levity but wish he was even remotely sad about me leaving. I ignore the pain.

Me: *Hahaha. Yesssss! Let's sweat it out!! For safety. Naturally.*

Honestly, I have never communicated with a man in this way before. He's being straightforward about who he is and what he can offer, and I'm making his inability to meet me emotionally *about me*. About my worth. Which is *so* wrong.

I can't see, in this moment, how much I'm giving my power away—attempting to control, fix, or change someone yet again. Taking responsibility for their emotions. Pouring my energy into what I can't change. Attempting to partner again with someone for their "potential," convincing myself my needs matter while their behavior keeps showing they can't meet them. Not because he's bad, but because I'm not choosing *myself* first. Same cycle, same result. Staying in situations that are terrible for my mental health. Rinse, repeat.

He is my only close physical lifeline as the pandemic swells, so I hold onto that lifeline with all my might. He makes the 45-minute drive up a few times a week from Cabo San Lucas. He is standing firm in what he can offer in my physical presence, and I am standing firm in ignoring my intuition—ignoring my need to stop hanging out and be truly solo for a while. The passionate sex is pulling this film of hormones over my eyes, making it nearly impossible to see things clearly. One can get ridiculously sidelined by the release of sexual hormones at the beginning of a new relationship. We lose our compass, biologically pulled to bond, flooded with pheromones, infatuated with the idea of being *chosen*—that we forget to slow down and ask ourselves, *Is this someone I actually want to choose?*

Looking back, it's crystal clear, I should have stopped hanging out with him if I had simply honored how my heart was feeling. But I was flat-out ignoring the obvious.

Little did I know, deep within me was a wound. The wound of feeling emotionally *unsafe* in childhood when I would ask authentic questions and be ignored. Trauma comes in forms big and small; we've *all* experienced some form of it. As it turns out, we often chase people who mirror our parents' behavior. In my case, my dad—always positive, always seeking activities and adventure, but never engaging in deep conversations. I didn't feel deeply seen or heard by the man I admired most.

Then there was my mother—repressed emotions, a note of narcissism, an inability to fully give love. I was confusing this type of behavior with lust and strong attraction, unknowingly seeking to heal that wound. My mom was emotionally absent, fairly cold. It wasn't safe to be myself or ask questions, when all I *had* were a million questions.

Did my parents love me? Hell yes, they did.
Did I have a pretty damn good childhood compared to many others? Hell yes, I did.

I love my parents very much. But like all of us, how we were raised affects how we show up in the world. We have this compulsion to repeat our past, a deep subconscious desire to enter the same dynamic, hoping this time we'll finally find secure attachment. A safe space. A resolution to the past.

I was totally incapable of seeing the red flags. Well—I *saw* them, but I overrode them with my own wounded desire to prove I was worthy of love. *I can win him over. I can show him I'm worthy.* I wasn't ready to forgive myself or begin the healing process from within. I wasn't ready to become conscious of my own behaviors and patterns. To forgive myself for chasing the familiar when all I really wanted was to find out what a healthy, safe, emotionally connected, vulnerable relationship actually looks like.

I was still deep in the un-learning process. And this is what that messy healing journey looks like. Frustrating to witness, isn't it? Perhaps you've been there too?

I was disrespecting myself every time I said yes to being with him, avoiding conflict to keep the peace while creating a war inside myself. Losing myself in an attempt to keep someone who was unavailable in the way I needed them. Abandoning myself in the process. Allowing loneliness to lower my standards.

I didn't yet understand that any relationship asking you to be a subdued, watered-down version of yourself in order to "function" is *not* the relationship for you.

It's a week before I'm supposed to return to Portland for good. Armando and I are spending it together, doing the usual: surf, coffee, sex, eat, repeat. Covid is spiking around the world and is the only topic in the news all week. The severity, the death tolls—it's on every channel. Lockdowns begin. The U.S. halts all traffic at the Mexico border.

My heart drops out of my body. I'm being laid off along with almost half the company. I have to hop on a call at noon for the details. It's March 20, 2020. I join the call, bracing myself. Miraculously, I'm *not* laid off. They announce that anyone receiving an email after the call is gone. I never get an email. Instead, they tell me I'm staying on—at 30 percent reduced pay. I breathe a sigh of relief.

Later that day, the texts start rolling in from my team:

"So sorry, Becca."

"Hope you're okay down there."

Confused, I email my interim boss.

No response.

I spend the entire weekend on edge, playing out a million scenarios in my mind, looping, repeating, wrecked with nerves. I feel physically sick.

On Monday afternoon, I get this:

Becca,

Sorry for the delayed reply. I had to dig into this further to understand what happened on Friday. Your position got grouped with the internation-

al team and a number of our international notifications were delayed until this week. Unfortunately, your position has been deemed non-critical and is being eliminated. As a result, you will receive a layoff notification early this week. The notification will come from HR with exit details.
If you have any questions you should direct them to HR.
Signed,
Name of my New Boss Whom I've Never Met

I was on the wrong list. There were four layoff rounds, but with a rapid mass layoff, they couldn't get it right. I am officially laid off. My boss didn't even bother to reach out until I emailed HR. This is an absolute heart-racing, epic mind fuck. The email isn't even signed with a "Sincerely" or "Take care" or "Thank you" or "I'm sorry." Or how about, *It has been brought to my attention that you're abroad, and we placed you there, and the border is shutting down, and it's a global pandemic. Are you safe? Can we help you get home?* No, nothing.

I immediately message HR and ask if there were any considerations in my specific case regarding my health and wellness—being south of the border, thousands of miles away, during a global pandemic—and their actions, in essence, abandoning me here.

I get an email back from my friend, or who I thought was my friend, who is my primary contact in HR:

"Hello, I am sorry for the late reply. I sent your initial note to legal for their visibility, I haven't heard back yet. Given the state of the world right now, I'm not sure that any considerations will be made. I will let you know if I hear differently, or frankly if I hear anything at all."

That's all I got. Even the note from HR expresses no concern for me or my safety.

Then they put a big fat layer of icing on my *We Don't Give Two Shits About You* cake and ask if I can travel to a FedEx or UPS to promptly send my phone and laptop back. Seriously? During a pandemic. I'm in a dirt road town in Mexico, you dirtbags. You've got to be fucking kidding me.

I read this while grabbing provisions at the tiny eight-shelf market in town. I'm with Armando. I'm beyond livid. I drop the orange I'm smelling. It hits the ground, bounces off my foot, and rolls away quickly—eager to escape my brewing outburst. I stop speaking mid-sentence. He watches as I slowly stroll out into the street. I stand there, stare up at the sky, and scream. A bloodcurdling scream like I've never screamed in my entire life. He comes out and gives me a hug. It's the first time he's actually consoled me. I guess to get what you need, sometimes you have to fucking scream for it.

Ironically, just two months after the massive layoffs, in the middle of the pandemic, it's announced that the company has a post-money valuation in the range of $1B to $10B as of June 2020 and is likely to go public for somewhere in the middle of that range. I see an article about the interim CEO's kitchen remodel that looks like it cost a couple hundred grand. Meanwhile, Glassdoor is filled with reviews like: *Comically bad compensation. Nepotism abounds. Micro-management.* The veil is so thin sometimes, isn't it?

During those same two months, I never heard anything back about legal recourse for laying me off abroad on the exact same day the Governor of Oregon issued a shelter-in-place order. I frantically think about trying to drive the 2,000 miles north, staying in hotels for 10 days, when there's a travel ban in California. I try to file for unemployment, but the intake system asks where I'm located. I click *Mexico,* and the system tells me I must call. I attempt to call for a week straight—nothing but busy signals. I spend about 28 hours on hold in total. The unemployment system is overloaded, payments are behind, and no one is answering the phones or social media messages to give direction on my case.

I file as if I'm in Oregon, hoping to speak to someone soon for clarification on this insane situation. Surely this is temporary? There's no way I can drive 2,000 miles back, staying in hotels along the way, only to arrive in Portland with no home to return to. Touring apartments and hiring movers, none of that is happening. Everything is closed. I have secure housing here in Baja, in this tiny town. The news is filled with images of hazmat suits. Everything is terrifying. Everyone is dying. We don't know how bad this will be. I ask my friends what I should do but it feels impossible in my mind and body to do anything but stay put.

Days later, they pile dirt at the entrance of my town to block the road, preventing anyone from getting in. There's no hospital here, and they want to limit exposure from unnecessary travelers. I hear that other small towns in northern Baja are turning back cars, saying they don't have the infrastructure or hospitals to risk the spread of infection.

I see men walking with machetes in the fields near my home. They don't seem hostile, but it's unnerving. I pick up some mace.

The next morning, Armando is informed that he'll be quarantined at work and must remain there for at least a month, if not longer. He works in the hotel industry. We spend the day together, and then he drives off back south. It hits me—I'll be here, alone in my little studio, for at least a month, maybe longer.

He sees I'm tearful but just smiles kindly as he walks to his motorcycle. He doesn't console me. I'm alone.

I wait a few days later, stewing, and I text: *No text as to how I am doing?*

Armando: *I know how you are. Why would I ask you how you are? I am sorry I am not what you seek or need right now. If by being what I am, I am what you need, well, I am glad.*

He has me spinning. The whole world has me spinning. I feel like I can't rely on anything or anyone. I need to just stop for a moment and get to know myself. Since everything around me is a total cluster, I need to finally find some security and identity within myself.

As I do some mind-numbing scrolling to ease my restlessness, I see an Instagram post: *"The Universe isolates you so you can find your soul's purpose. It may seem like you've lost friendships and relationships, but finding your path, passion, and purpose in life is worth more. For where your soul is, there you will find your treasure."*

To grow bigger, you have to endure the pain of breaking open and out of your shell. Looks like the Universe is telling me: *Stay put. And as a bonus, we'll chuck you off the never-ending corporate hamster wheel that's making you insanely stressed and miserable.*

Something deep inside of me was asking for a higher experience, and in order to get there, the Universe was willing to hand me the hard lessons needed to push me into becoming the type of person deserving of that life. To search deep inside for the answers.

It seems the treasure hunt was on in full force. *Thanks, Universe.*

Chapter Fourteen

One-way ticket.

I wake to find myself totally alone. Nowhere to go, no one around. It's a week into lockdown in my little dirt-road town, in my studio apartment, with only a small handful of other people quarantining here in the sprawling terracotta complex—sixty or so small homes nestled below a hillside sprinkled with agave, sagebrush, and a sea of cactuses waving a silent hello across the dusty desert landscape. The occasional rooster crowing outside my window is the closest thing I have to a neighbor.

A large, warped wooden door with a rusty iron latch guards the small yard I share with the vacant unit below me. On the side of stacked abodes sits a black metal spiral staircase that swirls upward to my second-floor entry landing, where my tiny outdoor kitchen and outdoor shower sit beneath a simple slanted palapa palm-leaf awning. A sliding glass door guides you into my little 10x12-foot room that holds a queen bed, two tiny nightstands that barely fit in the space, some shelves on the back wall next to a small window, and a small bathroom just past the foot of the bed, off to the right of the sliding patio door entrance. A colorful ceramic water jug holds down the back left corner where I keep my suitcase and a few bags of belongings.

Outside, the black spiral staircase continues upward leading up to the rooftop, where a simple metal table and four chairs sit under a bright aqua umbrella, offering some relief from the intense Baja sun. In the distance, I can see the turquoise sea, waves announcing their arrival loudly on shore. This would be my little quarantine nest for the foreseeable future.

I stop by the local four-shelf market, all masked up, to get my weekly provisions. There's rice, beans, some fresh fruit—albeit mostly bruised—a few root vegetables, some locally butchered meats sitting at room temperature, packaged chips, fresh eggs, and tortillas. That about covers it. My fridge is just like the mini-fridge I had in college, so I plan to make weekly runs to stock up.

Truth be told, I have zero clue how to cook anything beyond a grilled cheese or a can of soup. Luke always did the cooking for us. I attempted a few times, but it wasn't great, and he vocalized he wasn't thrilled to suffer through my learning curve, so I gave up.

Now, without any pressure to make things perfectly, I dive into experimenting. I find recipes, I practice, and to my surprise, I actually *enjoy* it. I dare say, I'm actually pretty darn decent at it!

The lockdown makes it hard to keep track of time, I often entirely lose sense of what day it is. Without work anchoring my routine, I feel lost in the rhythm of my days, so I put a little schedule in place to keep me focused. Morning coffee, then breakfast, followed by rooftop meditation, journaling, and a long walk around the hillside behind me. I carve out a nice little two-hour hiking loop—first climbing the steep hillside along the sea, then easing down into a lush oasis of farm fields below. It gets pretty hot by noon, so I try to wrap my stroll before my early afternoon lunch. I get back and shower under the warm Baja air, showering outside feels absolutely amazing. I soak in the warmth, the sun on my naked skin.

Lunch is followed by some reading or catching up with friends via social media or FaceTime, which is a godsend for my mental health. All of that is anchored by an afternoon siesta. I have no TV and little information on how the rest of the world is faring at this point in the pandemic, aside from the snippets friends and family tell me. I just know I am so grateful for my little, safe, remote place to hunker down.

I'm still figuring out unemployment, so I apply for jobs in both Oregon and Mexico just to be extra sure I'm following the job search protocols, even though I know there's not a chance in hell someone in travel marketing is getting hired anytime soon.

I prepare and eat dinner, settle into some nightly reading with classical music playing in the background, and then hit the sack. I'm surprised at just how much time goes into making fresh food and recipes each day, packaged goods simply aren't available. But I love it. I enjoy the meditation of mixing, chopping, and creating.

One day, I attempt to go for a surf, even though I'm told the beaches are closed. There's not a single soul in sight, and I can't stand just staring at the sea—I *have* to get in the water. I paddle out on my surfboard alone and catch a bit of whitewater a few times. After my third attempt, I turn around to see a National Guard truck on the beach, three guards waving for me to come in. I look around, then back at them, pointing to myself. *Who, me?!* They stare, unamused. I paddle in.

They tell me I must go home. I try to explain that you can close the beach, but you can't close the ocean. They show a tiny glimmer of sympathy before promptly telling me to leave and not return. "Pero, nadie está aquí?" *But there is no one here?* They simply point away from the sea.

Back to my little nest I go.

Out of nowhere, my very first Baja date, Mauricio, resurfaces with a text to see how I'm handling all the craziness and if I'm still in Baja. I'm just a few desert roads and farm valleys away from him, and he asks if I want to be added to a group chat sharing twenty-one days of Deepak meditations. *Heck yes, I do.*

The Former had no spiritual side, and I had shoved mine deep down, too. But after finishing *A New Earth* this week, that part of me is reemerging in the most beautiful and timely way. He speaks of what a destructive place Earth is, and how we could save the whole mess if we just let go of our egos, saw ourselves in each other, and accepted what *is* instead of constantly battling everything with judgment and expectations. Release those, and we can truly *live* in the present and enjoy this precious life.

I feel like I'm slowly unplugging from that destructive place. I'm beginning to feel immense gratitude for being let go from that prison of a job. I finally grasp how much I was holding onto it by a thread, choking on the societal script of success that no longer resonated with me.

I'm starting to realize—I'm not sure it ever really did.

Maybe the thrill of money and recognition in my 20s was satisfying, but as I climbed higher into my 30s, with bigger titles and salaries, I watched my happiness diminish. The more I earned, the more I felt I had to earn, constantly upgrading my so-called precious possessions. I couldn't see how much they weighed me down instead of lifting me up.

My life begins to merge with nature in a way it never has before. I find that I live outside more than I live inside. My only sources of light are the sun and a small, cozy bedside lamp with a slightly bent shade. The local mice love my outdoor kitchen—despite my keeping it as tidy as humanly possible. I see cockroaches in my sink and bedroom on the regular. So, it turns out I'm not really alone. The creepy crawlers used to freak me out, but I find they're not so awful.

One afternoon, I learn to make fresh cacao chocolate with nuts and local honey instead of the packaged stuff. I learn to cook all sorts of fabulously flavorful fish tacos. Another random afternoon, I decide to try a fried taco experiment, but I plop the fish down too rapidly and burn my hands as the super-hot frying oil splashes out of the pan. The burn is pretty bad, and no pharmacy is open. I forage for aloe in the field behind my casita, locating a hefty aloe plant nearly up to my waist. With my dull kitchen knife, I slowly hack away at a small limb from the bottom of the gorgeous plant until it releases. I carry it back, trudging through the vast field, dripping yellow aloe ooze onto the desert floor beneath my feet. Laying it down on my storage unit doubling as my kitchen table—like a heaping *Catch of the Day*—I dig out the insides and slather the cool gel onto my burn. The relief is almost instant. I am, in fact, *Doctor Quinn, Medicine Woman*.

Days begin to blur into a kaleidoscope of hiking, cooking, reading, and meditating. Without the news or media cramping my precious mental space, I realize how insanely harsh and fear-inducing it all is—something I hadn't fully grasped until I silenced it for a while. You also don't realize how often you get consumed in the stories of others instead of creating your own.

I accidentally hear the news for five minutes while in town picking up supplies, and my entire body tightens, constricts, my gut wrenching. I'm so much happier without the spin of the media and its forced, fearful rhetoric that feels so dramatic and disconnected. I push it out of my mind.

I'm learning to find luxury in the simple things: unrushed mornings, homemade food, deep sleep, time in nature, savoring a book, unplugged quality time, watching another perfect sunset, a tasty beverage in hand. Slowing down is showing me the depth I used to race past. In the stillness, truth rises—the kind I used to plow right through. I'm starting to see...life isn't meant to be conquered. It's meant to be *savored*. With nowhere to run from my thoughts, reflection flows in. Feelings return like long-lost friends, waiting patiently to be heard. I am connecting with myself in a way I never have in my entire adult life. And somewhere in the quiet, I begin to hear the whisper of my own heart.

Details become more vivid—the soft warmth of the summer breeze on my skin, the sacredness in the slowness. I find myself sitting under the sun, realizing how very little I actually need to be truly happy.

In the evenings, I walk outside beneath the black and silver-sprinkled sky of the Baja desert. The stars sparkle intensely, sometimes like an ebony blanket covered in precious gems. Other times, I'm positive the sky is a massive oil painting, still drying, with subtle terracotta and lavender glowing inky final reflections of the fleeing sun. The quiet becomes comforting.

Weeks later, which feels like two months later as time did in 2020, I finally hear from Armando: *Hey, how are you holding up?*

Me: *Life is so fucking deliciously unknown and beautiful!*

He didn't reply, and I didn't care to elaborate. The little bit of space that quarantine provided made me realize just how off I had been feeling in his presence. Sometimes, that in-between time of rest is when we truly learn who we are and what really matters in life. This pause was begging me—*please, don't numb your way through life anymore*. Breathe. Enjoy the stillness for once. You don't have to hustle so damn much. You were built for seasons, not an endless marathon of achievement.

This is the isolation part of healing I didn't know I so desperately needed. It's as if a force greater than myself was at play, getting me here, sitting me down, and placing me in a timeout. This precious time—my soul is desperately calling me to come home, to pay attention, to finally listen. I need silence. I need rest. I need to finally break free from the stream of thoughts and behaviors I had internalized and somehow mistaken for my own.

This time is also filled with some deeply uncomfortable moments, the nights when I sob under the stars, all alone. But I am so grateful for the tears. I am finally releasing some of the pain and loss of years past. I am finally learning so much about myself. I truly feel like I'm meeting myself for the very first time.

I meditate each day to stay grateful, to fall in love with the delicate beauty of life. Life can be difficult, messy, complex. But I am finding that meditation builds resilience to witness it all. Meditation is my lifeline. It cracks open my facade, offering a glimmer of awareness into my emotions, thoughts, needs, and triggers. I am creating calmness, clarity, compassion, and contentment from within. I notice how meditation shifts the entire vibe of my day.

I begin shifting small habits—how I spend my mornings, what I am reading, what I am watching, where I invest my energy, who I give access to my life. I notice how I have been talking to myself for years. *Hint: it's been ridiculously unkind.* If you're human, you've very likely been berated by this internal voice too.

I start being nicer to myself, thanking myself for the small acts of kindness I give myself each day—acts that had previously gone unnoticed. Simple things, like pouring myself a glass of water. *Thank you, self, for pouring this water.*

This precious quarantine time is allowing me to reset, to filter, to purge old habits and lingering beliefs, to notice the beauty in each day I had been plowing through. Could I have made this a horrible time? A time to feel panicked, alone, isolated? Damn straight I could have. But I choose to see the good, to begin altering the path of my one precious life in a direction that speaks to my soul. Something in me knows the loss of control, certainty, familiarity...everything I depended on dissolving, is something I desperately need for my life to fall into place.

Each day, each choice, I ask myself: *Will this choice help me move toward my true goals, dreams, and values? Or will it keep me in the past I am trying to outgrow?*

It's like the fake, scripted voice of what life, success, possessions, and appearances *should* look like is finally fading away. And my own voice is emerging.

I dare say, I think I really do enjoy what she has to say.

I dare hope we are writing a new script of success.

I spend this time still communicating with Armando, as he's the one person in my immediate quarantine bubble in Baja. And although I'm enjoying my solo time, I still feel so needy and dependent on his messages and the physical visits I've lost since he was put in quarantine. My side obsession with him is keeping me nicely distracted from diving too deep into a lot of the feelings I'm still not ready to face—like all the emotions from my divorce that I unknowingly haven't fully processed.

He finally manages to visit one weekend, and we enjoy our time together, but his inability to meet me emotionally and open his heart has started to really fracture whatever this pseudo-relationship is. I've had time now to tune into the rhythm of my own needs, even just for a little while, and it's clear this isn't flowing. I'm forcing it. We spend the night together, and the next day, I see him in bed, scrolling Tinder. My heart races, pounding out of my chest, heat overtaking me like a flash fire. I feel abandoned. Not enough. Unworthy. He can feel my invisible shotgun of anger bullets spraying his way, and he looks at me casually, unalarmed. Instead of the apologetic look I'm expecting, he just looks... annoyed.

He reminds me we're just friends. And I *know* this in theory—but in my mind, I'm still convinced that, at some point, he'll see what a wonderful person I am and change his mind about this evolving into a relationship. I'm simply not willing to meet him where he's very clearly communicated he *can* meet me. But there are tiny moments where he crosses the line of friendship, like making future plans and talking about traveling together, which keeps me holding on with hope. I'm convinced that if I show him my full heart, I can prove I'm enough. I'm unconsciously cutting myself, betraying myself, because I still haven't learned the lesson of how love *should* feel.

And so he leaves, after our weekend of cooking, hanging, and banging. He always shows a deep desire and excitement to be in my presence, to spend time—but now it's coated with a crusty layer of annoyance. Hell, I'm deeply annoyed with myself at this point. *Let him go, Becca. Move on. You can't change anyone...* my inner knowing pleads with me, again and again. I'm definitely not listening.

Little did I know, choosing someone too broken and traumatized by loss to commit is its own form of self-sabotage. A way of protecting myself from experiencing the loss of love again. So I unknowingly chase unavailable love to keep myself safe.

Two months into my isolation, a cute and friendly couple from Seattle moves into the small studio below me. They were in the middle of a world travel tour but got stranded in Baja. They're trying to find a secure base until the pandemic settles and the border and airports reopen so they can head back north. We share the same fence and outdoor wooden front door that leads to our little dual-studio compound. Bubble mates!

We share similar routines of hiking, meditating, and working out and decide we should have a rooftop margarita gathering. They find they are enjoying the simple, introspective time as much as I am. They had voluntarily quit their jobs and saved up for this year of travel, only to have it all canceled shortly after it began. I am grateful, it's nice to have a bit of company and the sounds of human life around me.

My hair has grown long, and I'm at a point where I can't stand it, so I ask Traci if she will cut it. She looks alarmed, worried.

"Oh no, I can't cut hair."

"I'm not picky," I laugh.

"Oh no, I can't. It's too much pressure! I'll definitely mess it up, and what in the world would I even cut it with?"

I smile broadly. "Easy. Kitchen shears!"

She looks at me as if I'm batty but sees the earnestness in my face. She glances around. We're in the middle of nowhere, Mexico, in a dirt-road town with no real interaction with society. She shrugs. "Sure, why the hell not?"

"Excellent!" We make a date for tomorrow, after my post-hike shower.

She's a bit nervous, but I reassure her, "Seriously, who is going to see it?"

"Armando!" she exclaims.

I laugh. They had seen—and, um, well, heard—the visits from my rugged, dusty Baja biker boyfriend substitute.

"I'm not worried about it." I hand her the old shears. She combs my hair out evenly and gently, shuffling around my head, trying to cut it straight. My hair gets jammed repeatedly in the rather dull blades. She walks around me several times, pulling and trimming here and there, doing her very best to achieve a quality result. She even grabs the strands on either side of my face, bringing them together under my chin like a proper hairdresser would to check the length, tilting her head to one side. She shrugs. "Presto!"

I look at the pile of hair on the dusty ground, then peek in the mirror. My longer locks are now a cute shoulder-length bob, perfect for the Baja heat.

"Looks fabulous to me! Thank you so much!" I give her a big hug. "I shall pay you in the form of a margarita."

She looks immensely proud, adding this new skill to her quarantine bartering resume. I'm also immensely pleased. It's a bit uneven here and there, but it definitely meets my needs. It feels wildly freeing. And wildly free.

The next morning, I hand-wash my clothes in my tiny stainless steel kitchen sink, as I've been doing since the lockdown. I think about how many people are stuck in tiny apartments throughout the world right now, and I am so grateful for my outdoor space. I am content with what little I have. When I can experience such simplicity, where nothing feels lacking—a wide-open world begins to expand, redefining my actual needs versus programmed wants. A world of *enoughness* versus the society I am unplugging from, the one that constantly told me, day in and day out, that I wasn't enough. That I needed a better house, car, appearance, job, partner, wardrobe—the list was endless.

How utterly exhausting. A maze with no exit.

I feel the societal narrative of lack, comparison, and competition fading away in my rearview mirror. Funny how, when I turn off the media, TV, and news—when I remove outside influence—I see those programs are purely fiction, no longer of my own making.

I start to recognize my ego and let it go.

Okay, maybe not *let go*, I'm not sure that's even possible. It's more like I'm learning to coexist with my ego, the way you might with a messy but well-meaning roommate. She talks too loud when I'm trying to sleep, leaves emotional laundry everywhere, and always has an opinion. So I named her Pia—short for Pain In the Ass. Now, when she acts up, I notice her, nod politely, and move on. She's allowed a voice, but she doesn't get the mic. Or the keys. Or the whole damn apartment.

I try to shift my mindset from negative to positive, to live from within for fulfillment, to stay out of victim mode. During my first month or two of meditation, I found I couldn't even do a body scan. I was unable to feel inside my body in sync with my thoughts. But now, I'm beginning to connect the two.

I can actually hear my own voice, and it turns out, she's really kind and caring—when her environment is gentle and nurturing. I get truly interested in knowing myself, spending time with myself. Asking myself, as a kind friend would: *Hey, love, so what are your true interests? Your true desires? What lights you up inside?* Not to please others or maintain a certain outward appearance.

I am finding security and identity within myself.

Thankfully, I'm beginning to see a separation between the repetitive voices in my head and the security of knowing my own heart.

The crazy, demanding voice isn't me!

One perfectly speckled, starry night, after finishing *A New Earth* and beginning *The Power of Now*, I catch my reflection in the bathroom mirror. I'm beginning to understand myself just a little more.

I look in the mirror, meeting my own eyes—deeply, patiently—for the very first time in my adult life and say out loud, "Why hey there, amiga. It's lovely to finally meet you."

I smile warmly at myself, lean in, and give the mirror a smooch.

A wave of warmth radiates from my chest down through my body. I stare up at the night sky, and tears of joy stream down my face. I am beginning to come home.

IT'S GONNA GET MESSY

The next morning, I wake up with clarity. A thought plants itself deep within me, rooted with certainty, arriving oddly out of the blue. I've been learning to listen to these thoughts, so I message my very first Baja Tinder date, Mauricio, who lives across the dusty desert landscape.

Hey, can you tell me more about this Kambô you mentioned on our date?

We chat via text about his extensive decades' worth of experience with Kambô ceremonies. He sends me a wealth of information, and I do extensive research online about this poisonous frog secretion, used ritually and medicinally. It has been studied for over three decades by prominent universities and has been shown to help with addiction, depression, anxiety, arthritis, chronic pain, and inflammation—among many other things. Of course, online you'll find plenty of negative commentary on its safety, right alongside countless studies showcasing its positive effects.

What I know is that it has a long history of use in South American traditional medicine as an indigenous tribal ritual, believed to purify the body of toxins and cleanse the mind and spirit of negative energy. It's ethically sourced and is also known to produce spiritual effects, releasing energy blocks both physically and emotionally.

I'm mostly interested because it seems to be a total body and emotional release. Hint: you vomit and go to the bathroom profusely—and I feel like I have the entire Hoover Dam of my past life I am ready to release. We plan to meet next week outdoors, properly masked and distanced.

Corporate Becca would be insanely hesitant, likely watching with popcorn and sideline sarcastic commentary for anyone voluntarily choosing to vomit profusely while allowing frog poison to enter their bloodstream. Baja Becca wants to let go of all judgments—of myself and others. I am ready to purge, cleanse, heal, and trust.

I arrive at my ceremony in comfortable, flowy linen clothes, my high black heels and dress pants uniform now part of a foggy past. The ceremony requires a twelve-hour fast, and my stomach is nice and grumbly. We begin the ritual with some delectable herbal tea, calming native music, and a sage smoke bath to cleanse my energy. I am instructed to quickly drink two liters of water. I set my intention: to release all the energy in my body that is no longer serving me.

The frog secretion must come into direct contact with my bloodstream, so Mauricio takes a small piece of wood, heats it over a flame, and makes three tiny ⅛-inch circular burns on my ankle. He looks at me; I nod, smiling. I'm ready.

He places the secretion on the burns, and I breathe deeply. He watches me closely. I feel light and at ease but no nausea. He explains that for some, it takes a little more, so after a couple of minutes, he adds two more burn dots and applies the secretion again.

About five minutes later, I begin to feel the rapid and intense effects of the Kambô. My hands and feet flush red, a wave of heat flashes through my upper body and face, my pulse quickens, and I feel a little dizzy. I look at my hands and feet, they begin to swell and pulse. I swear I feel my throat swelling too.

My god—I have frog hands and feet. I'm turning into a frog.

The wave of nausea hits quickly. My eyes are closed, and in my mind's eye, I am rocketing through clouds. I see a blinking red light—like the flashing light at the end of an airplane wing on a foggy night. Suddenly, I burst through the clouds and emerge into a black abyss where an endless sea of glowing electric blue orbs stretches before me in a perfect, invisible grid. They seem to go on forever, and as I focus on one, I get the distinct feeling it has intelligence. They all do.

And then, *boom.*

I'm leaning over my bucket, vomiting like a fire hose on full blast.

It's worth noting: this is not like the terrible drunk vomiting where your stomach twists and wretches it out. This purge feels different, like it's being pulled from my toes all the way up and out. My mouth simply opens, and it streams out in full force—not once, not twice, but five times.

When there's nothing left, I lay down under the shade of the palm leaves, staring into the depths of the desert sky, where gentle pastel hues are forming above me. I feel immense joy, calmness, and utter relaxation.

Mauricio treats my small circular wounds with a Peruvian tree sap called dragon's blood, *Sangre de Grado*, which seals the burns, minimizing infection and accelerating healing. He leaves me to rest with my tea. Before departing, he asks if I'd like a bit of *rapé*.

"Oh, you mean the tobacco you blow up your nose?"
"Yes."
"Sure, why the hell not."

He blesses the tobacco, places a beautiful wooden tool on the ground, and, given the pandemic, has me use a self-administering device instead of the usual direct administration. He instructs me on how to place it in my nostril and inhale the tobacco quickly.

Immediately, my entire head burns, and I gasp for breath as tears stream down my face. It's *painful*.

Okay—several hot seconds of *very* intense pain.

"Breathe, Becca. Breathe."

The pain is sharp, but after about twenty seconds, it begins to subside. He tells me we must do the other nostril for energetic balance. I nod, tears still flowing. I administer it quickly before I can change my mind.

"Breatheeeeee. Breatheeeeee."

I inhale deeply. The crown of my head feels like it has blown open, there's no other way to describe it. Energetically, it's like a door has burst wide breaking off its hinges.

I lay back down, letting the bliss and grounding sensation wash through my entire body. I don't think I've ever felt this light, this blissful.

Mauricio leaves me for an hour, and I stay there, a massive, immovable smile glued to my face. Flat on my back, palm leaves swaying above me, warming my skin.

I smile from my heart, listening to the music, listening to the desert.

"So, how was it?" he asks when he returns to find me upright and packing up my things.

I describe my experience and the visual of the flight through the clouds and the blue orbs of consciousness.

He smiles broadly, "Visuals like this are rare. What a beautiful release."

I smile back, calm as I think I've ever felt in my entire existence. "It was simply beautiful. Thank you." I wish I could give him a hug. I blow a kiss instead. I walk home through the dusty roads, ocean off in the distance, I feel so at home. So complete. Face beaming to the heavens above.

Thank you, thank you, thank you.

Chapter Fifteen

Calling me home.

I've been in my little cocoon of isolation for three months now. It feels like it's been at least a year. Besides the updates from my friends, I continue tuning out much of what is happening with Covid. Everything is still locked down in Baja and the rest of the world. Traveling north in Baja isn't allowed, nor is it advised in the States.

My seventy-nine-year-old dad isn't able to leave bed to send me emails—he only has a desktop computer and no cell phone—so our updates are frequent but short, shared over the phone as he struggles with his breath. I describe where I am and what my quarantine days are like. He does the same from his simple bedroom, where he watches birds flutter around the small pond outside. I know he's struggling, but he's always so positive and supportive of my adventures. He's living through me, and I'm not going to let him down.

My Airbnb host had given me a steal on this place for the last few months, obviously, with no one was traveling, but one of the women in the complex mentioned in passing that she had a place on the opposite side of Baja where I could stay for free for a month or two until things opened up. What I'd heard from Armando was that there were epic waves and isolated beaches over there. It would also be closer to him, and for all of my recent awakening and coming into my own, there was still a pull I couldn't totally let go of. He was one of the few people I knew in Baja.

I take her up on her offer and soon find myself packing up my little nest, heading east to an even more remote village on the Sea of Cortez.

My new little casa is straight out of a fairytale. I pull up to find an enthusiastic, bright purple dome—chipper and vibrant, like Barney himself. Inside, the walls are coated in a brilliant cobalt blue, swirled with soft white so it looks like the sky on a sunny day, minus the puffy clouds.

Through the front door, a massive wooden sleigh bed sits up on a platform to the left, overlooking the open living room below, draped in a white bug net. A stunning geometric metal chandelier dangles in the center of the dome, directly above a lovely star-shaped tile inlay on the floor.

To the right of the door, the shower is carved directly into the boulders of the natural landscape, allowing the huge rocks to sprawl naturally into the space from the outside through the curved dome wall. A bathroom with a massive tile tub is tucked behind the rocky shower.

The entire home is filled with incredible artwork, pieces that look like they belong in a museum, clearly collected from around the world. The eclectic collection is complemented by antique furniture and lush foliage, making the space feel like a fairytale sanctuary.

Each day, when the sun spills through the open skylight at the top of the dome, a crystal hanging in its path becomes illuminated, casting a huge rainbow spectrum of light across the ceiling. Damn, this place is completely magical.

The back patio offers a stunning view of the mountains, and the huge, double-hinged, rugged doors at the front and back can be opened wide to create a welcoming gateway for the desert breeze to flow through the space. There are a few other homes scattered around, but they are spaced quite far apart. I see no signs of life. There is literally no one around. This dreamy escape beckons me to go even deeper within.

I spend my days drinking coffee, walking barefoot, meditating morning, afternoon, and night, journaling my learnings, reading voraciously about spirituality, working on my photography, and experimenting in the kitchen. I'm still applying for jobs to comply with the unemployment protocol, but I haven't had a single bite, not even a reply to an application. This is an entirely new experience for me; I've never had to work very hard to find a gig. Losing any glimmer of hope for work this year, I'm beyond grateful for unemployment benefits to help sustain me.

I've come to realize that true work fulfillment arises when you choose a vocation you genuinely enjoy—something you're excited to dedicate your time and energy to each day. When you find joy in both the work you do and the learning journey it takes you on, and you share that passion with others, that's the real key to success. However, we're still living in a construct where we must exchange this bloody, made-up currency for things. Until we can miraculously find ourselves existing in a love-and-light barter system, exchanging time for energy, there still has to be a level of financial balance or at least an agreed equality of time and effort.

I'm also keenly aware of how fortunate I am to have the education that allows me the freedom to choose a vocation. Not everyone has that privilege. If that's you, my friend, how might you take action to find work more aligned with what excites you? What sparks your curiosity? There is always something new to learn, a fresh path to follow.

In my new remote environment, I go on long beach walks, spend time snorkeling in the delightfully warm sea, and gradually forget how to wear shoes or makeup. I wonder if I'll ever be able to pull myself back to reality after slipping even deeper into isolation. I lose track of time. I forget there is a world outside my little purple magical desert dome.

I'm convinced it's just me and the donkeys that wander into my driveway in the evenings, the bats that swirl through the open-air dome at night, and the occasional baby scorpions moseying about. I'm protected by the bug net over my bed, which sits on a platform at the edge of the dome, so the creatures simply become part of my habitat. My daily existence flows in rhythm with nature, my reference to time only guided by the natural light of the rising and setting sun.

Little pangs of guilt do pop up—the little devil of thoughts perched on my shoulder, whispering into my right ear with judgment: *You are* lazy. *You aren't actually doing anything. What are you achieving right now? You are merely wasting time.*

Then the little angel chimes in, lovingly whispering into my left ear: *You've already done enough. Don't wait for life to slow down, demand that it does. Carve out a pocket of joy each day. Recognize what makes you feel alive. Stop neglecting your well-being in favor of more achievement, more consumption. Life is happening now. Stop. Pause. Enjoy. Savor. Notice your life. Be present for all of it. Love, live, and gracefully let go of what is not meant for you.*

I'm still working on the *graceful* part, but I choose to listen to the kindness of the angel instead.

My bubble of slow, solitary days finally bursts. Four months into quarantine, the restrictions begin to lift, the border opens, and flights resume. It feels safe to travel again. It's the last week of July 2020, ten months since my divorce, and we still have some final logistics to handle. I pull myself out of my desert zen to deal with a bit of reality. On the last day of July, I find myself flying back north to Portland, along with only seven other passengers on my flight. Seeing other humans again, navigating travel logistics—it's a shock to my system.

The TSA process feels awfully prison-like, with search wands, body scanners, and weary, covered faces lacking a spark of life in their eyes. After all this time outside in nature, it feels stifling.

The plan is to help Luke move from Portland to Wisconsin. We still have the first home we purchased together back in Wisconsin, and it's time to sell, it's too challenging to co-manage from a distance. When I land back in Portland, I'm not sure what I will feel. I look around the city post-pandemic, and it is a shit show. Graffiti everywhere, a boarded-up downtown from all the riots, the waterfront full of homeless camps, people openly doing drugs in the streets. This is not the Portland I once knew.

Something in me clicks into certainty.

I ask if I can have my storage POD delivered to a parking space at a storage unit facility for the weekend, and the incredibly kind manager says yes. Before I put everything into storage back in the fall of 2019, I took photos of it all, so I quickly post everything on Facebook Marketplace. I head to the storage site, sit on the corner of my barely used, cute turquoise West Elm sofa, and proceed to sell absolutely everything.

Every part of my being is telling me to head back to Baja.

I have no permanent home there, no job lined up, and my truck is still in storage at the airport, packed with all my belongings. But my soul is telling me to go back to Mexico. It's the only place that feels like home.

For once, I finally listen.

I sit on the corner in Portland on a sunny Friday afternoon and sell my perfect French teak bookshelf, my vintage typewriter, the distressed wood dining table and chairs, my mid-century dressers that feel more like art than furniture—everything I've carefully collected in my entire adult life. I keep only a few books, childhood keepsakes, and some outdoor gear that's hard to replace. Fortunately, some friends agree to store a few of these remaining keepsakes in the corner of their garage for me.

And just like that, I let it all go.

As I reach the back of the storage unit, I start giving things away for free as the items dwindle.

"Here, would you like a gold meditation frog with your vintage dresser purchase? How about an excessively priced throw pillow from Anthropologie? A Pendleton blanket to go with those Nordstrom dinner plates?"

At the end, I snap a photo of myself standing in my completely empty pod, arms raised in triumph. I'm on a mission to release.

Something in me had always wanted to know what it was like to live with only what could fit in the trunk of my 4Runner, and now I was feeling bold enough to shed the material possessions and finally find out.

It's just stuff, after all. It can be replaced.

It all feels like it belongs to a previous life.

And so I let it go too.

We drive across the country to Madison and arrive in Wisconsin just a few days later. Stepping into the home we purchased a year into our marriage feels like walking into a stranger's house—the ghosts of our past whispering from the walls, reminding us of moments long gone.

We clear out the remaining items from the basement owner's closet of our cozy 900-square-foot first home and list it for sale. Naturally, we can't help but reminisce a little, and for the first time, Luke shares that he always felt our matrimonial path was about *me, me, me*.

I protest. "You did? But you never threw a flag on the field of play! You never flat-out said, 'No, I don't want to move there' or 'I don't want to apply for this job' or 'I don't want to journey down this path.' I *would* have listened!"

He says simply, "No, I felt I had no choice."

My mind is truly blown. And there, my friend, lies the importance of open communication. I never *felt* like I presented our moves or life changes that way. I didn't *feel* that way in my heart. I always thought I was doing it all *for us*, to better *us*.

Perception vs. perspective—you can't step outside your own unique perception to see the broader view of others unless you openly share your deep wants and desires.

Sigh.

Hindsight.

Afterward, I sell my fancy, oversized wedding ring for a ridiculously small sum. I don't see the point of it sitting in a box in a safe any longer, perhaps it will bring another bride some symbolic bliss.

As we sift through our excessively large Tupperware tubs in the basement, I thumb through old swimming ribbons, basketball trophies, and even older stuffed animals I couldn't bear to part with. I save two favorite childhood books: *Calvin and Hobbes* and *She-Ra: Princess of Power*. Then, I stumble upon a small golden metal treasure chest I had locked in childhood. With ease, I pick it open.

Inside, I find rocks, trinkets, a few photos, and at the very bottom, something shiny catches my eye. I reach in and pull out a small pile of coins. *Whaaaat?* It's a little stash of pesos.

A spark of energy flows through my entire body. A flash of knowing. A sign that where I am in life at this moment is *exactly* where I'm supposed to be. But how? How did a little girl from Wisconsin, who never traveled out of the country until her twenties and didn't set foot in Mexico until her early thirties, end up with pesos? I have no clue. But I *know* I need to keep exploring Baja. Not for a person, not even for the place itself—something deeper is pulling me back, and I don't know what or why. It's just a feeling in the depths of my being, an undeniable force calling me south.

This is when I begin to trust that pull inside me, to hear the subtle whisper and take action without needing to know all the details. Sometimes, we can plan our way out of existence. Instead, I choose to act. To simply follow the pull.

I can always pivot later.

The woman I am becoming will cost me people, relationships, spaces, and material things. But I am now choosing *her* over everything.

When I stop at my parents' house, I walk in, masked, to see my dad. I catch a glimpse of his 6'3" frame in bed, he has been fully bound to it for eight months. I don't think he weighs much more than 100 pounds. I haven't seen him since Christmas last year, and the shock of his physical deterioration takes my breath away.

I immediately turn around and step outside. Rounding the corner out of sight, I stop and collapse into myself, the tears erupting—uncontrollable sobs heaving through my body. My heart aches so badly I can barely stand it.

But I don't allow myself to feel the depth of my pain for more than a moment, I can't. I quickly tuck it back inside, wipe my tears, and put a big smile in my eyes before walking back in, mask on.

We chat from opposite corners of the room, my dad lying on the bed about fifteen feet away. I don't dare get any closer. He has gotten so much worse. The rare autoimmune disease is winning the battle; he has been in and out of the hospital.

I remain cheerful and upbeat. He musters all the cheerfulness he can, too.

We talk about the beautiful birds he's seen outside his window, the cranes taking off and landing on the small pond. We talk about the Brewers and their hopes for the playoffs. We chat about the Packers and how the last few games have gone.

We talk for almost an hour, but he is fighting to stay awake.

Quietly, I mention that I want to stay—that I *should* stay.

"Sweetie, what are you going to do here? Watch me lie in bed? Go. Go live by the blue waters, go surf, go chase your dreams. For me. I'm so proud of you." He smiles with complete love.

I can barely take it. The sob wells up in me. I hold it back. I stay chipper. "I'll call you lots and send photos of all my adventures. Love you so, so much!"

I can't go up to him and give him a hug for fear of any Covid exposure risk, so I wave from the doorway. I say goodbye to my mom, also keeping my distance, telling her, "He will get better." We look into each other's eyes, both so filled with fear.

I barely make it outside and around the corner from the front door before I drop to my knees. I sob and sob and sob. It's too much to process, too much to take in. My mind can't handle what I'm seeing, so I force myself to finish up quickly, allowing only a minute's release from the dam before tightly closing the doors back up again.

Luke is standing there and gives me a hug. Everything feels like it's spinning. I feel nauseous.

"Want to get a drink?" he asks warmly.

I look at him and wipe my tears. "Hell yes, I do."

I drink myself into numbed-out oblivion.

The next day, with my mission to lighten my load—physically and mentally—in both Portland and Madison now complete, I turn and head back into the unknown that is calling me home.

Chapter Sixteen

Careful what you wish for.

It's the end of August 2020, and I land back in Baja to try to secure housing near San José del Cabo. Our home sells, but it's 2020, and we time the market so poorly that we barely make the profits we'd hoped for. After taxes, expenses, and splitting what's left, it's a tough pill to swallow. Without a job opportunity on the horizon, I definitely feel the financial crunch and dip into my small pool of emergency savings. I'm still applying for jobs every single week and having zero luck. I still apply in Oregon for remote jobs as well as local jobs in Mexico, but marketing gigs are still a lost cause right now.

I manage to find a cute little studio casita with just a bed, a small bathroom, and a tiny single-seater table and chair inside. Outside, there's a plug-in electric hot plate, an electric tea kettle, a small stainless steel sink as my kitchen, and two lounge chairs with bright cobalt blue cushions that pop against the white rounded stucco walls behind them. The edge of the patio is anchored by a magnificent pink bougainvillea bush, and beyond that, the sea and a view of my surf break. It's not much, but I'm surprised by how happy and content I feel in my little space.

Can I continue to be happy with the wealth I'm building inside myself instead of all the material pursuits I've spent the last—gosh, next week is my 40th birthday—the last forty years chasing? I sure hope so.

Everything I own now fits in the trunk of my 4Runner, minus the items in Oregon with friends and one bin in Wisconsin under my parents' basement stairs. I've shed nearly all of my material possessions, yet at this moment, I've never felt richer. I'm starting to chase time instead of money. I feel physically and mentally lighter. The Baja sun and sea have made it so, inside and out. I'm learning that living well means finding deep pleasure in the valuable, even when I'm not feeling financially secure.

I begin to see that it isn't about becoming a "successful" person in societal terms; it's about becoming a valuable human to those I love and the community around me. It isn't about how much you achieve or accumulate, it's about how much you enjoy your journey each day. If you don't take the time to enjoy where you are, you never truly live. If it's always, *I'll be happy when...* then you're always going to be trying to "maximize outcomes" in an unsustainable culture that leaves its population in deep physical, mental, and emotional turmoil—and burnout. You wake up one day and wonder where the time went and what you exchanged for it.

I find more and more, as I begin to rewrite my own definition of success, that what I value rarely costs much money. The things I truly treasure don't cost a damn thing. Sunsets are free. Enjoying nature is free. Meditation is free. Hugs are free. Loving others is free. Deep conversations are free. Gratitude is free. Great sex is free. Exercising is free. Music is mostly free. The best things in life, the ones I value most, are free.

I spend my birthday surfing solo. A new friend at the beach sells me an old yellow beat-up surfboard with more patches and dings than I can count for $100. Tláloc is his name, I'm told, and the nose of the board is hand-painted with his likeness. Tláloc is the god of rain in Aztec religion. He was also a deity of earthly fertility and water, worshiped as a giver of life and sustenance.

I'm in love.

I meet some people in the lineup, and they buy me a birthday lunch. Later that evening, some surf friends meet me for tacos and mezcal. Everything is so rich, so delicious, so savored. It's a quiet, simple, beautiful birthday.

My mom and dad call to sing me *Happy Special Day*, each hopping on their home landline, one upstairs and one downstairs. My dad's having trouble with his lungs and can barely get enough air to sing, but you can hear the deep love in his voice. He sounds as loving and joyous as one can be while confined to bed. He keeps speaking of gratitude—for his TV and sports, the birds that visit him outside his window, the bit of food he can still get down, the Sunday church service he listens to from bed, and the daily prayers he receives from his Christian Science practitioner. My mom just listens, allowing my dad to dominate the conversation as he usually does.

He loves to randomly call and tell me, "It's a beautiful clear blue day, not a cloud in the sky!"

He asks how the surf is, and I describe the clear blue waters, the palm trees, the fish I saw by my feet that morning. He sounds so happy to hear about my Mexico adventures. I know he is with me in spirit.

"Love you, Dad."

"Love you, daughter dearest."

A simple quiet, "Bye, love you." From my mom.

We hang up, and I cry, as I always do after every call we've had this past year. Every time I see *'Rents* pop-up on my phone screen, signaling my parents landline number they've had for the last thirty-four years, I'm never sure if this is *the* call. I'm profoundly grateful for each remaining chat.

***

I continue to focus on my healing. For someone who grew up land-locked in Wisconsin, getting in the sea each day has done wonders for my soul. I've been an athlete my whole life, but learning how to surf has been the most humbling experience for me both physically and mentally. Every time I paddle out, it reminds me that I'm part of this beautiful, natural, immensely powerful energy that is so much bigger than myself. Yet it holds space and allows me in. It's one of my greatest teachers. It brings me back to the core of my being, patiently, every time I return to her. And as an added bonus, there really is nothing left of one's ego after being tumbled like a rag doll by a big-ass set of beautiful waves.

I'm not sure what I would have done without surf in my life right now. It came at the most absolute perfect moment. Surfing has taught me that you can either try ridiculously hard, forcing action, or you can wait and be patient for the right moment. By putting intentional effort into waiting, you can take off and ride in that perfect, blissful flow. If you put in heaps of effort without looking up and being aware of your surroundings, you just get exhausted without ever going anywhere—and likely piss off those around you who are trying to find their own lovely flow.

***

I've met a few people around town, mostly through the surf lineup. I meet a lovely woman, Nikki, at a yoga class, and she reaches out about an upcoming full moon sound bath and cacao circle. I have no clue what this is, but I agree to go the following week.

When I arrive at the gathering, I find it's in a beautiful beachside setting—twinkling tea lights strung overhead, a cozy circle of mats and pillows below, with a simple altar in the center adorned with flowers and a large steaming pot of cacao. I'm told that cacao, the raw form of chocolate, is rich in mood-boosting compounds like serotonin and tryptophan. It's a natural, nourishing way to spark joy, enhance focus, and give your heart a little love. Our small group of fifteen gathers in a circle, our ceramic terracotta-painted cups filled with warm cacao. The cool evening desert breeze kisses our faces. The native Oaxacan guide speaks about how this ceremonial cacao, sourced from her indigenous community, helps to gently touch and open the emotional center of our body, our heart chakra.

We sit on the beach, the fire crackling, the full moon glowing, waves rolling in, the night sky filled with stars and gorgeous guitar music. As the gathering comes to a close, the gentle harmonies of sound bowls fill the air, and I can't help but think of my dad—how he is clearly suffering, barely eating, body aching, unable to leave his bed for almost a year, withering away. I look at the full moon and ask with all my heart: *Please, help my dad go easily and peacefully when he is ready. Thank you.* I stroll home that evening with a full heart.

The next morning, after a surf, I return to my truck to see a missed call from '*Rents.* I play the message.

"Hey babe, it's me, Mom. Can you call me as soon as you can?"

My heart rate spikes. I fumble for the button to call back and accidentally drop my surfboard.

"Hi. He's... gone."

The bomb goes off in every cell of my being. My ears ring. I can't see clearly. I can't process it. I can't even process the environment around me. I reach my hand out and brace myself against my car.

"We were talking this morning. I went downstairs to do some prayer work, and when I came back upstairs, he was gone." She is fighting tears. I've never seen her cry. She sounds so small, so fragile.

I go into survival mode. Numb. All I can say is, "Okay. Let me get on the next flight. Love you." And I hang up.

I sob the whole way home.

I waste three days waiting for my flight. I just spend that time messaging with friends, family, and loved ones, sharing photos on social media, updating everyone. The only person I really know well in the area is Armando. Our communications had already dwindled to nearly nothing while I was up in the States selling everything. We had decided to just be friends—without benefits—before I left, as it was clear this in-between thing wasn't working, and our last hangs had been incredibly tense.

We've barely spoken in the last month, but I text him:

Hola. My dad died yesterday. And a real hug from someone here who gets me would help as I wait to fly north for the funeral Sunday. I think the willingness to face and understand uncomfortable emotions is the path to inner peace. Many of the overwhelming negative emotions I was experiencing while spending time with you were an accumulation of past pain that I hadn't properly processed. I needed to feel those emotions in one way or another to grow. I'm still learning, you being you helped me learn. We left things tense. Not sure how you feel, but I want to release that, not keep the past alive in any way or build identity around it. Would you have time to stop by?

His swift reply:

I am sorry to hear about your dad. I can't imagine how you must be feeling. I don't think I could give you a real hug, as, since some time ago, I decided to let go, release, and close the page with a nice memory of what we shared during that brief, nice time. My approach for inner peace is very different from yours, and I don't think or feel it would be beneficial for you or me to open that page again. Sorry if it's not what you would like, but this is what I need. I understand you are in a hurtful place, and I wish you the best as you go through your process, but an insincere hug from me might trigger something undesired in you. And again, I feel it's better for both of us how we are.

And then he blocks me.

In this moment, with the overwhelming grief of losing my dad, this feels like someone ripping out my already broken heart and beating it with a baseball bat.

Half an hour goes by. I stare at my phone in disbelief. In abandonment. In fear. In a pile of unworthy tears.

My reply:

I understand your needs. You are feeling for both of us what is better for you. It's okay, you have to take care of what you need. I try to show care to all who have shared time with me, short or long. I don't let go, I forgive. So I reach out to you in a dire time of need. Maybe this is the learning... that sometimes completely letting go is okay. Perhaps one day, you will let go of the past, and we can be friends. If not, I accept that. I hope there are no ill feelings. I will remember the brief, nice memories we shared and wish you well on your journey. Thank you for the condolences.

When people treat you like they don't care in the way you need to be cared for, believe them. When people throw up a strong boundary, respect it.

I get one gray check mark in WhatsApp for my reply. The message is never delivered.

I am not heard.

I never will be fully heard—not by this man.

Chapter Seventeen

Eating in a tomb.

Life becomes a few blurry days of such deep, visceral pain that I have never, ever experienced. I don't eat. I don't really move except from the bed to the floor. I barely sleep. I rotate between the floor, my bed, and my deck, looking at the stars.

I'm not sure how I get to the airport or board a plane, but next thing I know, I'm back up in Wisconsin. Luke greets me at the airport with my favorite snacks and a six-pack—my mom is too frazzled to drive to pick me up. I'm so incredibly grateful for his reassuring company when I land. After all, he was his dad too these last 15 years. We both are feeling the immense loss.

The week is a total blur. Because Covid protocols are still in place, family and friends are still distancing. We have a simple, five-minute ceremony outside at a small cemetery north of Madison, near the beautiful Devil's Lake where my dad grew up and where we swam together as a family each summer. It's just my mom, brother, his partner, my mom's sister, and Luke by my side. I physically lean on him for the ceremony, arms locked. I'm so grateful for his support, in all ways, during this time.

My mom says a short prayer next to my father's gravesite and reads his favorite passage from the Bible:

"*The Lord is my shepherd; I shall not want. He maketh me lie down in green pastures: he leadeth me beside the still waters. He restoreth my soul:*

he leadeth me in the paths of righteousness for his name's sake. Yea, though I walk through the valley of the shadow of death, I will fear no evil: for thou art with me; thy rod and thy staff they comfort me. Thou preparest a table before me in the presence of mine enemies: thou anointest my head with oil; my cup runneth over. Surely goodness and mercy shall follow me all the days of my life: and I will dwell in the house of the Lord forever." (Psalms 23:1-6)

I trail off in thought, thinking about how, up until the very end of his life, my dad was still sending me Christian Science articles and emails, always hoping I would convert back to the religion I was raised in. But there simply was no desire in me to do so. Deep down, I felt like I was letting him down, but I had to choose my own path. I was becoming increasingly spiritually curious—but not at all religious—which I shared with my dad toward the end. I hoped that brought him a bit of comfort.

Our ceremony is over in minutes, and a gentle man with the funeral company quietly asks if I want to take a look inside the coffin.

I stare blankly, ears ringing from the overwhelm of all the emotion stirring in me, not releasing.

"No. Thank you."

There is no way that his lifeless body is going to be my last view of my beloved dad. Watching over my shoulder as I walk away from his coffin, I can't comprehend that his body is in there. I never got to hug him one last time, which breaks my heart. I have the urge to run back, grip the coffin, and lie with it sobbing until my time on Earth is over. I stare blankly, lost in my fantasy for a moment, unable to move.

Someone gently grabs my elbow and guides me back to the car. We leave him there. I hold my gaze as long as I can on his final resting place as we slowly drive away.

That evening, we gather to have his favorite pizza for dinner at their home. I'm not sure it really tastes like anything, but I mindlessly chew. The house feels hollow, lifeless without his presence. It hits me what a blow to the family this is, he always carried so much of the conversation and positive energy. Always laughing, joyful, sparking discussion. Now, it's like eating in a tomb.

Dad lived a full life—he was 79, just under three months shy of his 80th birthday. But I simply can't stand being in my parents' home without him there. My mind can't process that he is no longer here. And the only bed available to stay in is the one where he passed away a week ago.

I. Just. Can't.

My mom understands. She stays at home, and we connect during the day for solemn visits along with my brother, all of us unable to say or express much. I decide to stay with Luke and his dad and am so deeply grateful for their love and company during this time.

We go to the pub a few nights to drown my sorrows, but I have to escape. I have to get back to Baja. Not for anything pressing, just because I know I can't be here. This is all too much for me to process. I need to get back to the ocean. To save myself from the mental spin I feel overtaking me.

I feel I need to return south to the ocean, to lose my mind and find my soul. Riding a wave is this emotionless, beautiful thing that pulls you into the present in a way that makes you feel really, completely *alive*. And I desperately need that right now.

The ocean teaches me I can be both calm and chaotic, gentle and strong. It shows me how to surf, but more importantly, how to ride life's waves. I need a place to just *be*.

This is why I love surfing so much. When I'm on the water, there is no time to think. I am simply in the moment, out of my own way, in that flow state where my mind connects with the movement of my body and the ocean's energy. When I'm out there, my mind is free from any other worries. I am present. It gives me space to heal.

I feel immense guilt for leaving my mother at this moment, but I have to escape.

Three days after the burial, I'm on a plane heading back down to Baja to try and heal my broken heart. Again.

Chapter Eighteen

One checkmark.

I land back in Baja in the afternoon and decide I must take myself out on the town. I deserve a nice glass of wine and a lovely dinner to soothe myself. I fear that if I go to my little studio apartment, I will slide into bed and be enveloped in a mental death spiral.

After showering, I put on one of the two dresses I own, curl my hair, apply makeup, and do a little research on a beautiful rooftop restaurant I've been wanting to visit—one that overlooks the Cabo Land's End arch and has spectacular sunset views.

I hop in my truck and am on my way to the restaurant. Just five minutes into the drive, I feel it before I see it. I glance in my rearview mirror.

Speeding up insanely quickly behind my truck is Armando, rapidly approaching on his motorcycle. The helmeted drifter, wandering Baja, running from the past—emotionally cut off after the separation from his wife and child. He truly is Mexican Mad Max. His metal machine comes within fifteen feet behind me, then quickly darts into the left lane to pass. His head remains dead ahead, no glance over.

Behind him is a woman, hair blowing in the wind, arms wrapped deeply and securely around him. Her chest pressed into his back.

My heart falls out of my chest. My breath quickens. I wince and try to breathe. My heart is breaking.

I tell myself I'm not enough. I'm not lovable. I'm not worthy.

I feel the tears welling up and debate turning around and going home. My spirit, trying to uplift itself, has just experienced a near-deadly hit-and-run, given my mental state.

I pull over to the side of the road and just breathe for a few minutes. *No. Fuck that. You're worthy. You're enough, dammit. You're all dressed up, you look beautiful, and I'm taking you out!*

I look myself in the eye in the rearview mirror. I breathe. *You know he wasn't good for you. He didn't make you feel secure. It's over now, thankfully. You learned a lot. Just let go and move your thoughts toward all the bright and wonderful things coming your way.*

I pull back onto the highway and keep driving the thirty minutes to the restaurant. A kind valet takes my car, and I stroll through the stunning hotel lobby that sits against the beach. Waves crashing. The sun is beginning its descent towards the sea. I feel relaxed again. Grateful.

I ride the elevator up to the top floor and am greeted by a lovely hostess.

"Table for one?"

"Yes, please. At the bar if there is a spot, thank you."

She smiles warmly and guides me back to the restaurant. We round a corner, and I take in the sun setting, the waves below, the absolutely gorgeous space, the wonderful music... and—holy mother of fucking God, please have mercy on me—Armando.

A mental shockwave hits me. I nearly have to sit down.

He's sitting at a high-top table off to my right with the same woman who had just flown past me on his motorcycle not half an hour earlier. I can tell he spots me. I have to walk past them, within two feet, to get to the bar. I have no clue if I'm smiling, grimacing, frowning, or snarling.

I grab myself by the emotional elbow and whisper to myself: *Keep walking, Becca. Smile. There ya go, great job. Keep walking.*

The hostess sits me at the bar, on a barstool directly facing them, just twenty feet away. She hands me the menu. The bartender hands me a wine list. My heart and head are absolutely pounding. I bumble out, "Un momento, por favor."

I stare at the menu, unable to process its blurry words. I could move to another table, but that would be so obvious—and they're all set up for larger parties and reserved seats. I could dig in, enjoy my dinner, and stare at them like I couldn't give two shits... I contemplate the situation for a moment.

I need air.

I force a smile at the bartender and tell him I'll be back as I stand and head for the hostess stand. I have to walk past them again. I keep my head straight ahead, forcing a smile even though my heart is imploding. My ears are ringing, and I'm pretty sure the room is tilting as the emotional shrapnel permeates my entire being.

I keep walking, straight past the hostess, who tilts her adorable head, looking at me quizzically, as I step onto an empty outdoor yoga deck just beyond the bathrooms. *Removing myself instead of forcing myself to sit with negative energy is growth*, I tell myself, offering a bit of comfort.

I call Luke and explain the situation.

"Seriously, I mean... what in the absolute fuck? Absolutely unreal. I can't even begin to process the probability of us both being at this restaurant, on this day, at the same time. There are literally over a thousand restaurants in Los Cabos. This place was over a half-hour drive for us both, and not a place Armando would ever go. It's fancy and expensive, and he sat there in his surf-bum wardrobe collection. What kind of cruel joke is the Universe playing?"

Truly, the likelihood of this happening is so impossible, it seems like a greater force is at play.

He chuckles, trying to add levity. "So, you staying for a battle round or heading out?"

"Hah. Even though things needed to end—a thousand times over—this still feels absolutely awful. Ugh. My heart is still so hurt. I've gotta get out of here. Unreal. Gah. I guess I'll just hit a restaurant close to home."

"Sorry, love. No fun at all. Get out of there and go treat yourself to the nice dinner you deserve." He says it warmly, with such a caring heart. I'm grateful for his comforting words.

"Thank you." I add some levity back and tease him, "How goes the visit with the girlfriend, is she getting carded?"

He laughs. We had been chatting about our new endeavors in dating—me savoring adventurous chocolate skin, him dating someone half his age who was just shy of the legal drinking age. You know, classic divorce shit.

"I just tell everyone I'm her dad, and that gets her in just fine."

I let out a sincere laugh. "Well, good luck with that."

"Yeah, you too. Hang in there."

I hang up, head right for the elevator, back to my truck to the surprised valet wondering why I'm leaving so soon, and I drive right back home. I take off the dress, put on my pajamas, drink a bottle of wine, and tuck myself into bed to marinate in my deep sorrow. Right before I fall asleep I get the brilliant idea to reach out. I message him that night as I fall asleep in my tsunami of grief that has just punched me down into total darkness: *You're a cruel, selfish human being and I fucking hate you.*

When you're aching to be seen, heard, or held, you're likely in the wrong place with the wrong people. Let go. Forgive. Not to excuse, but to free yourself from the belief that their actions were about you. Our messy, half-this, half-that connection was just two old stories colliding—full of past wounds and triggers. Sometimes it was about each other, but often, it wasn't. My alone time in the desert brought inner peace, but learning to relate to others on their own healing journey while still on my own? That cracks open a whole new layer of learning.

One check mark. My message was not delivered. It would never be delivered. I must accept that. Sometimes, the ache to be understood echoes into silence.

Chapter Nineteen

Under the full moon.

Grief is a funny thing. It can seem like it's letting up in one moment, and the next, it's everywhere. It's with you when you're out running errands. It's in the song on the radio. It joins you at the table when you're eating a favorite dish you once shared with your lost loved one. It's there to tuck you in at night, then decides to hop into your already overflowing, grief-filled bed, when all you desire is a decent night's sleep.

The grief is just too heavy for me to peel it off and get up right now. This is the most grief I've ever endured in my life, and I am not equipped to handle it. I have no choice but to wallow in it.

I am fortunate—or not so fortunate—to be jobless, so I have plenty of time, endless time, to sit in my grief and try to process it. If I had been stuck in my corporate job right now, there is no way I would have been able to return to work. I beg and cry and wait for the grief to lighten up. It does. And then it doesn't.

I lose track of all space and time. I stay in my little studio, drapes drawn, staring at the wall and crying for three weeks. The pain and abandonment I'm feeling, the uncertainty of everything, makes my head spin itself into a disaster of doubt, shame, unworthiness, fear, heartbreak. I swim in it all.

I think I fully realize that no one is coming to save me.

IT'S GONNA GET MESSY

It's the very next full moon when my dear friend Nikki, the one who brought me to last month's cacao circle under the full moon, texts me and asks how I'm doing with my grieving.

Do you need a hug? Come out tonight. There's another beachfront full moon cacao circle, breathwork session with a lovely local guitarist. Come. Come get some relief and company.

I simply can't.

She is kind but refuses to take no for an answer, gently urging me to come. I'm so sad and lonely that I finally give in.

I meet her there on the beach under the full, crisp, brilliantly white, most incredible full moon. I can't believe it's been a month since I last looked at the full moon at this very same spot and silently wished for my dad to go peacefully when he was ready—and the very next morning, he had.

I look at that same full moon as the sound healing host asks us to open our hearts and set an intention.

I stare up at the full moon, sorrow in my heart, but I close my eyes and wish with every single fiber of my being as I send a request out into the Universe...

Dad, if you're out there, please show me.

The evening begins with beautiful guitar music and gentle singing. We all take a bit of the warm ceremonial cacao that has been lovingly provided. This time, I learn a little more about cacao from our indigenous elder serving us.

Cacao is the name of the tree that produces cacao beans, which are used to make chocolate and other foods. Cacao itself is simply the raw, unrefined bean, it becomes cocoa after the bean is roasted. Our guide explains that cacao has been used for thousands of years in Mayan culture for medicinal, culinary, and ceremonial purposes. There are absolutely no psychedelic or hallucinogenic properties to it; the cacao herb simply works by bringing us back to the feeling of love, oneness, and connection. Both the Mayan and Aztec cultures have used it for centuries. In Aztec mythology, it's said that cacao was often used in sacrificial ceremonies to lift the spirits of those about to be sacrificed. They believed that with cacao, we are able to tune in and listen deeply to the callings of our hearts. They felt that this herbal drink helped open the heart space, allowing a deep connection to our innermost self, tapping into the profound power and wisdom stored within each of us.

I listen and drink it gratefully. It's like a thick, terribly bitter, but still somewhat tasty, hot cocoa. I nibble on the tiny, bitter chocolate nibs at the bottom of my mug, then lie down to connect with my breath and the soft, gentle Mexican acoustic guitar music.

I lay down on my little mat in the sand, surrounded by woven blankets. Breathing deeply, in tune with the music and the waves, I begin to forget all of my pain. As I lose touch with my grief and focus on my breathwork, relaxing deeper into myself, when I suddenly feel a gentle hand touch the top of my head and caress my hair across my forehead toward my ear.

For a brief moment, I am about to open my eyes, wondering *Why in the world is the ceremony guide touching me? This isn't part of the ceremony...*

Oh. My. God.

The viscerally familiar hand strokes my hair again—gently, slowly, lovingly. There is no mistaking this feeling, this energy, this hand. I have felt this caress before. It is, without a doubt, my father.

I gasp aloud. The air is sucked from my lungs, and I hold my breath. I dare not open my eyes. I dare not move. Tears spill from my tightly closed eyes, tears of purest joy, and then...

What happens next—there truly are no earthly words to describe.

Instantly, I am out of my body.

I am in total darkness. I am nothing. No body, no form. And yet, I am aware—aware of myself, of my consciousness. The darkness is eternal, expansive, warm, and welcoming. It is everything and nothing. It is utterly silent, like the vastness of space, yet it contains a blaring symphony of energy, pulsing through it, rumbling in the dark without sound.

I exist in the darkness, and I am also aware that I am golden light. A little bouncing cluster of sparkly diamonds of vibrant golden light. And I am not alone.

Before me, another cluster of golden light twinkles and pulses with delight. The light is like golden diamond stars, with streaks of warm light extending a foot or two above and below, clustered together in a loose form. Not the form of a human—but of an *energetic being*.

There is no mistaking this energy.
It is my father.
We are light. We are... There are simply no words in this physical world to describe it.
We *are*.
We are dancing. Sparkling. Pulsing. Our energy swirls together in Love, in this infinite void filled with eternal Life.
I feel all that eternal Life is, all that existence is.
And I am part of it.
I am *one* with it.
All Life before and after now—yet there is no before and after. Only now.
I communicate with him without audible sound. We are speaking without words, yet the exchange of thoughts is instantaneous and miraculously clear, passed between us directly in our minds.
Dad, is this what we are?!
He answers me without speaking. Again, our thoughts are exchanged instantly, without sound. His reply is childlike, enthusiastic:
Yes!! Isn't it so unbelievably wonderful? Aren't we just so incredibly beautiful? I am so very happy. I am completely at peace. I am home!
There are a million questions I want to ask him, but one rises without thought or hesitation—a deep, soul-calling question.
Dad... can I stay here with you?
And in that instant, I am dropped back into my body.
I actually *feel* myself return. The heaviness of it shocks me. A river of absolute gratitude, unlike anything I have ever released, pours out of me. I am absolutely out of control crying from pure joy. I can't open my eyes yet. I can't fully make sense of what just happened, but I can feel it—this immense, unconditional Love pouring through me. It's not just comfort. It's a soul-deep remembering, like something ancient and true vibrating in every cell. I feel safe. I feel still. I feel a peace so profound, it feels like home.
It *absolutely* happened.
I can't believe it.
He came to me!!!
I finally attempt to open my eyes. My friend Nikki looks over at me in the darkness, our faces illuminated by the fire in the center of the

circle and the full moon above. The ceremony is still in process. Her glimmering eyes ask silently, *Are you okay?*

I smile and nod, trying to bring myself back down to Earth.

My hearing is a little off. I can see everyone around me in the circle, but it's as if they are behind a glass window, their voices muffled. My body feels *insanely* heavy as I lift my arm to wipe my tears. I've never noticed just how heavy it is before. It takes a few moments for my thoughts to register with my body—and then, finally, it moves.

I slowly sit up, resting there in disbelief.

I'm not sure for how long.

Someone taps me, and I look up to see the group still in a circle, moving from person to person as each one shares their thoughts or feelings.

Words spill from my mouth without thought.

I *have* to share what just happened, if only to speak it out loud, to capture the energy and Truth for a single moment. I don't even know exactly what I'm saying. I try to express my feelings, my experience, but I can't fully hear myself. I'm sobbing. The lovely women on my left and right place their hands on my legs, my shoulders—comforting me.

I finish speaking.

Everyone is staring back at me, tears streaming down their faces, eyes full of love.

Then, I hear a voice from two seats down.

"A voice spoke to me several times," he says, his voice thick with emotion. "It simply said *Dad* and then *I'm Dad*. I had no idea why this was happening, or why it was coming to my mind so clearly. I now know why."

Tears stream down his cheeks. He smiles at me, nodding.

My friend next to me says she heard me begin to cry. When she looked over, she saw white light around me.

I stare up at the magnificent, crisp white full moon, its brilliance washing over me. My heart overflows with a wave of absolute bliss.

My perception of what this one precious life is all about has just shifted entirely—in a single instant.

I say silently to the moon, the sea, and beyond:

Thank you, Dad. I love you oh so very much. See you again soon.

I thank the facilitators. I hug everyone. I sit a while longer under the moonlight, my colorful Mexican blanket wrapped around me, staring in pure awe.

I look at Nikki. I feel more rooted in my body now. My hearing is normalizing.

"Nikki. Nikki... oh my god!!!"

I'm processing things a bit more, and my hands are shaking.

"I... I don't know how to describe what just happened. He came to me. He took me out of my body right here... just... just a veil over, I guess, is the only way to describe it. I was me, and he was my dad—there was absolutely no mistaking that—but there was no speech exchanged, we had no form but Light.

So he's right here, right now, just beyond a dimension we can't yet see through or experience. He is in this *same* moment in time that we are.

This life... it's all such a tremendous... gorgeous... painful... stunning... dream.

And we created it.

We are here by choice."

She smiles her gorgeous, motherly smile and holds my hand, squeezing it tightly.

"He loves you so very much. This is such a beautiful gift. I am so happy for you."

We hug deeply, for a long while. My heart could burst. It *is* bursting.

I head home, replaying every single moment in my mind and body again and again and again. I journal rapidly to capture every detail. I don't ever want to forget. I *won't* forget.

I will remember this night for the rest of my life.

It isn't lost on me that a good portion of my father's time here on Earth was spent trying to bring me back to spirituality, to the belief in something more. I *wanted* to believe. I wanted to believe for him and for me. But until now, I had never had such a visceral conversation with Truth. With Love.

In an instant—one instant of connection to the Divine, with my father as the bridge—I have felt what each and every one of us is a part of.

I am forever reborn from this moment onward.
My perception of reality has been forever shifted.
I will never be more grateful for a single gift in my entire Earthly existence.

Chapter Twenty

A broken system.

So, infused with this new wisdom, I immediately decide to head into the mountains of Mexico to meditate for the rest of my life, devote myself to a purely spiritual existence, and single-handedly elevate the energy and consciousness of the planet.

Yeah, no.

Not so much.

One would think that after a life-changing, supernatural experience—one where my dad literally moved through quantum fields to gift me with divine truth—life would get sweeter, softer, and remarkably better. And it did. For just a *hot* second.

The visit from my dad lifted so much of the grief I had been drowning in, almost immediately. I *knew* he was alive. More alive than he ever was in the way I used to interact with him, when we were both wearing these handy little meat suits our limitless energy currently inhabits. I knew he was happy, joyful, no longer suffering. And the icing on this eternal, scrumptious, galactic cream cake? The absolute knowing that he is with me, always.

The thing is, after experiencing something so profound—so deeply unearthing in the *best* possible way, lifting all my deeply rooted anchors around what I thought this reality was—I found that life here, in mental and physical construct land, got a little... tricky. A bit of a mind fuck around my purpose here, if you will.

The importance of material things, jobs, money, achievement, recognition... it all suddenly seemed so silly.

In the first month after my experience, I find myself telling darn near everyone I know, and don't know, what happened. I share my story with a woman at the gas station who looks like she's having a rough day. With a man in the grocery store queue. With a waiter at a bar. It gets a bit ridiculous, but I share anyway, through tears and an open, sincere heart. I just know so deeply that I *need* to share this experience with as many people as possible.

Maybe if I share it with someone who hasn't yet connected to Source, the Divine, God, the Universe—whatever you want to call it (they're all the same to me now)—maybe my story will help them on their own path. Maybe they'll truly *know* their Universal beauty, their interconnectedness, their limitless potential. Or maybe, at the very least, I can help plant the energetic seed of the idea, and with time, it will sprout in them.

The irony that I've now become *exactly* like my parents, who never stopped trying to convince me of a higher power when I was growing up, is not lost on me. Pops wouldn't give up on me. And now, I find myself doing the same thing. Hopefully, not as annoyingly as I felt they did back in my teenage years. *Ha*. Oh, the irony. The Universe has an uncanny sense of humor, doesn't it?

I find myself trying to slip back into some semblance of rhythm: into the small, earthly concerns of daily life. But after what I've seen, what I've felt, it's hard to care too deeply about silly relatively inconsequential Earthy to-do lists. Still, reality taps my shoulder. I'm unemployed. Still searching. Still applying. Still not getting a *single* reply. The great cosmic joke of trying to ground a soul that's just glimpsed the infinite.

I am in my small studio casita, alone. Blocked by the one person who knew me fairly well, Armando.

I turn to the surf and the sea, day after day, to ground me. The beaches have fully opened up, and I become a full-blown surf addict. Hours a day. Sometimes three, four, five hours at a time, until I'm so exhausted that all I have energy for is stumbling home, shoving some food in my face, drinking a bottle of wine, and passing out.

Rinse. Repeat.

I feel like I can't go it alone, so naturally, I turn to dating apps to soothe myself.

I hang out with a local musician whose hands move like the talented guitarist he is—he plays me most beautifully a few nights a week. But for once, I quickly notice this isn't fulfilling, and I stop reaching out. *Small win.*

Then I meet another local surfer, Mateo, in the lineup. He teaches me about numerology, pendulums, and asking your higher self for guidance. His car is completely beat-up, his simple apartment in the dusty desert landscape small and humble, with chickens outside as dawn's announcers. I love *all* of it. I fall for his kind heart, our shared infatuation with surf and the sea, and the fact that he has a spiritual side. We start hanging out regularly, just surfing, just being. Simple. Fun.

Then, out of the blue, I get a phone call from an unknown number. I answer.

The woman on the other end speaks in broken English, says something about the Unemployment Department, and asks if I was in Mexico for a two-week period in early November.

"Huh? No. What do you mean, *just* two weeks? Who is this?"

She sounds *entirely* like a scammer and not at all like a government employee. Something feels off. I tell her no, ask her to email me from her official government account if she really is who she says she is, and hang up.

A few minutes later, I get an email from a similar contact. I immediately respond: *Look, I need you to provide some credentials and your boss's information so I can validate who you say you are.*

At this point, I go into full panic mode. A friend had recently told me I can't apply for unemployment from Mexico. When I originally filed, I'd called the office dozens of times and never reached a soul, but I was positive I had followed protocol perfectly given my situation. It was a global pandemic, borders and transportation had shut down entirely. I was playing it safe, ticking all the boxes like a good little matrix minion, applying for jobs in both places, just in case.

How could they *not* understand my case? My employer had placed me in Mexico on a temporary assignment. I was still an Oregon resident. My driver's license was there, I was still paying taxes there, and I was supposed to be in Oregon—but then the company sent me abroad, and I got stranded. All jobs were still remote. I was following all unemployment weekly protocols.

I contact a lawyer for a consultation. He tells me my case is *insanely* odd but agrees that since my employer placed me in Baja temporarily, given my duration in Mexico and a bunch of legal technicalities and Covid concessions (which I won't bore you with), my residency is technically both Oregon *and* Baja. And also, he points out, I *never* would have been outside Oregon in the first place if my employer hadn't sent me abroad.

He says, "Just explain the situation. They'll understand."

So I get the unemployment agent back on the phone. She asks me again if I was in Mexico for that two-week period.

And I say, "No, I've been in Mexico since fall of 2019." Biggest. Mistake. Ever.

In that moment, she pounces. I can almost *feel* the hook in my mouth as she reels in the biggest trophy of her career, a fat promotional bonus shining in her future. She proceeds to slice me to bits—as does the entire system—in a battle that drags on for nearly four years and leaves me forced to repay every cent.

Ultimately, they claim they are not responsible for Covid and insist that I should have returned to the state, even though the very day I was laid off, the Governor issued a shelter-in-place order. Even though I knew travel posed a serious risk to my health and safety. Even though not a single person in my company returned to a physical office at any point in 2020.

Still, they say my *physical presence* was mandatory to receive benefits.

They hit me with a $10,000 fraud charge.

They demand I repay all unemployment benefits—plus penalties. A total of just over *$40,000*.

I contact my Oregon Senator relentlessly for months. This isn't right. And I'm going to fight.

Finally, I get a response from an assistant:

That's awful. This should not have happened. I forwarded your email directly to the governor's office to see if there is anything they can do to support you. They would be the next proper step because the legislature cannot do anything more without creating legislation to fix this very clear issue.

I get traction. Then the term ends. The senator and governor leave office.

I try. And try. And try again. Dead end.

Broken system.

And *this*—this teeny, tiny case of injustice in the vast sea of government injustices—is when I begin to lose all faith that the system gives even two shits about its people and our well-being.

I become infuriated.

Infuriated at a system so blatantly corrupt.

Our government is funded by Big Pharma. Wars fuel the pockets of our congressmen. Tax evasion for the one percent is rampant, yet they come after a little gal stuck abroad during a global pandemic who just needed some unemployment funds to buy some damn tortillas.

I am sick to death of a healthcare system that makes you both sick *and* bankrupt.

I am sick of them knowingly poisoning our food with chemicals just to further fuel the pockets of Big Pharma, the industry they're secretly in bed with.

I am sick of a society that worships celebrities on mega yachts, drinking absurdly priced champagne that could feed a family in Mexico for a *year*, while Nobel Peace Prize winners go unnoticed.

No one seems to give two shits about the teachers slugging it out in classrooms every day, making jack shit.

And I start to really hate the reality of this fucking *fuckfest* of a society that I seem to be seeing *clearly* for the first time.

The level of deception. The government and elite manipulating humanity. A sick chess game of human life. Of power. Of control. The *Matrix Machine* simply does not care.

So no. My transcendental, supernatural, deeply divine experience didn't make everything perfect and loving and blissful immediately. For a hot minute, it did quite the opposite.

Chapter Twenty-One

This human condition.

Around this time, things get dicey with Mateo. I am still hanging out with him, still sharing my bed with him nearly every night. And sure, he's fun. But I start to see it—he isn't emotionally available. He isn't capable of raw, open communication. He struggles with emotional intimacy. And all I really want, *need*, is that.

Shocker, I know.

The thing is, I was still searching for love outside of myself.

Our little fling ends one night with me completely *losing my shit* in the car, yelling at the poor guy about how much he reminds me of the Former. The next day, I send a million long texts, desperately trying to be seen and heard by someone who simply could not meet me there.

And then—total ghosting. Weeks of trying to get a reply. Nothing.

He couldn't truly see me. He couldn't truly talk to me about his feelings, or mine. And I was just so damn desperate for that. I was reliving the same dynamic. Again. Seeking unavailable love to prove my worth. *Again.*

But here's the thing—I was blaming him for not seeing me when I couldn't even see my damn self. I was still focused on changing others instead of changing myself: instead of learning how to feel loved, grounded, and safe from within. I wasn't accepting him for who he was. *Yet fucking again.*

My relationship compass, my personal compass, was still chaotic. Still crazy. Still vengeful. But—my cycle of noticing these patterns? It was getting shorter. And *that*, my friend, was a win in the midst of all the chaos.

***

A few days later, I took a little road trip north of town to get some space.

On the way back, after having a few glasses of wine, I am driving too fast. I come around a sharp curve in the dead of night—only to see a pack of *black goats* covering the highway.

There was no time.

I couldn't swerve.

I couldn't brake.

Thud.

The sick smack of flesh against metal.

Horrified, I pull over and get out. My bumper is wrecked, pushed far back, rubbing against the tire. But worse, when I look underneath, I nearly gag. Meat. Raw, dangling from the grill. The smell is *awful*. I choke back another dry heave. I stand here, frozen. I have no idea what to do.

I turn around, scanning the roadside for any sign of an owner, a wounded goat, *something*. As I make the turn, the tire grinds against the bent bumper with an awful sound. No goats in sight. No bodies. Not even a trace of them. Just my license plate, sitting alone in the middle of the road.

Strange.

It felt like *Back to the Future*, when the DeLorean disappears, leaving only tire tracks behind.

Where the hell were the goats? There should've been *something*, some sign they were ever there, besides the flesh still dangling from my truck. I swallow the lump rising in my throat. I feel awful.

I turn back toward home, pulling into a gas station on the way. Grabbing a windshield washer stick, I pry the bumper off the wheel enough so I can drive without it scraping. A group of Mexican men sit on the curb, drinking beers, watching the wonky white girl pretend to be a mechanic. I shrug.

They laugh.

I drive my ass home to zonk out. I'll figure out the truck in the morning.

***

But that night before falling asleep, I pour myself an excessively large glass of wine. Red liquid courage in hand, the rage at myself festers. Naturally, I decide to project it *outward*.

Armando flashes into my mind.

The devastating hurt of his abandonment, just after my dad died. The *exact* moment I saw him, speeding past me on his bike, another girl on the back, like I had never even existed. The way he looked right through me at the restaurant. No acknowledgment. No emotion. Nothing.

A fresh wave of *fuck this guy* rises in my chest. And that's when I hit an *all-time low* in revenge plotting. I decide—no, *I commit*—to getting the last word. He's going to hear me, dammit. He's going to *know* the pain he caused me.

I log into Tinder using my old work number. Then, I create the perfect fake profile. I use photos of my college roommate (sorry, Libby)—a wholesome white girl, exactly his type. My bio is basic: *Hi. Simplicity is bliss. In Baja to slow down and enjoy life a little more. Here to connect with and learn from others.*

Perfecto. I hit publish. The bait is set.

The next morning, Thanksgiving Eve, I check Tinder. And there it is. He's liked Libby. *Yesssss.*

I laugh to myself, noticing how much of his opener and icebreaker texts are nearly identical to what he sent me. It's almost like a system, robotic, like clockwork. We chit-chat for an hour that morning, a little more that night. The following evening, I weave a story about being out in town and randomly meeting his ex-partner-ish, *me*, at a ladies' event. In a town this small, especially among expats, it's totally plausible.

As Libby, I casually drop the bomb messaging him on Tinder: *So, this is crazy, I just randomly ended up talking to your ex Becca! We were chatting about the struggles of dating in Baja, and I showed her your photo as my promising new prospect. She literally gasped. How totally random and bizarre is that?!*

He replies: *Haha, wow. Small world indeed. Enjoy your night!*

I don't want to waste any more of my time. About an hour later, I go for the kill:

You know, deep into a few margaritas, I had to ask Becca why you two split. And I must say, as someone who has also recently endured the soul-crushing pain of losing a beloved parent, I wouldn't deny even a homeless man, smelling of booze and urine, a hug if he asked for one during that time... let alone someone I had shared what sounds like some pretty incredible adventures with. Regardless of what you two had, which I have no idea, that oozes narcissism to me. There are times when abandoning someone is understandable, but that? That wasn't one of them. I think this town may be way too small for me... anyway. I have your number. Thanks for the chat. I wish you well in lightening your own burden.

And with that, I click send.

A wry smile spreads across my face, slow and deep with satisfaction—not unlike the Grinch when he steals all the little town's presents. And not unlike the Grinch, that satisfaction is quickly followed by: *WTF, Becca? Seriously? You had to do that? You couldn't just let it go? You had to steal his peace now that he's moved on?*

A frown unfolds on my face at my mind's harsh scolding. Apparently, no. In this stage of heavy grief, solitude, and confusion, no—childishly lashing out seemed like a far, far better option than facing my own shit. Still, I wait to unmatch until I'm positive he's read it.

His response is simple: *...I have a feeling that only on Tinder do these odd things happen!*

I pass out for the night, glass on the nightstand. Honor hiding under the bed collecting dust.

The irony of the quote I see on Instagram the next morning smacks me in the face: *In the end, only three things that matter: how much you loved, how gently you lived, and how gracefully you let go of things not meant for you.* — Buddha.

Sigh. Apparently, I'm not there yet, Señor Buddha. The flaring ego still craves its King Kong moments of visceral, animalistic destruction. Such is the human condition.

The next day, once again pledging to do better, I head to a Friendsgiving gathering in town with my new dear Baja friend Beth, who's two decades older but feels like a sister. We have too much wine. I tell her what I did. She stares at me like I've lost it.

Oh, shit. Perhaps I am losing it. Actually, that's becoming more plausible by the second. I stare back with wide eyes and a grimace. "Yeah... that was really bad."

She raises her glass. "That's not nuts. It's fucking brilliant."

We clink. We erupt in laughter, but mine carries an edge—a brittle echo, one blink from breaking.

How am I the same woman who truly felt she found herself in the desolate isolation of the desert just a few months ago? Who's father hopped dimensions to show her true Love? Have I lost her already? I drown my thoughts with another glass of wine. *Shush down there, please. I'm getting revenge. He deserved it. He gutted me. This little final tease was fair.* Oh, ego. Seriously.

A few days later, instead of dealing with my truck, my friend Roberto and I head out for tacos and drinks. We start with a few beers, then some margaritas, then back to beers. At some point, we make out at the bar, even though we are very much just friends.

He pulls back, nodding in approval. "You're a great kisser."

I smirk, teasing. "Ya know, you are too." If only we were actually attracted to each other.

We laugh, pay the bill, and head out arm in arm into the warm Baja night. The city is alive, local music drifts through the streets, festive flags dance above the cobblestone roads. We pass a small, lively bar with a great DJ. He looks at me. "One more margarita?!"

I know I shouldn't. I know I'm already buzzed.

"Siiiiiiiii!"

After far too many drinks, I do something shameful—I head for my truck. Granted, I'm from Wisconsin, the land of professional drinkers, and I can hold my booze. But I've definitely had too many to be driving anywhere, certainly not in the breathalyzer-packed patrolled roads just north of the border. But this is also a place where people frequently drink openly in their cars and the police have bigger things to worry about. So I get in, find my favorite Spotify playlist, and start the short drive home on the narrow cobblestone streets.

Fifteen seconds in, the song isn't vibing with my drunken state, so I glance down to hit skip.

The momentum of my truck abruptly stops. A sickening crunch of metal fills the air. I snap my head up. The left front of my truck has slammed into the back right bumper of a parked truck.

Oh god. Oh god. Oh god.

I freeze. My stomach drops. The reality hits me in my boozy haze. I'm drunk, I'm driving, I'm a foreigner in another country, albeit here legally. Panic takes over. I throw the truck into reverse, mortified, and—ashamed as I am to admit it—I drive home. The entire way, my truck groans and screeches, the sound of metal grinding against metal. I don't even know what the front end looks like, but I can see my hood is crumpled. I creep through the quiet streets, sick to my stomach, unable to believe what I've just done.

I vow to go back in the morning, sober, and make it right.

For now, I can't even look at my truck. I pull into my little casita, park, stumble inside, and collapse onto my bed. Fully clothed, purse still slung over my shoulder, disgusted with myself.

***

I message Roberto in the morning about what happened, and he picks me up right away to go check out the damage and fess up to the owner. My head is pounding. I vow never to drink again.

He pulls up. "How's your ride?"

"I have no clue. I couldn't even bear to look at it. The thought of finding a reliable mechanic, the cost to fix it, plus renting a car in the meantime...ugh."

He parks, and we stroll over. The entire front left bumper is squashed and crumpled, right where the goat dent had been, but this one is far, far worse. The hood is bent and curled, the headlight smashed, the side panel twisted into the tire. Half the bumper is missing, leaving the raw metal frame exposed.

"My poor Rodney," I groan. Rodney the 4Runner. I'd had him for over a decade, of course he had a name. I've never been one to spend much on cars. I find one I love and stick with it. He's got nearly 180,000 miles and was running strong, until now. Seeing it in daylight, I have no clue how I even made it home. He's completely undrivable.

"Oh god. What am I going to do without a car here?" I drop my head onto Roberto's shoulder, fighting the urge to cry, to scream at myself for my stupidity.

I can't even deal with it yet, so we hop into his car and head to the street where the accident happened. We park around the corner and walk toward the truck. It's an old-school pickup, basically solid steel. Dents and dings cover the entire body, like scars from decades of use. I spot the damage, a broken taillight. And that's it.

Meanwhile, my truck crumpled like a soda can. Designed for safety, sure, but damn.

"Oh, thank god." Relief washes over me. "Do we knock on the door and talk to the owner?"

Roberto looks at me, his brown skin glistening in the morning sun. "Amiga, hell no. You leave some pesos under the wiper and call it good."

I glance at the old, beat-up truck and nod. He's right. I slip 500 pesos under the wiper, far more than needed to replace the light, and briskly walk away.

"Breakfast?" Roberto asks, squeezing my shoulder reassuringly.

"God, yes."

I feel like I've made things right for the truck owner, but I'm nowhere near making things right for myself.

Seriously, lady? You just turned 40, and you're still pulling shit like this? When will you learn? When will you stop drinking so much? If I'm honest—when will I stop numbing with alcohol and actually handle my own shit?

My dad once told me he struggled with drinking in his 20s—bar fights, reckless nights, even crashing his car after a bender. Maybe this is in my blood. Maybe I need to stop. Maybe this is my rock bottom moment.

A quote I saw floating across my screen this morning comes to mind:

"Courage is knowing it might hurt and doing it anyway. Stupidity is the same. And that's why life is hard."

Preach.

I know I probably should give up drinking. But I just don't want to. It's part of how I connect more easily with people. I love the bliss of a buzz, the way it makes me open, goofy, loose. Recent loss of my father aside, I typically never drink alone, but socially? A glass of wine over dinner with friends, a margarita with tacos—that's part of the magic of life on Earth, in my not-so-humble opinion.

Maybe one day I'll feel differently. But today is not that day.

The visit from my dad helped alleviate so much of the pain of his loss, but I am human, back in this realm, and the grief still drives me to drink, to numb. My mind has carved out a big, gaping grief hole, and I have fallen straight into it. The path to inner peace and enlightenment, it turns out, has some ego roadbumps. Who knew?

I can see it clearly—my grip on reality is unraveling. This is a time to question everything.

It's nearly Christmas, and flying is still a concern because of Covid. I don't want to spend the holidays alone in Baja, but my brother is worried about me traveling. I don't know what to do. I don't want my mom to feel too terribly alone, and I'd feel guilty if she did. So, I head home to Wisconsin.

It is, without a doubt, the worst Christmas ever.

December 2020. The rock of the family is gone. There are five people on my flight. The house is quiet. My mother is reserved as always, but I can tell she's grateful I'm there. It just all feels so awkward without my dad.

I catch her in a quiet moment in the kitchen, eager to share my experience with Dad, thinking she'll be proud or at least comforted. But all she hears, if she hears me at all, is that he came to me and not her. The depth of what I'm saying doesn't register.

My brother is still anxious about the pandemic, especially with my flying internationally. When I arrive, he says, "I'm sorry, but I don't want to share air with you."

I stare at him, unable to respond. He isn't an ass. We love each other. This is the fear and pain talking.

Christmas Eve dinner is eaten in separate corners of the living room, each of us sitting 15 feet apart. My mom seems totally numb.

After my brother leaves, I'm able to get face to face with mom who doesn't share the same concerns and earnestly ask her how she's doing. Tears well up in her eyes, a rare sight. She fights them back. She struggles to speak, "I can't believe he's gone."

I hug her tightly, holding on for a few moments. "I know. Me either." My own tears start to rise.

She pulls back from me and looks at me straight in the eyes, not missing a beat. "It didn't occur to me that you could be hurting too."

Blink. Blink. Blink.

I might as well have been stabbed. The comment is brutal, and I am in shock. The illusion that my mother and I had grown closer over the years is obliterated in an instant.

A fireball of pain and rage rises—I swallow it down.

I stare into her eyes, fighting back tears, overcome by a sadness I can't begin to explain. It is suddenly, horrifically clear that she lives in a world so detached from reality, so wrapped up in her own mind, that it never even crossed her mind that her daughter could be hurting too.

I can feel that she wants connection, but she doesn't quite know how to reach for it. Like a bird who's spent its whole life in a cage, unaware the door is wide open.

Looking back, we were all grieving so terribly, so profoundly, and none of us knew how to articulate the depth of our pain. We were all in terribly rough shape. I hoped, in some small way, my presence helped.

But I should have stayed in Baja. I knew it. Guilt and obligation carried me north, and this is what I got for ignoring my intuition.

A few days after the new year, I head back south.

Landing back in Baja I struggle with being on my own. I need a job to pay the bills and begin repaying my mound of debt. Marketing gigs are still impossible to come by. I'm lost. I don't know who I am or what this journey is supposed to be about.

And yet, deep in my core, I completely do.

Does that make sense? Have you ever felt completely lost, yet found at the same time?

Right now, I don't know how to merge my new spiritual knowledge with this dense reality.

What happened to the girl in the desert who finally learned to love herself? What happened to the girl whose father used his death to show her the magic of this one precious life?

She's currently locking herself back in her room, refusing to come out.

Universe, please take the helm.

Because Lord knows I've fallen back into old, archaic, asleep patterns—again. Eyes wide shut, steering this ship straight off the edge of an old Earth reality.

Chapter Twenty-Two

I am sorry.

I roll into a shiny new year, 2021, and vow to get my shit together.

At this point, I've seen enough of my own tricks, staring myself down in my raw, naked state. This is the murky mess I've led myself into, thanks to my own daft stupidity and deafness. Time for brutal honesty, confession, surrender, restitution, and apologies. To my damn self.

On New Year's Day, I baptize myself anew in the sea. I vow to listen to my intuition, to do something meaningful with what my father so lovingly and miraculously showed me. And I promise, again, not to drink so damn much.

But I also give myself grace. Direction is more important than speed. Sure, I'm still messing up, but I'm doing a little better each day chasing what brings me joy and letting go of what doesn't, learning my lessons just a little bit faster.

What more can a gal do?

I finally land a remote freelance marketing consulting gig—financial breathing room at last. It's with another corporation in the same space I was just in, and they offer me good money. I barely make it three weeks. Another controlling CEO. Another person telling me how to write copy, how to add dashes instead of bullet points, how to choose a "better" shade of blue like I'm a damn intern.

I push back, hard.

My consulting boss acknowledges the leadership is difficult. "Pick your battles," they say. "Tiptoe."

I. Can. Not.

And just like that, they don't need my services anymore.

Super.

Truly.

I have no idea what I'm going to do. But I know I can't do *that*. Not for one more second.

After losing my last three corporate jobs: one to the Great Recession, one to an acquisition, one to a global pandemic, I decide to dive into the thing that terrifies me the most.

I start working for myself.

I am afraid. But I have been dreaming of this for years—of leaving behind toxic corporate environments, of no longer wasting my life hours on someone else's vision, of never again being just another number, expendable at a moment's notice.

This is my shot. And if I don't take it, I will never forgive myself.

I begin building an online home decor business combining my nearly two decades of experience in e-commerce, branding, marketing, and design.

As soon as I commit to my vision, the universe meets me halfway. I land another freelance marketing consulting gig, this time with a local company in Mexico. It will keep the lights on and help me chip away at my mountain of unemployment debt while I work on my own business.

I'm still living in my studio casita, my "kitchen" a hot plate on the outdoor patio. And, to my delight, I still don't mind it. In fact, I quite like it.

No lawns to mow. No roofs to fix. No furniture to shop for, no plants to water, no weeding, trimming, or painting just to keep the illusion of the "dream of homeownership" alive.

I find I don't care about the size of my home or accumulating things anymore. What I care about is expanding my awareness. Learning to coexist more successfully with my ego. And connecting every day, a little more, to the Divine.

I keep thinking more and more about money versus value. Wealth, I'm realizing, is a pace, not a paycheck. I want freedom, time, and a purposeful calling for my career—not just mindlessly grinding away for someone else's dream. I think I finally see that if you live consciously and in service, no matter how much money you have, you possess true wealth.

But what I am also realizing is that my current relationship with money isn't a healthy one. I associate it with the old matrix existence I am trying to unplug from. I realize that if I want to thrive as I move from an ego-driven life to a more soulful one, my relationship with money has to shift, too.

It's been just three months since my dad passed, and I find myself desperately longing for that moment on the beach underneath the full moonlight when I was reconnected to him. I want to tap into that eternal energy again, that clarity, that infinite love. My god, where we all come from is so stunning, so divine, so limitless. I want my spiritual fix, dammit!

This 3D existence on Earth feels like a brutal kick in the teeth. Coming back into my body after experiencing the expansiveness my father showed me is like going from piloting an intergalactic spaceship—one that can travel anywhere in the universe with the power of thought—to being handed the first-ever version of a bicycle, sans shocks, shifters, and with a crappy metal seat. A million-watt jolt to the system, to put it lightly.

As I navigate the balance between shedding my past life and stepping into something new, I find myself in the surf lineup one day, chatting with a friend about his recent mushroom journey. Something pings me deep inside, that inner knowing I've been learning to tune into. I feel it in my chest, right around my heart. When something resonates, that space softens, sending out a gentle wave of warmth and comfort. Excitement, even.

Ah, yes. Brilliant.

Follow that feeling. That inner knowing, urging me to get curious.

It seems like the perfect time to explore psychedelics, but not in the way I used to. I dabbled in mushrooms a few times in college, but back then, it was just about getting messed up. I dabbled in quite a few substances, actually—ecstasy, cocaine, binge drinking, weed before it was legal—though I rarely smoke these days.

My surf buddy talks about the medicine and deep wisdom of mushrooms. I decide to watch *Fantastic Fungi* for a more updated perspective. It's a phenomenal documentary, detailing their incredible medicinal benefits and how Big Pharma regulated them out of existence so they could, well, make us sick and get rich.

Fuckers.

The greed at that level is unreal.

But beyond all that, I just want to feel what I felt during the full moon ceremony. That deep, unshakable connection with Love. I want my dad.

Lately, I've caught myself complaining about alleged problems—unemployment woes, recent Tinder disasters—but then, fortunately, I pull my head out of my own ass. I realize the life I'm currently living is one I *always* dreamed of. One that many people dream of. Sure, I've had hurdles, but they're nothing compared to the challenges some people face every single day.

I'm truly blessed.

Living simply in Mexico, enjoying the sea, soaking in the little things, surfing daily. I have time freedom, something many parents don't have, but their own path carries its own beautiful gifts that I won't experience. It's all about chasing what fuels your soul.

For me, wealth means filling my days with what sparks my curiosity, following that as my compass—not some societal narrative of consumption, comparison, and materialistic success. Society is drowning in not enoughness. Conditioning us to constantly think, *When I have this... When I do that... When I get that thing... Then I'll finally be happy.*

What an endless nightmare.

No one is allowed to live in the present. And when you don't do that—when you're always chasing, always waiting—you're not really *living* at all, are you?

I want to break the habit. I want to live deeply in the present. I want to soak in each moment, play like a kid again, and engage with the community around me every day. No more white-picket-fence separation. No more never-enoughness. Thank you very much.

I sit down on my little casita patio on a sunny afternoon, just a few weeks into the new year, and decide to take a nice, strong dose of mushrooms, courtesy of my dear friend Nikki. It's roughly 3.5 grams, and they're potent little fellas. I steep them into tea and guzzle it down. The taste, of course, is far from pleasant.

Perched on the edge of my simple casita's small patio, I settle into a camping chair beside my tiny garden. A palm tree sways above me, the sea stretches out in the distance about half a mile to the left, and below me, a somewhat busy road winds along the coastline. In front of me, rolling hills and a lush valley spread out like a dream. I have my headphones, my phone, and a little playlist I put together on Spotify for the occasion—*Hillside Chats*.

I smile, feeling the warm afternoon sun on my face. I ask my little friends now settling in my belly to show me what I need to see. Then, I wait.

After about 45 minutes, the garden before me begins to come to life. The vines of the fuchsia bougainvillea bush in front of me start to twist, move, and dance like a snake, its blossoms pulsing like butterfly wings opening and closing. Witnessing the life within it is simply *stunning*. I am completely mesmerized—more than by any symphony, Cirque du Soleil performance, or Broadway show I've ever seen. And I've seen quite a few.

The music in my headphones flows in perfect harmony with the bush, which moves and speaks, showing me the intelligence of nature, the life inherent in it, the same life that flows within *us*.

A soothing warmth spreads through my body, and a smile stretches across my face. I look out over the valley below. The entire stretch of palm trees sways in a perfectly synchronized yet unseen rhythm, as if at the bottom of the ocean, moved by an invisible current. Every tree, every green thing in sight, moves together in a choreographed dance. And yet, the man-made concrete buildings remain still, lifeless. The paved highway and metal cars sit rigid, stagnant, void of energy.

I turn my gaze toward the sea. The sunlight glistens on its surface like sequins on a dress, the water shifting, undulating, seducing—effortlessly comfortable in its vast, liquid, powerful, deeply feminine form.

I audibly *gasp* at the sheer magic of it all.

Tears flow.

I am suddenly *one* with the light, the garden, the sea. The sun's brilliance is almost blinding, its radiance divine. It's the kind of light you'd expect to see when passing from this life to the next—that sharp, cinematic flash we all imagine. And yet, here I am, basking in it. I slowly raise my hand in front of my face, turning it inward to examine my palm, then outward, wiggling my long, freckled fingers. Every movement is slow and deliberate. I am aware that I am moving my hand, but the hand is not *me*.

I feel the same divine connection I experienced when my dad visited me, only this time, it's another track from the same album of *Love*.

Time ceases to exist.

I sit in my camping chair, staring into the timeless bliss of nature, feeling as though I have been here for years. I am part of eternity.

Then, *You Can't Rush Your Healing* by Trevor Hall comes on in my AirPods, and my entire body *bursts* with emotion. More tears flow, this time from absolute, pure joy. I soak it all in. As the sun begins to set, the light slowly fades. Cotton-candy pink clouds drift across the horizon, making me giggle like a kid in a candy store. They are so *cute*. Then, they fizzle and disappear.

The desert air cools, turning crisp, almost chilly. The golden light dims to gray, and oddly enough, my soundtrack takes on a more somber tone.

The shift is sudden. Sadness creeps in. Loneliness. Abandonment.

As the light leaves me behind, I feel as though I am the only person left on the entire planet. Panic wells up inside me, an overwhelming sadness consuming me, pulling me downward.

I slowly slip from my chair, sliding onto my knees, then onto the cool concrete patio floor beneath me.

By now, it is completely dark. The stars emerge, sparkling in silent support, but they cannot comfort me. They can only twinkle enthusiastically down upon me and watch.

I am on my knees, folded into child's pose, my forehead pressed against the cold concrete floor. And then—

I *sob*.

A raw, unfiltered, ugly cry erupts from the very core of my being. It is a full-body release, pouring out of every pore. I have never felt a cry of this depth in my entire existence.

It begins deep in my abdomen, an ache so profound it feels ancient. When I exhale, I wail, releasing my pain into the night.

I sob and sob and sob, snot dripping freely from my nose onto the concrete, but I can't be bothered to wipe it away.

And then—

I begin to chant.

Three simple, powerful words, directed solely at myself.

"I am sorry."

"I am soooo sorry."

"I am sorry."

"I. Am. So. Sorry."

Over and over, I howl like a wounded animal in absolute agony.

"I AM SORRRRYYYYYYYYY."

And I go on.

And on.

And on.

And I *am* injured. I'm beginning to actually feel the pain—of losing my friend John, my home, my marriage, my job, my dad. And with that, I release just the tiniest crack of those pent-up emotions, all the hurt that's been waiting. Waiting to be held, so I can begin to heal.

I am sobbing, chanting the same words again and again. I emphasize different parts, as if offering them in just the right way out into the Universe will unlock a door to something lighter—a space in my heart without pain. I keep trying. Again and again.

Deep in my being, I feel like I'm apologizing for my humanness. For all my human faults. For my ego, for judgments, for expectations, for blame, for anger, for fear. For manipulating, for selfishness, for carelessness. For being an asshole at times. For hate toward others. For hate toward myself. For being a bad friend. A bad wife. A bad daughter. A bad sister. For withholding love. For all the human moments I am ashamed of. For *all of it*.

Then, a deep, intuitive flash hits me, illuminating all my relationship disappointments. In an instant, I see it all clear as day. The common denominator is *me*.

I suddenly *know*. I have been sabotaging myself from receiving love because, deep down, I didn't believe I deserved it. I kept blaming other people for painful relationship experiences, unconscious of this deeply rooted belief. I honestly, truly, deeply believed I liked myself. If you had given me a polygraph, I would have bet my own life on it. But now, looking within, I see it. I have been unconsciously choosing bad partners to fulfill this hidden belief, that I am not good enough. Not worthy enough.

Well, shit.

Suddenly, I hear a metal gate clicking shut nearby. I snap out of it, rip my earbuds out, and jolt up straight like a freaking meerkat. Dear Lord, I have forgotten where I am.

The gate to my little compound is right below me, leading to the main house and several other residences close by. Holy hell. They all heard me.

A flash of embarrassment and panic grips me, but then, the little fellas still in my system whisper, *It's okay. It's okay. Breathe.*

A quiet voice in my head chimes in. *Yeah, it's okay to cry. It's okay to let go. I bet they wish they could cry like that.* I let out a soft laugh. *Well, it's done now.*

I wipe the *epic* amount of snot from my face with my sleeve. It's disgusting, but I couldn't care less.

I pause. Look up at the stars.

And I smile.

I breathe deeply.

The heaviness has passed. The knot in my stomach, gone. The weight that had been pressing down on me, lifted. A massive anchor I didn't even realize had been pulling me under.

I pry myself off the ground and sink back into the chair. I glance at my phone, but the screen is so insanely bright I can barely look at it. I dim it to almost nothing and check the time, my playlist is on its second loop. I've been out here for only three hours. But it feels like years and years and years. I have been in the eternal time soup, connected to consciousness, fully immersed in the exquisite dance of calm and chaos. Such is life.

A rush of love surges through me, and I grab my phone, texting everyone: *I love you.*

Like Scrooge on Christmas morning, I tell myself: *I will do better! I will love more!*

I send message after message. Each *I love you too* I receive back makes my heart swell with warmth and gratitude.

Then, exhaustion washes over me. I stumble into the bathroom, splash my face with cold water, and lift my eyes to the mirror. They are soft, open, loving—and bloodshot from crying.

I smile at myself. "Why, hey there, amiga. Lovely to meet you again."

I stare at my reflection—this meat suit society says is ugly or fat or pretty or thin, based on some completely made-up rulebook of what beauty is, designed to keep us feeling not enough.

Fuck that shit. We are all stunning.

In this moment, I feel closer to embracing my real self than I ever have. I am releasing the weight of others' perceptions. I am finding *my* path to self-love.

I smile, realizing I barely recognize myself anymore. Since my experience with my dad, since more time in the nourishing sea, I've started changing. My once dark brown eyes have lightened to hazel, glowing with a golden ring. My hair is getting blonder by the day. Funny. I feel lighter by the day too.

My skin is dark and golden from the sun. I look healthy. Happy. (Minus the teary eyes.) I bow slightly to my reflection. "Thank you."

Thank you for being brave. For messing up but pushing forward. For trying to be better. *It's not easy, but I'm with you. Always.*

I smile, crawl into bed, and happily zonk out. It's 8:30, and I am done.

I'm quite pleased with my first psychedelic experience from a medicinal perspective, so different from my mid-twenties *let's get fucked up* mindset. The ease in my demeanor, the ability to see the world from a broader perspective, and the deeper appreciation of its beauty last the entire first month after and well into the next few months of the new year.

One day, while out grabbing coffee, I share this wonderful, transformative experience with my friend Nikki who had provided me with the heavenly mushrooms. She listens with a knowing smile, then asks if I want to join her for an Ayahuasca ceremony next month.

She explains that Ayahuasca ceremonies are sacred rituals that have been practiced for centuries, they offer an opportunity to connect with one's inner self, unlocking profound spiritual revelations, visions, and healing.

That same warmth of curiosity, excitement, and just a little bit of fear blooms in my chest.

"Why yes, I believe I do!"

She smiles—a warm, motherly smile that always instantly puts me at ease. She's the same friend who sat beside me when my dad visited me from that wonderful realm beyond our knowing on the beach. She's becoming my Baja spiritual expansion guide, and honestly, I wouldn't want anyone else by my side for my first Ayahuasca experience.

I wait the longest month of my life. That's how much I'm looking forward to this ceremony.

Finally, the day arrives. As the sun begins to set, I pull up to a small oasis just outside of town. The crisp sea air catches me off guard, I am entirely unprepared for how chilly it gets at night this time of year. People are gathering in a ceremony circle around a beautiful, gigantic tree, carrying sleeping pads, sleeping bags, thick blankets, multiple pillows, and snacks.

And then there's me.

I roll up with a yoga mat, a light blanket, and whatever I happen to be wearing—shorts and a handwoven cotton shirt from Oaxaca. At least I had the foresight to bring pants and a sweater, so I'm not totally clueless, but I probably should have asked more questions.

Classic me. I like to dive in with as few expectations as possible.

In true Nikki-mothering fashion, she has extra fluffy cushions and a warm, fuzzy blanket, which she hands over with a knowing smile. Gratefully, I create my own little Ayahuasca journey nest.

I'm excited. I'm ready.

I've heard so many different accounts of Ayahuasca, ranging from mild to utterly transcendental, so I have no idea what to expect.

Our gorgeous Mexican shaman hostess, Luna, begins moving through the group, cleansing each of us with sage. The smoke curls around me, clearing old energy, banishing bad energy, resetting my spirit, and opening my mind with a clean slate for a purposeful ceremony.

Once Nikki is cleansed as well, she fans out a deck of Oracle cards in front of me. I take a deep breath and pull one, setting my intention for the night.

One word: *Compassion.*

I read further.

"The Buddha realized that all life identified with form ultimately means suffering, and that non-attachment is the path to go beyond. Our human experience becomes a divine expression through compassion. Seeing the depth, feeling for the experience of others, sincerely caring about their happiness and well-being, is to know that everything is our reflection. This is the shift from fear to love."

At the bottom of the card, a question: "Do I give enough of myself to others?"

No. No, I don't think I do. I breathe deeply, press the card to my chest, and with all my heart and intention, I call in compassion—for myself, for others, for all of it.

We're about to begin, but before we start, we're each joined by our own adorable, colorful puke buckets—should the need arise. We set our intentions, breathing purposefully and deeply into them, holding them in our hearts and minds. I simply ask the medicine to show me what I need to see. It worked for the mushrooms, and hell, it knows far better than I do what I actually need.

One by one, we approach the shaman at the front of the group circle. I kneel before her and she hands me a small cup of ayahuasca tea, probably less than an ounce, but potent nonetheless. I take a moment to breathe into my intention, then shoot it down.

The taste is earthy, woodsy, and bitter, with a licorice-like bite. Do I detect a hint of chocolate? Decaying forest floor? It's not nearly as bad as I expected, though as I rise and head back to my nest of blankets, my mouth waters. The final note of dirty socks lingers on my tongue. I swallow. *Breathe.*

If you aren't familiar, ayahuasca is a plant-based brew that induces a mind-altering experience. It has been used for thousands of years in spiritual and medicinal rituals by Indigenous peoples of South America for healing and deep exploration. As its reputation has spread, retreats and ceremonies have become more common worldwide. Most people, like myself, attend these ceremonies seeking spiritual guidance, intellectual insights, or a deeper understanding of themselves. For some, the experience is dramatic—even life-changing—altering the senses and shifting one's perception of reality entirely. The active ingredient in ayahuasca is DMT, a hallucinogenic compound that occurs naturally in many plants and animals. Some healers believe the DMT in ayahuasca activates the DMT that may already exist within us, unlocking something ancient, something hidden, perhaps just a key to a secret garden within.

Either way, I'm ready.

Once we've all taken our gulps and settled into our places, the ceremony begins. Traditional shamanic icaros, songs from Peru sung in Quechua and Spanish, float through the air blending with soft jungle sounds and the rhythmic shake of Luna's rattle. A fire roars at the center of our circle.

An hour or two in, I am deeply relaxed, cross-legged on my mat, a warmth surrounding my heart. The music is sublime, but beyond that, I don't feel much happening. I crack an eye open to peek at Nikki—she's smiling, eyes closed, fully immersed.

I glance around at our eclectic group of twenty, a mix of Americans, Canadians and Mexicans. And then, I notice, almost everyone seems to be having a much more intense experience than I am.

We've got the moaner, the yeller, the singer, the crier, the sleeper, the pacer, the giggler, the preacher, the dancer, the hummer... and me, just observing it all.

Maybe that's the point.

At first, I'm annoyed that they're keeping me from going deep into my own experience. But then I ask myself, *Well, what the hell can I do about that?*

Nothing. So, I let go.

Annoyance shifts to compassion, suddenly, I feel for everyone in this circle. I feel a profound release of self, a deep connection to the group as a collective. I'm part of their journey now. Their experience has become my experience too.

I lower my gaze to the ground, watching as the dirt and grass slowly coil together like a snake. I lift my eyes to the sky, and the clouds are alive—dancing along their own puffy highway, transforming with ease as they travel wherever they need to go.

A long-buried emotion rises to the surface: a deep mistrust of other women, a quiet sense of unsafety woven through my female friendships. As I drop into the feeling, it carries me all the way back to childhood. I see my tiny self looking up at my mother, tears in my eyes, begging her to say she's sorry—again and again. I don't remember what for, but I *know* this fear of feminine energy traces back to her emotional distance... and likely her mother's before her. Moments later, I'm pulled into another memory during elementary school where I'm suddenly reliving the day all my girlfriends turned on me. The teasing lasted for months. It was brutal.

Ugh.

I try to shake off the terrible feeling of them laughing at me in the bathroom: Brittany reaching under my shirt, trying to snap my bra and sneering, "Oh, look, Becca doesn't even have a training bra yet." Yeah, no, I don't. My mom doesn't take me shopping for things like that.

I had to read the directions on the Tampax box by myself, struggling to figure out where to push it in, how to find the right angle for a bodily map I'd never even studied. When it wouldn't cooperate, I shoved a super-thick pad into my swimsuit just so I could swim my race the day my period started for summer swim team. I waddled around the pool with a towel wrapped around my waist right up until the start of the race, feeling terribly awkward—praying no one would notice as I took my mark on the starting block, or worse, that it might pop out while I was swimming.

I'm snapped back to the present moment as the woman next to me begins to sob. *I feel you, sister.*

The entire experience is a whirlwind, my emotions intertwined with everyone else's around me. I flash in and out of moments in time. I feel deeply connected to the group, as though we're all experiencing the pain and beauty of this moment together. Their pain is my pain. Their joy is my joy. I'm no longer annoyed but instead fully immersed in their emotions, as if I've become part of something greater than myself.

Compassion leads me deeper into my own journey. It floods through me, this visceral knowing that we all come from the same creative Source. Skin tone, countries, languages, religions, all just man-made labels that divide our infinitely connected energies.

The sun has left us now, and darkness envelopes our little circle. I slowly turn my head to check on Nikki, and my eyes promptly bulge out of my head. Her entire head and face are *swarmed* by mosquitoes.

For a moment, I wonder if I'm hallucinating, there must be fifty of them. I gasp.

Leaning over *very* slowly, I inch into her space, careful not to disturb her experience. I wait. Maybe she'll sense me.

Sure enough, after half a minute, she tilts her head slightly in my direction and pries open one lovely, zenned-out eye.

"Nikki!" Oops. Too loud. I whisper softer. "Ummm, Nikki! There are mosquitoes *everywhere.*" I stretch the letters out for emphasis. Half a dozen have landed *directly* on her face and neck, while the rest buzz eagerly, hoping to make landfall. She opens both eyes now, moves them around without shifting her head, and takes in the swarm. Then, her gaze returns to me. She shrugs.

"Not much to be done about it now, is there?"

And with that, she turns her head back to center and closes her eyes again.

We're in an arroyo by the sea, and it feels like they're emerging from the ground itself. I start swatting around me. The shaman's assistant is walking around the circle. I make eye contact, my eyes bulging further. I silently beckon him closer with a frantic scrunching motion of my index finger.

"Mosquitoes!" I hiss in a loud whisper. "*Everywhere!*" My head jerks twice to the side in Nikki's direction. I mouth, SAVE HER.

He smiles. Nods. And walks on.

Gah!

That's it. I throw my blanket over my head and drop into the darkness of my cocoon. The music drums loudly around me. My cohorts are yelling, crying, dancing. The dampness of the Earth creeps in—it's *so* chilly out.

You know what? I tell myself. *I'm just going to close my eyes for a moment until the mosquitoes pass.*

Next thing I know, a metal sound bowl tolls loudly three times, signaling the end of the ceremony. I pop up. *Crap! How long was I out?*

I look over, Nikki is buried under her blankets too. At this point in the chilly night, it looks like everyone has retreated into their blanket nests.

We close with an *excessively* long sharing circle. Some people launch into their entire life stories, and I find myself wishing we had a beeper and a time limit. Compassion has its limits too. I'm absolutely freezing and ready for bed.

We finally wrap around 1 a.m., and as Nikki and I happily head to the car, our arms overflowing with our cocoon-making supplies, she turns to me.

"Well?" she asks.

"Eh. I mean, it was incredibly beautiful, and I did feel a wonderful sense of calm, so viscerally connected to the group... but the mosquitoes!"

She laughs. "Holy hell, they were awful! Yeah, the medicine wasn't that strong for me either. Oh well."

We reach our cars in the darkness. She gives me a squeeze. "Text me when you get home."

"Will do. Love you."

I feel a little bummed that I didn't experience anything massively profound—no wild hallucinations, no strong energy from other realms. But I have to admit, the sense of calm and compassion for myself and others was truly wonderful. I also have to acknowledge that I did have some pretty high expectations based on stories from friends, the potential to sprout wings and travel interdimensionally was apparently on the table.

However, as I drive home, I see the beauty in the simplicity of the message I did receive. It's one that has continually surfaced on this spiritual awakening journey.

My true nature is Love.

And I am connected to everyone on this beautiful life journey through that same interconnected Love. Everyone is forever and always connected to me. We are an eternal, soulful community currently playing this nutty game show called *The Human Experience*—where infinite beings of light ignite in fury over cars riding

IT'S GONNA GET MESSY

their asses in traffic or cry in the shower over these very real things we have so brilliantly created, called broken hearts.

The following day, I realize the ayahuasca medicine is still strongly with me, perhaps even stronger than the night before. I'm feeling tired but content and barely leave bed. I read, write, listen to music, and allow myself to rest and recover.

Then it hits me. It's been exactly a year since I was laid off. A year and a half since I started over on my own in a foreign country. It feels like the woman I was no longer exists. When I show people a photo of Corporate Becca vs. Baja Becca, we look like two incredibly different people. And in many ways, we *are* different people.

I've come to realize that the hardest two years of my life are the very years I am now ridiculously grateful for. I've traded possessions for presence, and I've never felt more abundant. Emptied my life of things and somehow filled it with meaning. I've been running after sunrises, not salaries. I chose slow mornings over margins. I'm finally living inside the moment, not just passing through it. I'm not ahead or behind—I'm exactly where life *is*.

I've tried to shed, daily, what brings me down. Shedding the visible to discover the invaluable. I am simply aiming to chase joy. On my terms. No one else's.

That doesn't mean I haven't failed or fucked things up. Obviously, I have. You've been reading just how messy it's gotten. Romantic relationships are still a struggle as I come into a deeper knowing of my own worth. And sure, there have been some very mentally challenging down days.

But I'm beginning to see the beauty in the learnings. The evolution. The reason we're on this big, lovely rock. As I lay in bed reflecting on yesterday's ceremony, I say a silent prayer. A profound thank you. To this precious life. This perfectly imperfect divine existence.

Chapter Twenty-Three

People-pleasing train.

In the coming weeks and months, I begin to fall into a beautiful rhythm of my own with life in Mexico. I don't feel the need to escape, to go anywhere else. For the first time in my life, my adventurous travel spirit simply wants to stay put.

I continue to surf daily—it remains my meditation, my church, my healing space. And, if I do say so myself, I'm becoming a damn solid surfer, charging on overhead waves and feeling the epic stoke of riding them. I explore different surf breaks up and down Baja, uncovering hidden coves, unknown gems in welcoming rural communities. Surfing keeps me in a beginner's mindset, staying curious, exploring the uncomfortable, fueling my spirit.

I'm getting better at taking life's curveballs to the face. I can see the sparkle of wisdom forming on the horizon, just like a wave, and I know each lesson will sharpen my reaction time in the future. I'm building my wisdom muscles.

I work hard at building my business, but I balance it with nature. I work the hours that work for me as a night owl, and though I've never worked harder as an entrepreneur, I feel deeply fulfilled.

I soak in live music around bonfires on the beach with friends. I go to sound baths and fall into a beautiful practice at the most magical yoga studio—a tiny white dome yurt nestled amongst palm trees. I go twice a week regularly, something I've never been able to sustain before. I breathe. I chant in ancient tongues. I connect with five other local Mexican souls in our cozy studio that just barely holds us all inside.

I buy crystals—*all* the crystals. I become that lady who gives them away to those I think need their energy. I no longer recognize my closet. It's filled with summer dresses, delicate lace, floral prints galore. I'm in love with my simple, toss-on, feminine wardrobe.

I'm learning to merge the fiercely independent woman in me with the soft, feminine, vulnerable side I stuffed deep down to protect myself during my corporate life. I meet amazing women on similar journeys of letting go, reinvention, and renewal. I dance with them under the full moon in beautiful flowing dresses, in awe of their beauty, strength, and courage.

It's odd, though—when people tell me they see those same qualities in me, I don't totally see them in myself just yet. And that's how I know I have more healing to do.

Speaking of healing, I still have a few romantic stumbles left in me. There's one bad drunken night.

I'm hanging out with, yes, yet another Mexican surfer buddy. We drink *way* too much (I know, I know), and he starts making out with me. I'm too drunk to say no.

Don't get me wrong, I wasn't forced. But deep down, I don't really want to sleep with him. In that drunken moment, I want to please him. I want to be desired. So I escape out of my body for a while.

And an absolute siren emerges in the bedroom that night.

Some sort of primal celestial seductress takes over, demanding, contorting, moaning, writhing. I almost wish it had been recorded—not to share, but for my own posterity, for when my body no longer bends at such angles. It must have been quite the show.

In the morning, we wake, and he gazes at me, starts telling me how wonderful the night was—

Then, an *insane* pounding on the door.

He peeks behind the curtain. Looks back at me, eyes wide. Puts a finger to his lips. We wait in silence, my heart pounding along with the pounding on the door. He finally goes to the door.

I hear her yelling, "Who is in there? What are you doing?"

Well, shit. Oh god, oh god, oh god.

I quickly get dressed and wait for the emotional spectacle to end. I feel positively dreadful, for her, and for myself.

He comes back in, and I roll my eyes, heading for the door, making sure the coast is clear.

Jesus, Becca. Do better.

Yeah, well... I may have, just *may* have, had a little romp with another man a month or two later. After 15 years of feeling mostly unseen in my body, having someone deeply drawn to me, *wanting* me, felt intoxicating. Like I said... these men? Are. Delicious. Pure temptation. And honestly, my sex drive? Never been higher.

He's a dead ringer for Mateo, the Mexican lover who ghosted me, though I don't realize it in the moment. But subconsciously? I'm trying to get over Mateo by getting under his exact physical *doppelgänger*, searching for some kind of closure.

It also occurs to me that I've now been ghosted twice in my last two pseudo-relationships. So perhaps, just *maybe*, it's me and not them. You don't say?

Okay, okay. We've established the monster under the bed is *me*.

I keep falling into the same trap—choosing people who can't meet me emotionally, then bending over backwards trying to *win* them over. It's a losing game I keep signing up for. I don't fully understand my own emotional wiring yet, the roots of my old wounds. But the real pattern runs deeper: I'm still learning how to love myself. I say I want deep, steady, available love—but some part of me is terrified to actually receive it. My thoughts about myself don't reflect that I'm worthy of it yet. So I'm still attracting only the love I'm capable of giving myself.

I am, in essence, creating my own reality. Fun stuff.

Turns out, my thoughts about my worthiness are a magnet for unavailable partners. But really, how am I supposed to feel confident in love when I've never actually experienced a thriving relationship? Cue the spiraling self-doubt.

What I'm absolutely certain of, is that the Universe is wildly generous when you release judgment, let go of expectations, and just give with an open heart.

Well, my friend, as you're keenly aware—I'm still working on that part.

Around this time, I find myself venting to my close female friends about my string of relationship woes. One friend listens patiently, her eyes soft with compassion. Then, in the gentlest tone, she says, "Becca... you might have just a *smidge* of codependency."

It's funny, not funny, but up until that moment, I thought I had escaped my childhood unscathed.

I believed it was only my brother who had struggled with anxiety and OCD because of it. That I had been aware enough of the situation to not let it affect me.

Sure, Mom was cold. Sure, the Christian Scientist thing was rough. But I was fine. It was a pretty darn decent childhood. It *was*. And... it *wasn't*.

I have to look up codependency because, until now, I thought it only applied to spouses of alcoholics—à la *Codependent No More* by Melody Beattie. Not so much. So I dive into some extensive Googling.

If you're not familiar with codependency, as I wasn't, it turns out it's an unhealthy relationship dynamic where one person becomes so focused on taking care of, fixing, or controlling the other that they neglect their own needs. The relationship becomes *enmeshed*. There aren't clear boundaries or a sense of being separate, unique, independent people. And just like that... things start clicking into place.

Codependency is built on low self-worth—feelings of inadequacy, relentless self-criticism, and high levels of guilt and shame (the feeling that there's something fundamentally wrong with you). Some signs include difficulty setting functional boundaries, owning your own reality, acknowledging or meeting your own needs, and experiencing and expressing your emotions.

It's another way of describing relationship addiction, when a person believes it's their job to "take care of, fix, or control" another. Or, in my case, to improve them, to make them shine as beautifully as I *think* they can, even when it negatively impacts my own mental, physical, or financial health. It's putting all your focus on helping someone else, becoming so attuned to pleasing others that you ignore your own feelings, avoid asking for help, suppress your honest thoughts, absorb other people's emotions, get lost in people-pleasing, and feel deeply afraid of disappointing or upsetting others.

As a result, codependents have an unhealthy need to be needed and liked. They seek validation from others to feel worthy and lovable, often sacrificing their own needs, interests, and goals in the process.

Perfectionism also runs rampant in codependents, who can become controlling, nagging, and critical of others as a way to create a sense of security in their relationships. Emotional numbness. Anxiety around other people. Excessive self-editing. Dissociation. Feeling empty.

Codependency stems from trauma, whether personal experiences or generational patterns. This often includes things like being told or shown you're unlovable, being judged harshly, being blamed for things beyond your control, being ignored, being hurt by people who claim to love you, being told your feelings don't matter, not feeling safe to be yourself, regularly feeling scared, anxious, or on edge, and experiencing caregivers as inconsistent or untrustworthy. When emotional needs aren't met, a child learns to adapt to survive, but the patterns linger into adulthood.

Even now, your self-talk likely reflects the messages you absorbed in childhood. Many people realize that their inner critic sounds *exactly* like the voices of their parents or siblings. Without even realizing it, we internalize these negative messages and reinforce them over time, repeating them to ourselves until they feel like truth.

To learn more I read *Too Much* by Terri Cole, where she defines a "high-functioning codependent" as someone overly invested in the emotions, outcomes, finances, and relationships of the people in their lives—to the detriment of their own inner peace. It's not just caring for others; it's feeling *responsible* for their emotions and actions. Others' moods affect you profoundly. You don't know how to be separate from the people you love. You covertly try to control outcomes. Watching someone struggle is unbearable, so you try to fix it—not just to help them, but to *relieve your own pain* in the process.

Damn. Nailed it.

So, what caused *my* codependency?

My very real, and also perceived, abandonment. The inability to form secure emotional attachments to reliable caregivers. Experiencing significant rejection at a young age.

I felt all of that growing up.

You know, like so many of us do.

The realization finally registers in my core—my mom being emotionally unavailable, largely incapable of showing love, her constant negativity, my childhood fear of getting sick and feeling physically unsafe at home. I spent 18 years stuffing down my questions, joyfully pretending to be a good Christian Scientist. I didn't want to let anyone down growing up, so I silenced my true emotions, and my fears.

Codependency is an emotional addiction, an endless search for security outside of oneself. When core emotional needs like affection, warmth, or safety go unmet in childhood, those needs don't disappear; they often resurface in adult relationships. This can lead to "repetition compulsion"—a subconscious pull to recreate familiar emotional dynamics in hopes of resolving them. If you were loved but also experienced volatility or emotional distance (like with a father who adored you but had a temper or limited emotional depth), it can create a mixed message: Love is safe, but it can also turn volatile. So you might be drawn to partners who are similarly inconsistent or emotionally unavailable—trying to finally "earn" the love you once craved.

For my entire adulthood, I've unconsciously looked to my partners to make me feel secure and cared for. Even though I projected total confidence, I now see I was always feeling unsafe in my relationships, performing for affection like love was a prize to compete for. Codependents feel like we have to do everything ourselves, like we can't count on anyone. Our relationships become enmeshed. We lose our sense of being separate, unique, independent. And we stay loyal, even when that person might not deserve our loyalty, even when it drags us down. Low self-worth, feelings of inadequacy, relentless self-criticism, shame—the belief that there is something fundamentally wrong with us—this is our norm.

We need to be liked. We need to be needed. We seek validation that we are worthy and lovable. So we do whatever it takes to make others happy, often sacrificing our own needs, interests, and goals in the process.

Holy. Mother. Of. God. This is me. All of it. This is why I stayed so damn long. This is why it felt *impossible* to leave my Former. This is why I keep choosing unavailable men.

The speed and intensity with which I now fully see myself, my behaviors, my patterns, hits me like a freight train.

I'm not sure what parts of me will be recognizable when the dust settles.

Or maybe... I'll vanish completely. When awareness hits like a wrecking ball, what remains of who you once were?

Chapter Twenty-Four

There she blows.

The hangover from the codependency realization has me feeling shocked yet grateful—like staring into a full-length mirror and realizing, like the Emperor's New Clothes, I've been parading around totally bare all along. My armor was all a façade. I realize: maybe it's time to start dressing myself instead of relying on the court. To prioritize my own needs and boundaries, and let others take responsibility for their own damn lives.

I decide to treat myself for this realization breakthrough as a way of being a little more loving, accepting, and patient with where I'm at in my relationship shortcomings. So I order my first custom surfboard—a 7'2", 50-liter beauty that acts like a mini longboard with her wide nose and buoyant body. She's special because she's shaped just for me to match my skill level, body shape and surfing style. Which makes her feel like more than just a board, she's a symbol of me showing up for myself. I name her Bella, and she is so damn beautiful. My card to myself reads:

"You're doing your best. You've gathered wisdom at every step. What's meant of you is on its way. When the time is right, your love will be met, held, and multiplied in places you've yet to imagine. Life has a rhythm. Let it all go, trust the timing."

And so I do. Again.

In the surf lineup, getting used to my new beautiful ride, I find myself chatting with a friend about my last ayahuasca experience and I mention how I felt it wasn't as profound as I had expected. He shares about another upcoming ceremony with an entirely different energy, so I decide to try it one more time to see if I can downshift the experience.

Lately, it feels like psychedelics—mushrooms, ayahuasca, bufo—are becoming trendy tools to chase constant bliss. To be clear, that's not my goal. I've seen people burn out trying to fast-track healing with back-to-back ceremonies. You can't rush this work or use plant medicine as a band-aid. I'm approaching these experiences with intention—to reconnect with the supernatural energy my dad helped me access, and to help soften my ego, heal, and remember the sacred beneath the surface of everyday life.

So I go once more, this time with another dear Mexican surfer buddy, Emilio. The ceremony is entirely in Spanish and filled with masculine energy—mostly a Mexican male crew in attendance, led by a male shaman. I'm the only gringa there, and with the blonde locks, I stand out a smidge.

Much of the ceremony is similar to my first, but this time I feel a profound connection to nature, the stars, and the gorgeous ceremony music. I don't have insane hallucinations or otherworldly experiences, but I do feel an intense, almost visceral oneness with the Earth.

After my first cup, they offer a second dose for anyone not yet feeling the effects. I walk up to accept it. Twenty minutes later, that second dose proves to be too much for me—because just as the beautiful, strong hallucinations begin, I promptly have to run to a cactus and purge.

I spend the rest of the ceremony feeling beautifully connected to all things, enjoying the music, and eventually falling asleep as the long night of songs and singing wears on.

Maybe I'm not meant to have the wild experience some people report with aya—and that's okay with me. My two journeys have been beautiful, simple, and exactly what I need.

The next day, back in bed, having a day of recovery and rest, I find myself writing in my journal—a reminder to myself:

Hi love, you know that time you were broken and hurting, but then you showed up yet again to give yourself another chance? That was beautiful. Do that again. And again. And again. Don't chase anyone. Don't beg someone to stay. Know your worth. Save your heart space for the people who matter. You'll know them because they'll make loving you easy. Accept what cannot be changed. Leave what isn't for you. Above all else, please, love yourself unconditionally. You deserve it, and that is the key to getting all that you desire.

We all deserve to feel that self-love, my friend. Embracing the mess, that's the heart of healing. One moment you see it all clearly and reach the castle, and other days you're back in the moat, knee-deep in the townspeople's shit, wondering where the hell your crown went.

There is no perfect level of happiness to achieve. Life comes—and therefore, healing comes—in waves. One moment you're dropping in and feeling the immense bliss of matching your own frequency to the ocean. Another moment, the ocean is pummeling you into darkness, deep below the surface light, and you pray for a little help and guidance to bring you back up. And then, out of pure, nutty human curiosity, you paddle out again.

This is the beauty of the rhythm of life.

The sea helps me daily, sending me forgiveness, compassion, grace, permission, opportunity, healing, and love.

I need to plant my own garden and decorate my own soul instead of waiting for someone else to bring me flowers.

Putting myself first isn't selfish—it's necessary.

Life slowly rolls into the middle of the year. I've decided the best way to heal is by hopping off dating apps completely. I'm done waiting to be chosen—I'm going to choose my own damn self. No more making myself uncomfortable to make others feel comfortable. I'm done worrying about finding a partner and finally starting to worry about feeling comfortable with myself, my triggers, and my reactive behaviors, so I can close the cycles for good.

I dive into that work. I swear, deeply, that I don't need anyone at this moment in my life. And then, *bam*, just a few months later, I meet Danny at a bar when a random guy decides to come up and harass me after I kindly explain I'm just out for some solo time, grabbing a beer and some wings. As he proceeds to call me a bitch for setting a boundary, Danny—who happens to be out with friends, bellied up to the same bar—quickly steps in with his easy smile, effortlessly chatting the guy up about the ballgame on TV to redirect his attention, while simultaneously giving me a kind look and an eye roll, silently apologizing for the guy's poor behavior. A true Canadian gentleman.

I thank him, and suddenly our circles start overlapping. A few weeks later we end up at the same bar, sitting at the same table of mutual friends. He's cute, gentle, kind, intelligent, has a great sense of humor—and like my father, he's deeply spiritual. We get into a long, deep conversation, but after one too many margaritas, we end up in a tipsy tiff over our spiritual beliefs. Funny how, even as you awaken to the realization that we're all just spiritual beings having a human experience, the ego still pops in like, *"Actually, I know our purpose and how the Universe works."* Classic.

Newly awakened folks like myself often find themselves coaching, preaching, dissecting others' behavior and "enlightening" them from their little tower of "awake and aware." So here I am, downing tequila and preaching all my spiritual knowledge and experiences. Oh, ego.

But for once, instead of diving straight into sex or commitment, I set my relationship expectations aside and just allow myself to enjoy being together as friends—albeit with a healthy dose of attraction and flirtation. I'd never dated a spiritual man before, and the pull was intoxicating. From our first chat, he also seems emotionally available (*finally*). And, well... he also drinks like a sailor. Whelp, you can't have it all, can you?

If you think this is the part where I learn to cut back on booze, spoiler alert: it's not. Oh no, this girl doubles down. Danny and I spend the summer partying like it's 1999—and I act like it in the best and worst possible ways. We start hanging out all the time. We have happy hour, we have bloody mary hour, we go to parties, we go out dancing late into the night.

I find myself one sunny Baja afternoon at a hotel poolside day club, twerking it out with a huge crew of Black ladies celebrating a bachelorette party. They cheer me on, pour champagne down my ass, and we move and chant and dance and grind in pure, ecstatic, playful joy. Their hair is a sculpted masterpiece of curls and waves, their rich ebony skin glowing, their energy carrying the gravity of something soulful and ancient.

Shit, I hope to have a fraction of that universally gifted swagger someday. I'm just so damn delighted they lovingly welcome me into their circle to dance and chant and celebrate together.

Danny and I spend warm evenings drinking wine and talking until the wee hours about spirituality, life, love, evolution, the direction of the planet, the space-time continuum, chess, quantum physics—the total gamut. We talk and talk and talk, vulnerably, from our hearts. We never seem to tire of listening to each other, holding space for each other. It's like falling into a thousand-thread-count hotel bed after a month of camping in the Baja outback without a hot shower.

We begin to connect on a soul-deep level. I feel the possibility of love and joy and expansion—without expectations.

One night out with our amigos, after nearly two months of flirtatious friendship, I find my very long, very drunk 5'9" frame attempting to curl up in his lap like the sweet kitten I am *definitely* not. And then, boom—we're having the most deliciously sloppy makeout session in front of the entire bar. I promptly make my way back to his bed for an equally delightful clothes-tossing romp with my wonderful new friend-with-benefits.

We spend the next month hanging out around town and guzzling far too much alcohol, but screw it, I'm having a damn fine time and not crashing into anything. He's sweet like honey and toasty warm like mezcal straight. And I'm chuggin' away because, for once, I feel safe. Safe to be myself. Safe to be seen and heard. I'm smiling more often, remembering to be grateful, laughing until my belly hurts.

My birthday is approaching in a few days—and apparently, so is a hurricane. Baja's hurricane season runs from mid-August to mid-October, and my birthday lands smack in the middle on September 10th. We've already dodged two storms the month before, but this one looks like it's really going to hit.

On my birthday eve, the whole town is busy preparing—gathering water, gas, candles, and provisions. As the storm rolls in, the sky begins to shift. That perfect Baja blue is quickly swallowed by an ominous, smoky gray cloud steamrolling across the horizon. The sea transforms from turquoise to murky gray, the sun swallowed by darkness. The waves begin to protest, foaming and frothing in anger, swelling in size and intensity like an army rallying its forces beneath the surface.

The wind rushes through the palm trees, whispering a strong warning: *take cover*. I'm still living in my tiny casita on the hillside overlooking the sea, and the owners want to close up the hurricane shutters—which would leave me sitting in a small, dark room, save for the faint light from a single tiny window.

Danny texts to check if I'm safe, and when I mention the situation, he kindly invites me over to his bunker-style casita, tucked into a little knoll in the hotel district.

I grab a few things and make my way over just as the storm really starts to hit. I'm so grateful for company—and for this cozy space to wait it out.

It's a Category 3 hurricane, projected to make a direct hit right here in San José del Cabo. We watch through the window as the awning rips off the patio roof, terracotta tiles fly like frisbees, and the tall, thin palms bend violently—looking like toothpicks about to snap. The wind keeps picking up speed.

Friends up north text me happy early birthday wishes, asking what I've got planned for tomorrow. I send them a few storm videos in reply—looks like it's going to be *quite* the party.

Just as our pasta finishes boiling, the power goes out. We hunker down in the dark with our wine and pasta, the wind howling, windows rattling, water starting to seep in under the front door.

Over the next hour or two, it gets so intense I can't imagine the wind getting any stronger—and yet it does. For about thirty minutes, I'm genuinely scared.

We know how lucky we are compared to the countless families living out in the barrios in simple structures with tin roofs. I can't even fathom the night they must be enduring. We bow our heads and send them a prayer.

I eat my pasta in the dark, full of gratitude for everything I have.

And then—about an hour later—absolute, total stillness.

We step outside. The sky's clearing, the air is still, and the palm trees are frozen in place—like someone hit pause on the storm.

"Well heck, that ended abruptly," he says. I nod, wide-eyed and wiped.

But then it hits me. "That ended *too* abruptly." Rookie move. I pull up the radar. "Ohhh, good Lord... we're in the eye. Part two's coming."

"Well, shit."

Back inside we go. Forty-five minutes later, the wind's back—louder, wilder. The roof creaks. Sleep's not happening. We lie together listening, limbs tangled and skin damp, snuggled despite the thick tropical heat. By 1 a.m., the wind dies down and—thank God—the power kicks back on. Sweet, glorious A/C. We're lucky. Some of our friends won't see power again for a month.

Light pours in the next morning. I barely slept a wink. I look outside at the debris everywhere. My dear friend Dawn had asked a few weeks back if I wanted to join her at a yoga, breathwork, and Bufo retreat outside of town on the coast for my birthday. I message her that I'm at a friend's place and wondering what the roads might be like. We decide we'll chat in an hour or two.

Dawn messages back: *I'm in the same boat. Totally pooped. I'm at a friend's place that has power. Didn't sleep at all. House is a wreck and my husband has a ton of work, so I'm feeling guilty about leaving the kids on top of the storm issues. Let's talk in a bit... if the power comes back on, I'd feel better.*

She eventually gets power back at her house, and part of us wants to leave this mess in the rearview mirror, while part of us wants to stay and help clean it up. We decide to say screw it—the retreat center will be a safe spot to rest and reset, and at the very least, it'll make for an amazing birthday adventure!

When I finish packing up my few things, I give Danny a kiss and a long embrace. "Thank you so much for sharing your space. I think if I'd weathered my first hurricane alone in my little casita, I would've lost it."

He smiles broadly. "You made the whole thing enjoyable. Enjoy your retreat, be safe on the roads—I can't wait to hear everything when you get back."

My heart melts.

Not long after, Dawn rolls up in her SUV, and as we make our way out of town, we begin to see the full extent of the destruction.

On the way to our retreat center, we see roads washed out, metal highway signs twisted like pretzels, roofs torn off, downed palm trees everywhere, and flooded arroyos transformed into raging rivers. Everything around us looks like a complete disastrous mess. I immediately wonder if we've made a mistake making this two-hour drive to the coast—but we continue on.

As we get further from town, the damage becomes less and less. We arrive at our seaside retreat center to find the location totally unaffected by the storm. I look at the beachfront pool, the cute restaurant filled with locally sourced nourishing foods, and the cozy, colorfully decorated rooms.

I look at Dawn with a huge ear-to-ear smile, both of us nodding fervently in synchronous agreement: we made a damn good choice.

Chapter Twenty-Five

Kiss the frog.

As my year of tinkering with psychedelics was coming to an end, *Bufo Alvarius* (commonly called *bufo*) had been mentioned by friends in Baja, but I didn't know much about it. Actually, I knew nothing—except that it's in the DMT family. What I did know was that I trusted Dawn completely, and my intuition whispered, *Go with her guidance.*

I'm learning that squirmy feelings and tugs in my gut are usually signs urging me to follow safety guidance—to leave, step back, or escape a situation entirely. But those intuitive heart tugs, that flutter of warmth expanding in the chest? That's my emotional higher-self nudging me to lean into the projects, paths, people or passions I feel called to pursue.

Following that flutter of intuitive interest, I find myself at this retreat, on my birthday, after some gentle yoga, breathwork, and nourishing food leading up to the ceremony. We split into smaller groups of four—Dawn and I made sure to stick together, along with two other attendees, Valerio and Marie. We snag some colorful Mexican blankets and carry them down a long, vertical path of whitewashed, weathered wooden stairs zigzagging to a cozy, private beach spot next to the Sea of Cortez.

Dawn goes first. Our shaman is dressed in earth-toned woven garments, colorful ceremonial beads adorning his strong neck. He has wonderfully kind eyes, grounding energy, and a profound feeling of love radiating from his heart. I feel completely comfortable and safe in his presence.

He takes out a small clear pipe and a lighter, and I have an immediate judgmental reaction: *Umm, this sacred medicine is taken from a crack pipe?* Seriously, that's exactly what it looks like.

I settle my ego. *Shush already. Trust.*

Dawn is saged by the shaman, then sits down on her blanket, sets her intention, and he lights the pipe for her, placing it to her lips and holding it as she inhales. She draws in deeply. He counts out fifteen seconds, and she's instructed to hold the smoke. She releases it, and about five seconds pass before her body goes totally limp. She falls back into the waiting hands of the shaman, who slowly lowers her onto the beach blanket.

Her color fades from golden tan to a paler white. Her chest begins to heave aggressively, arching upward like a rope has lassoed her sternum and is yanking her toward the sky. Her head throws back, and then she begins to writhe, moan, and chant in tongues.

This is *not* the relatively quiet, polite, and conservative Dawn I know.

I glance at Valerio, stretched out on the blanket beside me, my eyes practically bugging out of my head. He stares back, equally wide-eyed and concerned.

I start to panic. There is *no way* I can do this. Nope. I'm positive—I am *not* doing this.

But after a few minutes, she starts to calm. The arch in her back softens, the chanting fades, and the color returns to her face. A gigantic smile spreads across her cheeks, glowing and blissful. I've never seen her look so content.

Still cradled by the earth beneath her blanket, she slowly sits up—eyes still closed but unmistakably aware, slowly breathing the experience in.

The whole thing lasts about twenty-five minutes, and then my Dawn is back—more grounded, centered, and glowing in a way I've never seen before. We lock eyes. She smiles, radiating a calm that feels cosmic. There's a new sparkle of knowing in her gaze.

I relax a little.

IT'S GONNA GET MESSY

Valerio decides to give it a go next. His journey lasts barely fifteen minutes, and the whole thing seems pretty chill and uneventful for him.

Screw it. This is your psychedelic year of experimentation. You're here because your curiosity and intuition have called you here. You're conflicted, but you know the doubts in your mind are the mind, the ego, trying to keep you safe. Remember why you are doing this, to connect again to the incredible energy your father showed you that exists right here and now, that is a part of you, for you to access whenever you need it.

I look at Valerio's beautiful blue and turquoise blanket compared to my pale cream one, and he catches me eyeing it. Without hesitation, he lovingly gets up, folds it, and hands it to me. I'm so grateful—blue was my dad's favorite color, and for some reason, I instantly view this particular blanket as my anchor for the journey ahead.

The shaman comes over.

I'm sitting on the beautiful handwoven blanket, legs curled up to my chest, feet in front of me, toes curled in the sand. The dusty pink and green mountains and the turquoise sea stretch before me, grounding me. I'm ready.

He lights the bufo in the clear pipe and brings it to my lips. I inhale deeply, and he tells me to hold it for about fifteen seconds. I hold it in as long as I can—thinking how all those years of bong rip competitions in college might finally be paying off—and just before I begin to exhale, the scene in front of me shifts.

The mountains turn into sacred geometric shapes, fractaling into a kaleidoscope of intertwining, vibrating, brilliantly glowing triangles. The sea morphs into flowing, colorful metallic lines, and what can only be described as angelic, gliding beings. The shaman begins to drum and chant—and then a split second later, I lose control of my body.

I am free-falling backward toward my blanket and the grains of sand beneath me as he whispers ever so softly in my ear: "You're going to feel like you're dying."

Well shit! Seriously? Do more research, damnit!

Sure enough, I *do* feel like I'm dying. I see the shaman's face above me being overtaken by the most intense flash of golden-white light—like in the movies when a nuclear bomb detonates and the entire horizon is engulfed. Everything becomes muffled.

I fall into his arms and am gently lowered to the blanket. I have no memory of what happens next with my body, but Dawn later tells me I fought for a moment or two—my arms swimming, literally pulling at the air in front of me, trying to keep myself tethered to this reality...

And then, *poof*, gone.

I am completely gone. I am light. I am in an eternal sea of light. I have no body. I am nowhere. I am no one. I am no thing. There is nothing but warm, golden, searingly intense white-gold light all around me—and I *am* the light.

I am in total bliss. I am simply my Soul's essence, back in eternal time. I am my truest form. I am Love.

Dawn watches over me as a massive smile spreads across my face, my body completely relaxing. I begin to giggle—a warm, rolling, bellyish, content giggle of absolute, pure delight.

This sea of pure bliss is where I remain—for, by my best Earthly estimate and sense of time, about 1,000 years.

I am simply *there*, with no memory of where I was before. I simply *am*. And I am so content with that.

Somehow, at some point, living in this eternal space, in this endless moment that felt like it spanned ten lifetimes, I begin to hear far-off echoes. A gentle, muffled drum softly guiding me back to my body.

I slowly begin to feel my arms and legs again. As I slowly open my eyes, the shaman is above me. I did not expect anyone to be here. I'm not sure what I expected. Nothing. Everything. Both, maybe.

The sunlight is fading, but there is his face, and tears of pure, gorgeous joy and delight are streaming down my cheeks. All I can manage to say is, "Beautiful."

As I come into the present moment, I am keenly aware of the weight of my body, returning to it—just like when my dad visited me. I lift an arm like a puppet controlled by strings, but it flops back down to the sand beside me. I lift the other arm, and it quickly drops to the sand again. I smile at the novelty of it all, feeling confused. This meat suit thing is so dense, so heavy, and—ugh—I can feel my lower back, which apparently comes equipped with aches and pains? I look to the heavens. *Can I have an upgrade?*

The warmth of the sun has just set behind the mountains, and as its light slowly fades, the sky responds in celebration with radiant pinks, oranges, and purples dancing across the horizon. I notice the luminous water in front of me, and I immediately strip down to the swimsuit I had on underneath my clothes. I slowly walk toward the edge of the sea.

I step into the warm, gorgeous liquid as it envelops my toes. I vow to myself: *You're reborn, in this moment, let it all go, allow it to fade away, there is only now.*

I sink into the warm, salty water—up to my waist, then my chest—and finally dunk my head under. The delicious, weighty, gooey, loving water caresses me. I can hear the life below the surface—the crackling of coral, the swirling of the sea, a whale in the distance. The water feels like a nurturing womb, holding me entirely in endless love, without expectations. I enter yet another reality entirely.

Oh my God, this truly is heaven.

I come back up thirty seconds later and see the shaman standing on the shore next to the water, looking down at me, making sure I'm alright.

I smile up at him. Still a little slow with my speech, I tell him, "I was gone...a thousand years." I try to find the words, but it's impossible. "It literally felt like a thousand years passed. I wasn't sure what would be here when I came back. I didn't know there was a back. I didn't know there was a forward. It simply all *was*, and I was completely content."

He smiles a knowing smile, bows his head without speaking, and slowly walks back to the group for our last friend to go.

As we walk back up the whitewashed wooden stairs to the retreat center for dinner, Dawn asks me, "How was it?"

"It was just... so incredibly beautiful and powerful. You know the movie *Interstellar*, when time on the water planet was entirely different than on the ship? When Cooper and his team spend what feels like about three hours down on the planet, but when they come back to the ship, they find the captain old and gray—and for him it was 23 years in Earth time? It was like that. I truly felt I was gone for multiple lifetimes."

What I didn't know upon partaking is that bufo, otherwise known as 5-MeO-DMT, is one of the most powerful psychedelics known to man. It's reported to be 5–10 times more potent than DMT. Bufo is derived from the *Bufo Alvarius* toad, also known as the Colorado River toad. The secretions are collected from the toad and dried to form a powder, which is then smoked from a pipe. Bufo has many uses by Indigenous tribes, the main being to connect with Divine power, heal from physical and mental suffering, and prepare the dying for death. In recent years, it has also been shown to assist with mental health issues such as depression, anxiety, PTSD, and addiction.

Well, I suppose I'm glad I learned this afterwards, but I loved the experience. I now know what death feels like, and I have to say, it was an instant of intense fear followed by an eternity of something absolutely glorious.

Life is our greatest teacher, and the more we trust in the process, the less we judge our experience, the less we judge people, the more we find ourselves living our greatest adventure—and letting go of telling other people how to live theirs. This was an epic experience I'll never forget, one that came the closest to taking me to the realm my father brought me to—sober as a judge—that night under the full moon.

It's odd, though, because even though my father took me to infinite time and space, where I traveled with him was total tranquil darkness, and Bufo was a blazing, fiery light. But the feeling of bliss and oneness was exactly the same.

At dinner, our conversation drifts from the day's profound experiences to motherhood. Unexpectedly, guilt and shame rise in me because I didn't choose that path. Sometimes, it feels like women who don't become mothers are seen as lacking, even selfish. Society sells us the idea that womanhood is earned through partnership and procreation. But Dawn gently reminds me, nurturing isn't reserved for mothers. It's not a role, it's an energy. And I can offer it freely to those I love, wherever it's needed.

This year, for the first time, I've felt that nurturing feminine energy bloom in me—soft, strong, undeniable. And I wonder: is this regret truly mine, or just society's script? Sitting with it, I know—it's not my truth I'm mourning, it's the pressure to conform. Fulfillment can take many forms: deep friendship, creativity, personal growth, community. We each get to define what makes our life meaningful. And with her insight, and my own permission, the shame dissolves.

The next morning, we all share a healthy breakfast, a round of sincere hugs as we head our separate ways, thanking each other for sharing this incredible experience. As Dawn and I hop in the car and begin the two-hour drive back into town, I find I'm so excited to tell Danny all about my journey. As someone who's never touched a single drug in his entire life, he listens intently—smiling, encouraging, asking great questions, and feeling genuinely glad I had such a transformative experience and birthday. I love that he's never touched drugs despite all the societal pressures he's felt over the years. They simply don't call to him.

I find myself flowing through the end of the year in a wonderful rhythm. Suddenly, I notice my underwear, a toothbrush, a change of clothes, and then—one day—my surfboard at Danny's place. It's nearly Christmas, and we just effortlessly shift into living together officially as boyfriend and girlfriend, though we'd already been spending nearly every day together anyway.

I was proud of myself for still being willing to risk getting hurt—loving another human being again without fear. Have you ever felt a connection with someone, not just attraction, but something deeper, something woven into the richness of their soul? That's what it feels like with Danny. The thing is, at this stage, I can see my triggers, but I can't quite dive deep enough yet to understand the root causes. What I need is to finally vomit up some of the suffocated emotions from the fifteen-year relationship that left my insides unknowingly bruised and bloody. Little did I know, I was now standing at the top of the high dive, all ten toes curled over the edge.

The partners we attract are often reflections of our repeated cycles until we learn our lessons and guide ourselves toward a new start, and there is a glimmer of hope here that I'm not stuck in the rinse-and-repeat cycle again.

I get the most random email from the CEO of my old company saying he's heading to Los Cabos to host a small gathering at an all-inclusive for a handful of key employees, with a bunch of excursions: zip lining, canyoneering, Baja car racing, kayaking. And by George, I say fuck it, I go and have a damn good time.

I see now: everything happened exactly as it was supposed to. Would I have had the courage to ditch the corporate life that was making me so insanely stressed without a nudge from the Universe? I would have—but it likely would've taken me a few more years, maybe until I hit total despair, to finally set myself free. Just like with my marriage.

Unfortunately, sometimes we have to take ourselves to the breaking point before we have no choice but to make a change. I am no longer chasing what doesn't serve me. I am finding the courage to let go of the people, places, and things that pull me backward.

As the year winds down, I attend the posada—a holiday party—for the small Baja company I now consult for under my own brand. This little company feels more like family than business. My work is valued, and it lights me up. With my e-commerce store up and running, I've realized something over the past year: I love the messy beginning: the blank page, building the brand, shaping the voice, crafting the offer, mapping the marketing, setting up the systems. The part most people avoid? That's where I come alive. Once things settle into routine, I lose interest.

I let that business idea go, reluctantly at first, labeling it a failure in my mind. But with time, I see it for what it truly was: a valuable learning experience that showed me what actually excites me—helping others launch their own business. So I pivot. I start offering guidance to conscious entrepreneurs ready to leave the corporate matrix and bring their passion projects to life. It's heart-centered, purpose-driven work—and it finally feels aligned.

As the holidays roll around, I decide not to travel back to freezing Wisconsin this year. Boundaries. Instead, Danny and I spend Christmas with Baja friends in the sunny warmth instead of the icy snow. I apologize to Mum, but I'm choosing what I need right now—not following what feels like obligation. I'm surprised to see she seems to understand my desire to stay put.

I find myself falling into the Baja time warp for the better part of a year—partying, spirituality chats galore, lots of outdoor play, and, unfortunately, a fair bit of ego battles. After moving in with Danny, we begin to face the expectations of what a relationship is, versus what it meant to simply enjoy each other's company. It's so odd—put a word on it, a label, "relationship," and suddenly the expectations shift.

What I don't understand yet is that an unhealed person can find offense in pretty much anything someone else does. A healed person understands that the actions of others have absolutely nothing to do with them. Well, I'm still not there by a long shot when it comes to love. It turns out I've been carrying a lifetime of unhealed trauma I didn't fully understand—but now, I was beginning to. And it was all finally vomiting out.

We're arguing quite a bit, but I know I'm growing—because I stop pretending to be unbothered. I stop Pollyanna-ing my way through discomfort and burying from memory the things that upset or worry me. I tell Danny the truth when he asks how I'm doing. I finally let all the fears and tears out instead of stuffing them down. I ask for what I need instead of giving the silent treatment or hoping he'll read my body language.

Relationship maturity is the ability to sit with uncomfortable emotions and have the hard conversations—the ones ego would rather avoid. Real growth begins when we face those truths, both within ourselves and with each other. I used to chase happiness outside of myself, not realizing that made it impossible to truly find. What's beautiful is that even in the mess, we recognize we want to do this work together. We begin healing old patterns—not through codependency, but through compassion—learning to see past the behavior and into the feeling beneath it, the unmet need. Instead of reacting to symptoms, we start tending to the root.

Actually, most of our ego-driven arguing would occur on holidays. When you pile the societal expectation of what "should" happen on a holiday in a relationship, add in excessive booze as fuel for the fights—that's a deadly cocktail right there. Unfortunately, it's one I've drunk before.

On our first New Year's Eve, for example, I have expectations from all the wonderful societal scripts we're told—that when the clock strikes midnight, I should have the most epic kiss with my new love.

As the bar begins the countdown, Danny pops up to help a waiter, a friend of his, carry a large tray full of glasses filled with champagne. The clock strikes midnight, and I sit there by myself as everyone cheers and makes out with their loved ones. A minute later, he makes his way back to me.

Danny can tell I'm mad. His good friend at our table can tell I'm disappointed—and he knows why. His friend whistles and somehow manages to rally the attention of every drunk person in the bar. The entire place erupts into a second countdown, just for us. Everyone screams, cheers, and pops a fresh champagne bottle so we can have our kiss. And I just stare back at Danny, still seething.

I stand up, look him in the eye, and simply walk past everyone to head outside to get some air, trying not to cry.

What. An. Ass.

What a drunken ass *I* am.

I can't see the goodness in the moment, because we've been drinking for hours and I'm damn near blackout drunk. He follows me outside with friends to watch the fireworks, and then I start to cry. We live just a few blocks away, and I walk home alone—disappointed, angry, and oh so drunk.

What I didn't know in my drunken blur of expectations was that he could see the server wasn't going to make it to the table in time for midnight on his own, so Danny hopped up to help him out. What a lovely thing to do for a friend. Only in my spinning, tequila-soaked brain, he had abandoned me.

Expectations, my friend, are the killer of happiness.

We make up the next day after a long, sober chat where we're finally able to understand each other's views. The importance of the midnight kiss *was* on his radar, but he saw someone in need. His logic went: *I don't need the kiss, I need to help my friend so this table of people can have a great celebration.* My problem? That solution left *me* out of the equation.

He hasn't been in a relationship in eleven years, never been married, and so we find he has quite a few of his own set-in-his-ways behaviors to work through. He admits it wasn't the best move.

We begin to see we're definitely yin and yang when it comes to the types of relationship baggage we each carry—the stuff that needs to be hauled up and sorted through. Still, this manages to be a truly gorgeous year of lust, love, and healing for us both.

We help each other with self-acceptance. We face our relationship with money, *in* a relationship. Together, we heal childhood ties and traumas with our parents. We both learn patience, and proper communication with someone we love, to truly listen and be heard. Without ego. Without name-calling. Without withholding. Without shutting down.

(When we're sober, wink wink.)

We still haven't mastered getting to understanding *in* the heat of the moment, but most of the time, we land there eventually. Sometimes it takes a few days to see each other's unique perceptions—to step outside our own lenses, which are so often filtered through whatever personal shit we're going through, or have gone through in life.

I'm learning most arguments aren't really about what we think they are. They're because we all have our own unique perception of reality that no one else can fully access. To grow, we have to be open enough to consider a wider perspective. To understand that someone else's experience of the same moment might be completely different—and still be true. It isn't easy.

We talk things through *ad nauseum*.

So. Many. Times.

But in this one year, we truly work through a decade of trauma together.

And amidst the trauma vomiting (which, let's be honest, is *a lot*), there is so much rich goodness between us. I feel like I'm flourishing. I've found a wonderful balance of work and play. I'm getting pretty dang decent at surfing, two years into learning, and I'm in the best shape of my life. At 42, I feel more alive and stoked on life than I ever did at 22.

We go to rooftop moonlight dance parties with strangers who become friends by sunrise. We attend birthday parties and a dear friend's wedding. We spend cozy nights reading, having endless slow conversations about life and spirituality over coffee. There are romantic beach dinners, local music, artist gatherings, sunset yacht rides, epic whale-watching tours, hikes into the golden evening light.

Ridiculously long morning snuggles. Wonderful sex. And making out to my heart's content.

We buy crystals at the farmers market together, picking out the ones that resonate with us most. He teaches me how to play chess. And fine, I'll admit it, I'm *still* working on not being a sore loser. That level of zen may never be achieved, but I'm trying with all my might.

I'm drawn in because Danny is *gentle* with me.

Intimacy, I'm learning, is about safety. And the peace I feel in his presence is something I've never felt with a partner before. Don't get me wrong—the sex is delightful and oh-so-fun—but it's the emotional intimacy I've been starving for. To be fully listened to. To be truly heard. To feel profoundly safe.

My heart and soul are wide open to love again, to breathing in life. I take down a little of the fortress around my heart. I find a little more faith in love. I slowly begin to heal all the times I've emotionally betrayed myself, rebuilding trust within.

I appreciate the ease in his voice, even when we disagree. His attentiveness when I'm struggling. The proud tone in his voice when he talks about me to others. A man who takes care of me in ways money never could.

If only I weren't still stuck on the societal-programmed idea that, for a man to be a man, he has to provide financially. But I am.

Valentine's Day rolls around, and after a dressy dinner at a nice restaurant, the bill lands. I pause—waiting in that awkward space where old-school expectations still linger, where the man is supposed to take care of the check. When he doesn't, I give him the look and, frustrated, pull out my card first. Only then, out of guilt or obligation, he puts his down to cover it.

The thing is, I'm finding out we view money completely differently. I come from a corporate background: steady income, savings plans, budgets, and an eye on the bigger financial picture. He's lived his whole life self-employed, guided by a "make it, spend it" mentality. And I mean *all* of it.

I'm tired of feeling like I'm carrying the financial load. I'm not looking for a sugar daddy, I never have, but I do want a partner who sees saving the way I do. And yes, someone who wants to pamper me a little sometimes. Especially on Valentine's. That spend-it-all approach? It stresses me the hell out.

Like my spiritual father who struggled with finances, Danny believes divine Source will take care of him—without too much thought about action or planning. Me? I think Source *will* take care of you, *if* you take consistent action and effort toward your dreams.

My father felt the same way Danny does, and as a result, finances and career ambition nearly ended my parents' marriage. Actually, it probably would have, if divorce had been something they felt they could do. That—and my dad's deep desire for adventure—while my mom was content with a simple, repeatable schedule at home.

In *our* case, I'm the adventurer. Danny prefers the repeatable and steady rhythm.

And yet—this is the first man who has truly listened to me, seen me, and held space for me like no one else on this planet ever has.

The Universe really does have the most wicked sense of humor when it comes to teaching your life lessons, doesn't it?

The finances, the adventurousness, the comfort—these are major things for me. Plus, in my new expat surfer life, coming from land-locked Wisconsin, I'm totally water- and beach-obsessed. And he... can't stand the beach. The sand on his feet bothers him, and he hates the water.

I explain this to friends, and they look at me like I'm completely nuts.

"You? You're dating a guy who doesn't like the water and the beach?"

He did have a near-drowning experience as a kid, so I get the not-going-in-the-water part. But not even sitting on the beach with me?

I begged him to come just once to watch me surf. We'd been together six months and he'd never come, despite my asking. I offered to bring a chair, an umbrella, drinks, snacks—everything. He still refused. Said it's just not his thing. He's perfectly content doing his daily coffee and crossword. *Not even once—for me?* I was so upset.

My friends noticed the mismatch and would gently point it out. I'd reply, "It's okay. After spending nearly 24/7 with my ex-husband throughout our marriage, I now know it's healthy to have separate interests and time apart." And while I *do* believe that, I could still feel the lie underneath.

This was his boundary to set—and I was largely accepting of it. But my own boundary? Having a partner who would at least come to the beach with me now and again. Like, twice a bloody year.

We were butting boundaries, hard.

Everyone saw the shaky ground, but they smiled, nodded, and said, *"Totally."*

As we all know, when a friend is swimming in the depths of love, the whistle of the lifeguard can't be blown. You just stay a few strokes away with the life preserver, waiting until they're ready to reach for it.

This is when I began to understand that the ones we love most aren't always meant to walk beside us forever. Sometimes, they're simply who we need in a particular season—no less significant, no less real—just not destined for the distance.

We're taught by society that love must endure until death, that anything less is a failure.

But true love isn't measured in permanence or bound by expectation. It isn't something to possess, nor a contract to uphold.

Love, in its purest form, is rooted in freedom.

Chapter Twenty-Six

This one's on me.

It's the week before Easter, and we've been dating for four months, though we've been hanging out for about a year. One evening, I randomly blurt out to Danny, "Let's get tickets to Mexico City!" I was ready to roll on a trip at a moment's notice. But it was too quick for him—he said he needed to think and plan a bit more.

"Look, I'll plan every last detail. You just have to get on the plane!"

I know I need to find a fellow travel adventurer, and towards the end of my marriage with the Former, he *did* get much better at enjoying travel... maybe the boyfriend will too?

Eventually, he agrees. I find a hotel, and then we go from there with a fairly rough outline of things to do and see. We take off for Mexico City the next week.

If you've never been, Mexico City probably isn't what you imagine. In neighborhoods like Condesa, Polanco, and Roma, we stroll through lush parks shaded by jacaranda trees, admire stunning architecture, and pop into world-class museums and cafes that feel both cosmopolitan and deeply rooted in culture. It's massive—twice the size of New York—but somehow manages to feel surprisingly intimate. I'll even say it: in these areas, it's cleaner and more walkable than many other capital cities I've visited.

Granted, I know I'm experiencing a particular touristy slice of the city. These neighborhoods are vibrant and well-resourced, and while they represent one beautiful facet of Mexico City, they don't tell the whole story. Like any major city, CDMX is layered. Many parts face real challenges—economic inequality, violent crime, limited access to essential services—and that reality lives alongside the beauty. Both exist. Both are true.

On a whim, I land us a table at one of the world's top-rated restaurants—a phenomenal, four-hour experience, worth every indulgent sip and bite. Despite my offering to pay, and I do, frustration creeps in. Once again, I feel I'm carrying the financial load, and the afterglow dissolves into tension. I chalk it up to relationship struggles—something to work through with better communication.

In my new spiritual awareness, I try to ignore this old financial equality frustration. He provides in many other ways. Why can't that be enough?

But the truth, my friend, goes beyond just finances—and it's clearer than I want to admit in this moment: I'm living a story I've lived before. He is rooted in comfort, and I am built for growth.

We return to Baja and find ourselves rolling into the middle of the year, living in a balanced blend of mornings for surfing and afternoons for work and coffee breaks together. Literally: rinse, repeat. Life is suspended in the Baja time warp again, where everything just moves so much slower.

I get back into a good rhythm and carve out time for myself to grow—using evenings for yoga, dabbling more in holotropic breathwork, trying out four-minute ice baths, and exploring deeper meditations.

Breathwork has been wonderful for my healing and for achieving deeper states of consciousness to better understand my self-awareness and emotions. I'm getting better and better at meditation, too. Each time is still a challenge to quiet my mind, but I'm learning to surrender more quickly.

I'm intrigued to see if I can reach that heightened state of awareness I experienced through psychedelics via meditation. I've read that it's possible. I've certainly felt a glimmer of that intensity through breathwork as well. I'm fascinated by all these healing modalities and wish I could ditch the matrix work altogether, simply focusing on healing, raising my vibration, and becoming a better human.

July of 2022 rolls around, the month when I usually visit family since Wisconsin is toasty warm and gorgeously green at that time of year. Living in Baja these last nearly three years, I've become a total desert brat. I'm in a puffy jacket once it drops below 60. I used to make fun of Californians in college. I *get* it now. Sorry about that.

I don't think twice about asking Danny to come home to Wisconsin to meet the family over the 4th of July. Granted, this is the first guy I've brought home since my divorce two and a half years ago, and for a split second, I put some pressure on myself about what this means—but I promptly shake it off. He's totally excited to come along, and I want to show him where I grew up and introduce him to my amigos up north.

I show him the lakes, the supper clubs, the friends, the foliage, the beer, the cheese, the art, the old stomping grounds, my home—and yes, the mother. Gasp. We even stay with her for two weeks, and I'm pleased that she actually really likes him. Everything goes rather swimmingly. Over the years, we've gotten closer, but I've only seen her twice since my father passed at the end of 2020.

I shared the story of my father coming to me on the beach when I was in town last July, but she didn't seem to hear me. I was so disappointed. I thought such a profound spiritual moment would make her proud.

I'm feeling conflicted about how much I should keep trying to connect with her. I decide to try one last time. She's not toxic—she's just wounded. We all are. There are boundaries, and there's also giving people grace. So, we sit down for brunch to share the story once more, this time speaking slowly, carefully, pouring my entire heart and energy into sharing this moment with her. She stares back, really listening, and for the first time, we see each other. Tears in our eyes, a knowing flashes between us, connecting us in the understanding that he is still with us. We see the love for each other and know we've both done the very best we can on this messy human journey. I love her very much, and I know she loves me so deeply, even though she doesn't always express it. In this instant, we heal all the stories and traumas of heartache from our past.

The same happens with my brother during this visit, not that we were as distant as my mother and I, but still, we didn't fully connect. This visit, we're able to talk openly from the heart, and he's more awake than I ever realized. We bond over the magic of our dad's visit to me on the beach and the profound spiritual growth we've both experienced over the last year, as we mourn the loss of our father that we both loved so dearly. He meets Danny, and they get along just swimmingly. My heart could burst. The tension we've been feeling in Baja is temporarily forgotten. My brother has the most gorgeous, kind soul. He shares that same sweet heart my father had, and on this visit, I feel how much I wholeheartedly appreciate and care for him. I love my brother to infinity and beyond.

After breakfast, I get a short email from my mom saying that once she returned home, she turned on the TV to a random sporting event. The first thing that appeared on the screen was a player with his name on the back of his jersey, crisp and clear: Thomas Young. My dad's name. She expresses in that moment that she felt such a profound connection to the Divine, the strongest she has felt in a very long time. She sends her deep love and appreciation for our chat, and my heart melts. *Thank you, Dad. Thank you for bringing us all closer together.*

I head off the next morning with Danny to visit Luke. In my last two visits home, I've hung out with the Former along with his new girlfriend. During those visits, we all truly had a great time.

So, this time, I bring Danny up to his house in Northern Wisconsin to hang with the Former and his fiancé. It's so funny; people cringe and ask, "You're all going to hang out together?!" Apparently, most think it would be awkward, but it really wasn't at all.

Well, at least not for me.

Danny is totally game for a hangout, which I love. I'm elated to hear of their engagement, as she is a far better partner for him than I was, although, admittedly, after a decade and a half together, it is a little bizarre to wrap my brain around the idea of him being married to someone else. We all seem to get along beautifully—until we don't.

We've all been drinking heavily, and I've been asking them to come visit me for years. They vaguely mention a trip in my southerly tropical vicinity—but not to see me. I get super sad and stay behind in the parking lot of the dive bar we're all about to stroll into, so I can process my emotions for a moment.

They head toward the entrance, but then the Former sees I'm upset and walks back for a chat. I say to him, all teary-eyed, "I love you guys, why won't you come visit me?" I mean it.

He looks at me, simultaneously compassionate and annoyed, "We're busy and have a lot going on, and it's harder with her kids. We've been looking at the Caribbean, as well."

Tears rolling, I press on, "But you've traveled to a lot of other places and it's been over two years—Baja is better than the Caribbean!" I know I'm grasping. I just want the truth, even though deep down, I already know it.

Somewhere in the drunken haze, he suggests maybe she thinks I still have feelings for him. "REALLY?!" I burst out laughing and half-stomp toward the bar, ready to set her straight.

He stops me, "Don't have that conversation."

I scrunch my eyes and glare at him. Something in my spidey sense feels off. My gut says maybe he's not exactly shutting down that story behind the scenes.

I decide to drop it, and we walk into the bar, my eyes still watery. As I sit down at the bar, I turn to her and say sincerely, "Sorry—I just love you both and wish you'd come visit."

She stares back at me, frozen. It's too much. And, she likely finds it ridiculous that her future husband is consoling his friend and ex-wife in the parking lot. Well, I do learn later that's exactly what she's thinking.

I finally realize: she's here for him, not for me. I really wanted us all to be friends. Sometimes, no matter how much you wish it, that just isn't in the cards.

I ask Danny for his thoughts on the whole matter. He pauses for a moment, then says thoughtfully, "If it weren't for you, I likely wouldn't be friends with the guy."

I'm shocked. Interesting. I think on that statement for a while and see it all from a new perspective. I suddenly can't figure out how I got here. Why are we still hanging out? Do I even resonate with him now? The rose-colored glasses vanished in an instant, and all I could see was a magnifying glass of apathy.

"Huh. Fair," I reply, staring ahead somewhat dumbfounded.

Without our history, I am no longer the woman I was when we separated—let alone the girl who first met him in college. That version of me feels like a distant echo, a face in an old photograph I recognize but don't quite remember living inside.

I try to see him with new eyes, stripped of memory and meaning. Honestly, if we were strangers passing on some quiet street in rural Wisconsin... I'm not sure we'd stop to talk. I'm not sure we'd be drawn to one another at all. It's hard to say given our history, but I also realize I have never fully allowed myself to acknowledge, until now, that there was physical and verbal violence woven throughout our relationship.

It was, as you now know, quite ugly at times. I simply deleted those bad moments from my memory. Control alt delete coping mechanism, remember? That's not to imply I regret our time together, or that I don't care about him—not at all. We were meant to be together, to teach each other, to love each other, and eventually leave each other. Even the challenging times are here to teach us—especially the painful ones.

Funny enough, even after all that understanding, I *still* couldn't let go. Did I mention those codependent tendencies I was trying to overcome? We didn't let go until a full year later, when his new wife finally said she was no longer comfortable with us being friends. Divorce isn't just losing a partner—it's grieving an entire extended family, nieces and nephews, a dog, a life. The loss is brutal, even as it eventually becomes freeing. I dove into friendship to soften the rupture, but you still have to wade through the sea of memories before reaching the other side.

I was upset at first because I felt her personal boundary wasn't compassionate or considerate, that she didn't care she was tossing out all the work we had done to end the marriage with love. But sometimes, you have to respect others' boundaries—even if it means letting go of the painstaking efforts of carefully, consciously uncoupling, along with nearly two decades' worth of life history.

Sometimes, these boundaries have absolutely nothing to do with you. Sometimes, like I see now, they're a hidden gift in disguise. Her boundary became the ending I hadn't yet admitted I needed. Rolling straight into friendship after divorce doesn't leave room to fully process the loss or reevaluate how you want this person in your life. So I begin to mentally prepare for the final round of grief still to come, when it will be time to fully let go. Friendship, history, and all.

Just before cutting ties, I received the most beautiful gift from Luke—a simple, heartfelt text:

Hey, I hope you're doing well. I've been reflecting this week on my life, and I just want to say thank you! I am a better person for knowing you. You helped me grow so much as a person over the fifteen years we were together. I didn't know who I would be, or where I would be, if you and I hadn't joined our lives together. I'm sure I'd be in a good place, but maybe not as good as I am right now. So, again, thank you. I appreciate you and I love you.

This sent such a profound wave of warmth through my heart. I send my gratitude back for all the learning from our journey in life together. Such is life, love, and loss sometimes. The key is to appreciate how these things once served you, granting them the respect they deserve before letting them go. That love is never ever lost—it simply means it's time to close the chapter. Just because the band breaks up doesn't mean it didn't once make good music.

I was, however, feeling incredibly upset that I didn't get to see my dog Duke that I still shared with Luke on this visit, and this brought up how to make seeing him work moving forward, with her new boundaries of me no longer being welcomed in their lives. Then, a few months later, Duke died very suddenly, within days, from a mysterious and rapidly spreading cancer. I didn't get to say goodbye. It was soul-crushing, but it was almost like he and the Universe were both whispering, *It's okay, let go.*

And so, I do. Finally, fully and completely. We have not spoken since.

Chapter Twenty-Seven

Shady shadows lurking.

Danny and I land back in Baja after the trip north, and a week later, on my drive home from a yoga session, I suddenly hear a voice, clear as day: *Write the book.* It's hard to explain where it came from. It was like it was spoken out loud right here in the car, yet also in my thoughts.

I pull over for a moment, take a deep breath, and ask aloud, "Dad?" I hold my breath, waiting, hoping.

Nothing.

For a moment, I sit dumbfounded on the side of the road, staring blankly ahead. Still, I know exactly what the voice means. The story of me and my father. I'm supposed to share it. This very story.

On my drive home, the fear creeps in pretty quickly: *What, you? You're no writer, you've never written a book!* But somehow, I also know that voice is a lie.

"Stop it! Plenty of idiots have written books. Zip it," I say out loud, defending myself.

At this point in my life, I don't take clear guidance from Source lightly—and this is the first time I've heard it so distinctly. Since my out-of-body experience with my dad, something has opened up. I've been sensing things I never did before. Feeling energies. Receiving Divine messages I used to miss. Not whispers, but truths that shimmer with certainty.

I share this with Danny, and to his credit, he fully supports me following the call. We both need space, and deep down, we know it. I've been unconsciously leaning on him to fill a self-love void only I can fill, and putting that kind of weight on someone you love never ends well.

Things were peaceful in Wisconsin. But the moment we landed back in Baja, the old arguments picked up again. It's starting to feel like too much. Like the message I've been avoiding is finally getting louder.

It just so happens that a friend of mine, Hudson from back up in Oregon, is preparing to move down to Baja to a coastal town just an hour north on the Pacific side. We originally met briefly through Tinder the weekend I sat on the corner selling everything in Portland. We snagged a surf, shared an intimate afternoon, and found we profoundly connected as adventurous friends looking to escape the vibe in America. He messages me that he needs someone to watch their new lovely garden home until his mom is able to fully move south for her retirement in Baja.

Sold!

I pop up there the following week, packed to write and be solo for a month. I find Hudson's mom's future home to be just a picturesque white garden house by the sea, nestled among blooming gardens, fruit trees dripping with gifts, and plentiful palm trees galore. It's divine. His mom is on a short visit to inspect and see her new home for the first time.

We watch a gorgeous sunset together, and I'm feeling all excited and ready to begin writing the next day. Then, I wake in the wee dawn hours to the startling silhouette of a man right at the foot of my bed, standing over me. I blink and make out what looks like my purse in his arms. Hudson is sleeping on the sofa to the left of me; we see him at the same moment. I'm too shocked and groggy to have a single sound escape my gaping mouth. I am completely frozen. I can't move.

Hudson pops out of bed in an instant, and before I can even fully process the situation, he is chasing the stranger out the door and down the staircase. We had left the screen door open to let in the cool evening breeze.

I go stand on the balcony. The dawn light is barely forming, so everything is still cool, gray, and misty. I can't see more than about ten to fifteen feet in front of me. My heart is racing, pounding out of my chest. I'm barefoot in my pajamas, and I don't know what to do. I look at the long staircase leading down into foggy darkness; I can't even make out the bottom of it. I don't know if there are more people down there. Do they have knives? Weapons? I think of the worst-case scenario, and so I stay frozen, unable to act.

He returns in a few minutes and grabs me by the shoulders, still breathless from chasing the intruder. "Hey, are you okay?"

I stare blankly back. "I... I can't believe he came into the room while we were sleeping!" We cautiously walk over to the main house to see his mom on the balcony in her room upstairs, looking down at us. Safe, thank God.

Hudson says, "We've been robbed. He took Becca's purse, but we're not sure what else."

She is so sweet and innocent, looking down at us. Her short white hair is tousled, a lovely floral shawl draped around her shoulders. "Oh no, oh dear!" I see her eyes and heart sink, and mine sinks along with hers.

We search the house and find that the invader had slit the screen on a small living room window and jumped inside, taking my surf backpack, everyone's cash, any electronics he could find, and even the keys to my friend's truck. We go out to the truck to find the keys dangling in the ignition, and the silent driveway gate had been opened.

"Holy shit, he was going to steal the damn truck too!" I say, astonished.

We call the local police, and in my somewhat decent Spanish, I explain the situation. They let me know they'll be there in about half an hour. We all sit in the main house, and my friend offers to make me some breakfast, but I tell him, "No, thank you. I'm not hungry."

I begin to feel so overwhelmed. I just want to head back to my place in San José. I wait until the police arrive, chat with them a little bit, and help my friends explain what happened. They file a report but say there's not much to be done. They take our numbers and say they will call if anything comes up. And that's that. I give them both big hugs and explain I can't stay there alone to watch the house. They of course understand. We all exchange big hugs, focusing on the immense gratitude we share that no one was harmed.

"Let's talk in a few days." I offer a tired smile as I leave, then get into my truck and lock the door. I barely make it out of their driveway, but I make sure I'm out of sight before I begin to sob. I start my hour-long drive home, still in shock. I phone Danny to tell him the story.

Once I arrive, he gives me a huge hug, and I ask for a bit of solo time to process it all. He heads out for a while, and I simply collapse to the floor, curl into a ball, and cry a trembling, full-body cry for about an hour or two. I'm mentally and physically exhausted. My heart breaks for his mom, who has just spent months preparing to move down here on her own expat adventure, only to have this happen on her first visit to see her new home. The experience sends an invisible crack shooting through my core, like a fracture running through ice—slow and steady, then dangerously fast. I didn't know it then, but that extreme invasion of safety would linger in my psyche, quietly haunting the edges of my sleep for years.

A few days later, I get a call—a neighbor of Hudson's found my purse in a ditch several streets away. I drive back up, and to my surprise, everything's still there: wallet, lip balm, bag, all my credit cards. No cash, and my AirPods are gone. The hardest loss was a handwritten note from Pops. That one stung, but I remind myself—he's with me always.

Hudson, his mom, and I sit down over breakfast to talk through it all again. They're still set on staying in Mexico, so they start arranging for a new house sitter and dogs on-site, which will be helpful in deterring intruders. Word spreads quickly in the community, and we're told there have been several recent break-ins. I admire their resilience, even as I worry for their safety. People say it's rarely violent, just cash and electronics. They join a neighborhood watch, meet more locals, and hope it won't happen again. I dearly hope so, too.

On my drive back home, I'm thinking, *Well, sister, what now?* I feel totally deflated. The idea of even attempting to write a book seems totally absurd now. I'm listening to *Super Attractor* by Gabby Bernstein on Audible as I drive, and I happen to be right at the part where she's speaking about being able to ask your higher self and angelic guides for a sign. She explains that asking for a sign means you're willing to collaborate with the Universe. She mentions that she asked to see a very specific symbol— blue butterflies. I shrug, glancing up to look myself in the eyes in the rearview mirror. I've never done this, or even thought to do it, but I'm feeling so lost. It feels like the path to writing a book is being blocked, so maybe that's not what the voice intended after all.

I pause, take a few deep breaths, and open up my heart. Then I silently ask my higher guides with all of my heart: *If I am meant to write this book, please show me a sign in the form of... hmm, my dad loved birds so much... a hummingbird.* I can feel the humble ask resonate deeply in my chest, a subtle pulse of warmth around my heart. I surrender to the question and send it out to the Universe to decide. I have to admit, I feel better. The pressure is off, and I'll just trust to be guided. Because, at this moment, I have absolutely zero clue what steps to take next.

I head back south towards home but make a stop at my friend Beth's house to pick her up for a friend's birthday party dinner we had planned for that evening. I stroll into her place, and she's just finishing up writing a note on a birthday card.

"Oh shoot, you managed to find a paper card? Was I supposed to bring one?" Birthday cards are a bit of a rare gem in Mexico.

"No worries, sis," we call each other sis since people have repeatedly asked if we are sisters, as we look similar. "You can just sign this one and put the sticker on the back." She hands me the card and then a small sticker. I stare down at it.

Tears come to my eyes. It's a round sticker of a golden hummingbird. "Oh my God!" I cover my mouth, and she catches the tears welling in my eyes.

"What's wrong, sis??"

I tell her the story. She smiles, "He is with you. He loves you. Keep the sticker. Write the story."

But there's something else. I can think of nothing else all night at dinner, clutching the sticker and looking down at it. I leave a little early and drive quickly home. The moment I get inside, I toss on the lights, run to my room, and open up my jewelry box. I dig for it at the bottom. And there it is, a little white strip of paper made to hold two stickers, but only one sticker is on the strip, the other long gone. The sticker that remains is the exact same golden hummingbird sticker that my friend just handed to me.

He loved cards and he *loved* stickers, and he put them on the back of every single card he ever gave me, which numbered in the hundreds by the time he passed. This was the last sticker my dad gave me, and I had been saving it. It had simply been missing its pair. He loved the Papyrus signature golden hummingbird sticker. It had been a favorite he used over the years on the cards he gave me. It has been stashed at the very bottom of my jewelry box since he passed.

Stay with it, daughter, you can do it. I'm with you. He whispers to my heart as I stare down at it, the sticker my friend just gave me perfectly completing the blank space on the half-filled strip he'd given me. The tears and joy and love in my heart burst all at once. I can hardly believe it. I'm so ridiculously grateful for this quick and clear sign.

I wake the next day, but I feel paralyzed to begin getting my thoughts down. Writing a book wasn't even remotely on my radar. I don't know how to begin. I have a lot of beliefs in my mind about what it means to be a writer, how one goes about it. My dad was a writer of young adult adventure books on the side of his full-time job. He always dreamed of becoming a big-name author. He did get his first book published, *Island of the Innocent*, and that delighted him beyond all measure. I believe he gave away more books than he sold—handing out flyers to waitresses in restaurants was his favorite marketing tactic, which made my mother want to shrivel up and hide. He went on to self-publish two other books: *Scathe* and *Eternal River*. In all his books, he spoke of spirituality, of time as a man-made construct, of our true nature as infinite beings—and how dreams, too, are a form of reality. He believed that even this moment, right now, is a beautiful dream.

I get it now, Dad. Thank you so very much for loving me so dearly and transcending time and space to personally show me.

I want to make him proud. I want to make myself proud. So I build a towering wall of expectations around that pressure—and in doing so, I freeze. The writing goes quiet for a while.

Over a gorgeous seaside birthday dinner with Danny the following month, with a surreal burnt-orange harvest moon rising out of the sea at sunset, palm trees swaying in harmony with the breeze, I decide my year of psychedelics isn't complete without one more nice big dose of mushrooms. I need to thaw out and reset again after the home invasion. Danny supports me in going, so I return to the little town north of Cabo San Lucas where the home invasion happened and stay at another friend's home, nestled in another part of town, surrounded by a stunning palm grove that feels secure on the second story, with lots of locks for protection.

I sit one quiet afternoon on my friend's sofa, settling in with my journal, a cup of tea, calming meditation music, and a few fresh fruit snacks. Then, with a deep breath of gratitude, I gulp down three potent grams of my little teachers—gifted to me by my dear friend Nikki, who assures me this batch is especially powerful. I love the way they challenge me in their own unique way—gently nudging open the doors of self-inquiry, revealing the truths and deep learnings I need to see beyond the narrow lens of my thinking mind.

I smile... and wait.

I decide to stroll outside and sit in front of a gigantic agave plant and cactus garden to get the medicine moving. The grounds are lush with desert plants and vegetation. As I stare at the landscape around me, I notice the ground of hexagonal patio tiles begin to shift beneath me. I'm no longer sitting on the tiles but conscious of them shifting dimensionally. One tile pops up, the one next to it pushes down, then another, and another, like a ghost playing patio tile piano. The cactus garden moves and sways, and the entire landscape becomes illuminated with a rainbow iridescent glow.

Then everything somehow shifts, and I'm able to see the garden in front of me, but past it, through a shimmering invisible curtain, like a veil, I see another... I don't know what to call it—dimension, I suppose. There are people walking around, but their skin is purplish-blue-gray, they are taller, more muscular, and all their features elongated. Human, but not human. There are creatures eating the vegetation—not quite dinosaurs, not quite hippopotamuses—something in between but also large and muscular, with spikes around their necks and a vibrant sage green. I try to hold my gaze to not lose them, but I can only see them for a few seconds before they fade away. It feels like a glimpse into eternal time. Into all the people, places, things, and timelines happening everywhere and all at once. I get the feeling they are living, right now, with me, somewhere else on a different physical plane, on their own journey.

Behind that curtain feels like a glimpse of pure creation—divine, expansive, fleeting. I head back up to the house and sit on the balcony floor, mesmerized by the sacred geometry of a succulent. Nature's design feels intentional, intelligent. I study the swirls of my fingerprints, like stone layers etched into the Grand Canyon—proof that these bodies were crafted with the same loving care. At my feet, an ant colony moves in perfect unison, lifting a beetle far larger than any one of them. No words, no confusion—just purpose. I slip into their world, awed by the silent harmony. Above me, towering palms look on like amused guardians, each one holding a face, a knowing. The whole universe feels alive—almost amused—watching me.

One towering palm asks silently, yet clearly in my mind, if they could watch me eat the fresh mango I had gathered from the garden.

I stare up and smile broadly, I can't help but laugh, "Huh? You want to watch me eat the mango? What sort of strange fetish is this?" I say aloud, looking up at the giant, wise palm trees swaying in the light Baja breeze.

In silent communication, they reply, *You have no idea the delicacies you are able to enjoy there—the smells, tastes, touches, sounds, and sights. We would kill to taste that mango.*

I think about it. I stare at the ripe mango, its soft skin with reds, oranges, yellows, and greens flowing together like a precious watercolor painting. "You don't say?" I flash a big grin, willing to play along. I slice into it and take a massive bite, sugary mango juice dripping down my chin. *Oh my God, this is the best thing I've ever tasted.* It does taste incredibly good. They look down, *See! Yes, enjoy, dear one. Enjoy it.*

This fruit gluttony goes on for quite some time, the same music looping, and I begin to feel like I've been on this porch, living this way in this little desert nest in the sky for a hundred years.

I look to the heavens and see faces in the clouds—intelligent beings. They are stretching their necks down to see what is happening here as well. I'm like, *Who are you?!* They stare back, and it becomes apparent that Earth is quite the show. Beings from all sorts of times and dimensions are watching us, intrigued to see how this whole game is going to play out. Like the intergalactic Super Bowl. *Wow... I had no idea.* They confirm with their silent yet knowing gazes.

Then, I find myself at an intergalactic podium of sorts. I'm standing at the podium, and there's an oval stadium of seating sinking below me, like the Colosseum, spiraling down and down and down, forever. It's filled with spectators—beings, souls.

A deep, resonant voice from within—silent, but somehow loud as hell—says, *We have something to share with you. Three things, precisely.*

I say aloud, "Um, okay... wait. Oh no. Am I Scrooge? Are you the Ghost of Past, Present, or Yet to Come?"

The voice does not appreciate my humor and insists this time: *Get a pen.*

Uhhhh, right, right, a pen. I look around and spot my journal and pen just in front of me on the kitchen table. Slowly, I grab them and find a fresh, clean page, clicking the pen to life.

The voice asks, *Are you ready?*

"Yep, I'm ready!" I enthusiastically say aloud.

The voice says simply, *One. Chill out.*

"Huh?"

The voice clearly states again, very calmly but firmly, *You and everyone else down there need to CHILL out.*

Oh. Yeah. I would agree, I think to myself, nodding in silent agreement. I physically write it down in my journal: *1. Chill out.*

The voice says: *Two. Music is medicine.*

Ohhhhhhh. As the magnitude of that hits me, I understand the gravity of these words I am being gifted with. I speak it aloud, and ever so slowly, I write it out: *2. Music is m-e-d-i-c-i-n-e.* I finish writing, looking eagerly out into the stands below me, pen poised in my hand, waiting to hear the wise voice from the void above the Colosseum for the final insight.

The voice says after a long pause: *Three. Be Uniquely You.*

I stare out, not writing yet. They elaborate, with humor: *Be yourself, share the unique gifts that only you can offer, but don't be an asshole about it.*

I laugh aloud. *3. Be Uniquely You, but don't be an asshole.*

IT'S GONNA GET MESSY

Got it! I look down at the page, smiling broadly at the wonderfully simple yet incredibly impactful message.

And then the massive Colosseum below me begins to fade. I say aloud, *Thank you!* out into the vanishing void. I stare down at my paper. *Wow.* That about sums it up. I love my little Intergalactic School of Life session.

I decide to finally look at a clock: *five* hours. I'm shocked. I actually start to panic just a tiny bit, as this much Divine time for my little meat suit mind is a lot to handle, to endure. My Earth mind isn't meant to know what eternal time feels like; it operates in seconds, minutes, hours, days, months, and years. These little constructs we've come up with to make time relevant. But by my meat suit estimations, I've been living in this house approximately 900 years. It truly feels I've been on this porch too many lifetimes to count. I am ready to return to human time. I send Danny a text, *I am certain he is dead and gone and there's no one left on the other side of my phone's keyboard that will know me.*

I wait a few minutes. It feels like forever. And then I see the three rolling dots... *My God, he's still there!* I type quickly: *You're still there?!!!*

Danny: *Hey, you ok?*

Me: *I love you.*

Me: *I'm sorry I'm such a pain in the ass sometimes.*

Me: *I can't talk right now, but I'm thinking of you. I've been at this house for 900 years. I'm still here. You're still here. This shit is hard, but I love doing it with you. And so many beings are watching, and they say, keep going, you're all doing amazing things. I love you.*

Danny: *Love you too, boo.*

Me: *Me too, a lot.*

Danny: *That's the most wonderful news to hear!*

Me: *I can't even begin to explain how long I've been here, lol.*

Me: *Okay. I love you, gotta go back to cosmic class for a bit.*

Danny: *Haha, ok ok, go! Keep me updated.*

I stop texting and return to my eternity house. I see an absolutely gorgeous, absolutely gigantic moth stuck in a little pool of water on the concrete floor of the porch, its wings saturated, crumbling on the edges. *Oh no, oh no, oh no, oh no, oh no.* It is suffering, my heart is breaking. I try to help it with my fingers, but that is hurting the edge of its ever-so-delicate wings, making them crumble a little more. *Oh noooo!*

I search for some flat sticks that I can slide under its wings to pull it out of the water. I find some that work and slowly slide them under it, little by little, with painstaking tiny movements, until I shuffle and slide it out of the water's entrapment and onto the dry concrete a few inches away. It can't fly; its wings are too heavy. I make sure it's in a spot where the sun will hit it first thing, and I pray it will be okay. I think the dry Baja desert breeze will help it on its journey, and the wings should dry by the morning.

I message Danny: *You still there?*

Nothing.

I message again not even a minute later: *You still there?*

Danny: *Yep babe, still here.*

Me: *Okay, phew. Thank you. I'm grateful you're there. I'm sorry when I overreact or critique you. It's because I'm scared to fully open up to love. The critique is often a reflection of how harshly I speak to myself. I'm protecting my heart. It's not about you. It's about what I'm still healing in me.*

Danny: *That's ok. That's a really big thing to realize.*

Me: *Love you lots.*

I go on and on for a bit, back and forth with texts filled with a lot of 'love yous' and 'are you there?' and 'thanks for being my anchor, you won't believe how long I've been gone.' I talk about how I'm ready for the experience to end, that the duration has been challenging. I ask if he can come up later that evening, as I'm feeling a bit isolated. Then I text: *Actually, never mind. I should rest. I love you, don't worry, I'm good, see you at home tomorrow.*

I lay down on the sofa inside and simply wait to finally reintegrate. The duration of this journey has definitely been a challenge for my mind. It has shown me the simple delicacies of life, the fragility of life, the complexity of time, space, and reality as we know it. And it has shown me just how simple it is to find purpose and joy in this incredible dream. As twilight turns to dark, I choose my old reliable compass for my thoughts in these moments: *Compassion.* For others, and for myself. Sure, I'm imperfect—we all are. There is magic in the deep, heartfelt curiosity we all carry for the meaning of this precious life—the shared quiet longing to learn, to love, to evolve, to grow.

I give myself permission to embrace the whole messy entirety of my journey—road bumps and all. I am giving it my all to let go of my unhealthy thoughts, patterns, and behaviors. I'm trying, sure, maybe with a step forward and a few steps back, but overall, progress is happening. I stare out into the night sky through the large picture window above the sofa, the vast array of twinkling stars applauding all our efforts here on Earth. I continue to listen to my tunes, and slowly, eventually, gratefully—I drift off, hoping for a peaceful night's sleep. Turns out, I still have a lot of anxiety after the home invasion, and I spend most of the night restless, jumping at every little sound. I gratefully manage to grab an hour or two of shuteye before the early dawn glow signals a new day.

***

The warm Baja light intensifies and envelopes my little nest, signaling it's time to pack my things and head back home. I look at the space with fresh eyes. The palm trees are now just palm trees. The mango is just a mango, not a golden ticket to ecstasy. We humans can see 100% of the visible light spectrum—which sounds impressive, until you realize that visible light makes up only about 0.0035% of the entire electromagnetic spectrum. That means almost everything that exists is invisible to our eyes.

I look around without my enhanced vision—we're moving through a world that's mostly hidden from us... and yet, we think we see the whole picture. It's wild.

I head out on the patio to see how my moth is doing, and I find it on the ground with the life force no longer pulsing through it. I am so saddened that it didn't make it. Its body remains beautiful, but the soul has clearly moved on. I pick it up and place it in a bird's nest on my friend's mantle as a token of appreciation for allowing me to use her space to rest and heal. The utter beauty and fragility of this life strikes me in my heart—one day you are fluttering about enjoying the breeze, the next moment you just so happen to land in a little puddle you can't escape, even though freedom is only a few inches precious away. And just like that, you're out of this game called Earth School.

We are often fearful of death, assuming it is radically different from life. But, like a beautiful wave, that energy has to return to the ocean. In truth, they were never really separate at all. There is something so wonderfully unique about the way each wave is expressed, yet ultimately, it comes from the ocean and goes back to the ocean in one fluid, rapid, and graceful expression. This lovely moth, all of Earth's creatures, us too—everything. We are not so different from the waves, my friend. I vow to appreciate the little things more, to savor them, for each little smell, taste, touch, sound, and sight is truly a beautiful gift.

On the way home, I feel called to reach out to John's grandmother, who raised him, to see how she is doing. She messages me: *Each day without him is so hard, but I am glad he is at rest. He had a very strong personality, and I feel his presence, especially when I see things or do things we had done together in the past. I find pennies on my coffee maker, less frequently as time passes, but there is no physical explanation for how they appear.*

I beam with joy. That would be John. Very much alive, very much still a jokester, and very much onto his next adventure. We all aren't so far behind him. We have to forget who we truly are to feel the sun on our face, the warm cookie on our tongue, the cool ocean wrapping around our toes, the bloom of fresh flowers—and yes, even the gut-wrenching ache of loss. It's all part of the deal. The gift of being human is that we get to feel *everything*. Wouldn't you choose that, too, if you were a being of infinite time? To feel time itself. To taste the illusion of scarcity—just to savor your creation a little longer.

So here we are, my friend.

We have to entertain ourselves somehow. And let's be honest... after a while, even Netflix doesn't cut it.

Driving south, I think about Danny and how, after nearly a year together, we both sense—we're likely not a long-term match. But deeper than romantic love is understanding, and for the first time, I feel truly seen. This relationship has healed so much in me. I've learned that words shape reality, carry energy, and should be used oh so carefully. I still expect too much financially from a partner, but really, I just want a co-creator—not to be the one steering alone.

Yet in clinging to that expectation, I rob myself of the quiet strength it takes to give without needing anything in return. I wasn't capable of that yet—few are. The less we own our flaws, the more we project them onto others. I could see where we clashed, but I ignored it, choosing the comfort of love over the discomfort of truth. Once again, I'd chosen someone who values comfort over growth.

But this time, I see it sooner.

I'm learning that there's love in holding on, and there's love in letting go. I'm just not quite ready to let go. So I weigh logic against my heart, shuffling through pros and cons, trying to quiet my intuition. Life, I'm realizing, is both a masterpiece and a work in progress—growth and acceptance happening in concert. We can't predict the journey, who stays, who leaves, or what shapes us. But every moment adds to the beauty of becoming.

Psychedelics have been life-changing. I'd do them all again. And when I need a shift, I know they'll call me back. But they're not the destination, just a window to what I already know. Now I wonder—can I reach those states through meditation and breathwork?

And so, as it goes when you lean in with curiosity, excitement, and trust—I already know my next path on my journey is perfectly unfolding for me exactly as it should.

Unfortunately, after my epic mushroom journey, I am still stuck in the quicksand of not writing for two months, refusing to crack my fingers free and type. It occurs to me that the idea of a silent meditation retreat has been popping up here and there in conversations for well over a year. I recognize something is calling me to seek more silence. I hop on my laptop, do a quick search, and I open up six different website tabs on retreat centers I'd like to possibly go to. I quickly get a little overwhelmed by where to choose to go, as I'm shocked to see there are actually quite a few options around the world. I pause, breathe, and go within, silently asking again for a sign to guide me. I look at the first website in my lineup of open tabs. I read a few sentences on the first retreat center, but it doesn't hold my interest.

On the next tab, I scroll down, and on the third scroll, I see one of the teachers, and right there, on the instructor's neck, a large colorful tattoo of a hummingbird. Eager to end my self-inflicted suffering, I keep reaching for the healthiest, happiest, most healed and confident version of myself. I know it's time to stop forcing, stop gripping so tightly to control—and instead trust that everything is unfolding exactly as it should, in its own perfect timing. I need to remember I'm part of a greater symphony, a larger energy. My only job is to allow it to move through me. To stop fighting the damn current. Enough looking outward. It's time to pause, be still, and go deeply within. I want to go all in on myself, my goals, my dreams, my passions, my healing, and cultivating my own damn inner peace. I chose to chase *me*. To know myself beyond aspirations, attachments, achievements, or anyone's approval. I am plunging deeper into the great adventure of becoming.

Danny and I talk about the constant tension. We both know things aren't flowing anymore. I tell him I need space and time alone to focus on myself—and he supports that fully. We know it's over. We just can't say it out loud yet.

So, I surrender and follow the trail of my hummingbird guide to Chiapas.

Chapter Twenty-Eight

A stranger Thanksgiving.

As the plane descends, I catch my reflection in the window and smile—just three years ago, I dreaded solo time, and now I chase it. I'd assumed the airport near Tuxtla Gutiérrez would feel more international, but it's tiny, tucked between mountains, with five taxis and a single shop. After politely declining a wildly overpriced quote from a sweet old driver, I pile into a shared van with locals, tourists, and a scruffy dog for the winding ride up to San Cristóbal de las Casas. The driver piles all our luggage and gear on the roof and secures everything with a spider web of frayed ropes that look like they have seen better days, then we're off for the hour and a half ride.

The van rocks with the curves, and the Mexican beats on the radio, I slide back and forth into my fellow passengers as the air cools through the glass. We climb higher, the views unfolding—stunning valleys below, misty cliffs ahead, and storm clouds raining with directed purpose like a helicopter dumping over a forest fire. We arrive as the sky dims, and an older Brit named George chatters away about the city's culture, 7,100-foot elevation, and Mayan roots, deemed one of Mexico's *Pueblos Mágicos*. Whether his facts are accurate or not, he's endearing.

As we roll into the bus stop on the south side of town, I watch women in traditional wool skirts and bright blouses walk the cobbled streets, kids in tow, flip-flopped feet peeking from layers of warmth. Graffiti art colors weathered walls, blending past and present. I hop out and give my body a nice stretch, and the driver a thank you. I walk to my hotel, a cozy space filled with terracotta tile, antique wood, and thick walls holding the mountain chill. Such a welcomed change in climate from the hot, sunny, and dry Baja California Sur. I settle in my room and take a short, needed siesta before heading out to explore the city and grab dinner.

That night, bundled in scarf and gloves, I wander. The streets hum with music, soup steam curls into the air, and I find a bowl of local *Sopa de Chipilín*, rich and earthy. Then, hot cacao—thick, warm, transcendent—fills my hands and heart. I stroll through amber-lit shops, grateful for this quiet pause before my silent retreat begins. The future can wait. I'm doing my best to simply be here, to savor this sacred, present moment.

***

I wake to the smell of bacon and coffee drifting through the crack beneath my old wooden hotel door. My nose is cold, my body heavy from a restless night in a new place. I burrow under the comforter, grateful for a day with no agenda, and drift back off to sleep.

By noon, I finally roll out of bed, toss on a sweater and jeans, and wander into the sleepy streets of San Cristóbal in search of sunlight, coffee, and something warm to eat. Colorful flags flutter above the cobblestones, and the air hums with a slow, easy rhythm. I've found the city to be wonderfully walkable. My hotel sits just on the south side of town at the edge of the primary downtown area with all the quaint shops and delicious eats, but from there, it is only thirty minutes from one end to the other—that's walking at quite the leisurely pace.

I stumble upon a stunning breakfast café—lush with plants, light spilling in from skylights, the smell of herbs and espresso dancing in the air. I settle into a corner table, sip smooth Chiapas coffee from a handmade mug, and savor chilaquiles piled with salsa, eggs, crema, and cheese. I pause to realize how comfortable I've become in my own company—how different it feels now to sit alone without shame or distraction. Once, the words "just one?" from a host would shrink me. Now, solitude is something I seek. Nearly three years into life in Mexico, I've shed the frantic pace of the States—the race, the rush, the pressure to prove. Here, brunch stretches long, the check never arrives unless you ask. Here, I'm learning to define success in moments of stillness, to see the power in pause. I thank myself—for choosing differently, for listening, for letting go of the old playbook that never fit. I thank the Universe for nudging me toward a life that feeds my soul, not my ego. *Gracias. Gracias. Gracias.*

This is how my first days getting acquainted in San Cristóbal de las Casas are spent—in delectable, grateful gluttony. Thanksgiving Day arrives, and it's time to meet the pre-arranged group taxi outside of a little convenience store on the edge of town. We're heading deeper into the mountains for the silent meditation retreat. I can see about five or six people waiting outside, and I'm eager to meet the strangers I'll be spending my first-ever solo Thanksgiving meal with. I find a motley crew of travelers that look to be in their mid-late twenties and maybe early thirties. I admit, I think about my age for a split second—but then I remind my aptly named ego, Pia (short for *Pain In the Ass*), to kindly behave herself. With that, I stroll over eagerly to say hello and introduce myself to my retreat mates.

On the ground, leaning up against the storefront glass and surrounded by their large backpacker bags, we have Alyssa from Canada, Michele from Belgium, Betty from France, and Philip from the States. Standing next to me as I walk up and plop my bag down is the very tall, lanky Nick from England.

Alyssa stands and walks over. She's adorable—mid-20s, pale smooth skin, long brown hair, just under six feet tall, sweet and soft-spoken with her gentle Quebec French accent. She immediately asks, "How old are you?"

I smile, laugh. "I'm forty-two."

She exclaims, "Wow, you definitely don't look 42! This is excellent news." She snuggles in next to me, leaning her head until it touches mine. "You can be my retreat mom while I'm away from home!"

I chuckle. "Look, I can happily be your good retreat friend, but most definitely not your retreat mother."

She tilts her head playfully to the left, then to the right, smiles, gives me another hug, and says, "Yes! That will do quite nicely. Even better." She bounces back to her spot on the ground and stretches in the sun.

Michele is classic backpacker chill. She stays seated on the ground in her flowy bohemian pants, lavender floral tank top, and extremely worn leather hiking boots. Her brown hair is happily disheveled in a bun on top of her head. She smiles warmly, with a hint of trepidation. "Where are you from?"

I smile. "Well, I've lived in quite a few states in the US, but I'm originally from Wisconsin—and I live in Mexico currently."

She nods as if knowingly, then asks, "Where is Wisconsin?"

I laugh. "Just a bit north of Chicago, Illinois."

She grins, nodding broadly. I like her immediately.

Betty from France is standing nearby, munching on *cacahuates*—peanuts—and asks mid-chew, "Have you done a retreat like this before?"

She's so tiny next to my five-foot-nine frame, I'd guess just shy of five feet tall. Dark brown hair, Disney character-worthy doe eyes, and remarkably large, voluptuous lips, hips, and a booty to match—truly curve-a-licious, top to bottom. I immediately nickname her *Betty Boop* in my head, with affection.

I say, "I haven't, have you?"

She shakes her head, smiling coyly. "I'm equally excited and nervous to give it a go."

Nick is towering over us both. He looks like a European basketball star, maybe 6'5", and he's already chattering excitedly with Michele. In his soothing British accent, he peers down at me and proclaims,

"Well, this is going to be quite the bloody adventure, isn't it!"

I love his boyish grin and childlike excitement—it's charming coming from such a large human. We all laugh, swept up in that pure anticipation, the kind of nervous buzz and giddy thrill that only comes from embarking on something truly unknown with a group of strangers.

I mean, truly—I saw the hummingbird sign and did *zero* research on what I was getting into. I'm simply trusting.

Philip is still on the ground, lounging in light jeans and a long black wool sweater, wearing a shit-eating grin layered with a kind of chill I've only encountered a few rare times in life. His long, dark, curly hair is tied in a loose bun at the back of his head. He looks like the spitting image of Jon Snow from *Game of Thrones*, and I can't help but wonder if he gets mistaken for him constantly—but I keep that thought to myself.

He finally breaks his silence and says, in an accent I can't quite place, "Should be a damn fine time."

I tilt my head. "Where are you from in the States?"

"Pennsylvania," he replies with a slow, easy smile and a relaxed drawl.

"Huh, you sound... Southern?"

He chuckles, the slow, intentional laugh of someone much older than his years. "Well. People from the middle of the state like myself really do have an almost Southern accent. Definitely different from West Virginia or what you'd think of as an 'Appalachian accent.' Any Pennsylvanian can tell you there's a huge difference between the state's two most well-known accents: Philly's hoagiemouth and Pittsburgh's 'n'at'-laden talk. Most probably can't tell you the difference between the other three, which technically makes Pennsylvania the most linguistically complex state in the country, thanks to our five distinct dialects."

Smart *and* easy on the eyes. I love his calm energy, his groundedness, the way wisdom settles around him like a well-worn coat. Hard to believe he's only 26.

"Well, ya don't say," I reply, mustering my best southern accent and shaking my head, impressed. I'd had no idea—I'd only ever spent a long weekend in Pennsylvania and definitely hadn't picked up on the subtle drawl during that brief stay.

Just then, two tiny taxis roll up, the drivers confirming we're the group for the retreat center. Upon hearing yes, they both enthusiastically shout, "¡Vámonos!" *Let's go.*

We split into two groups. I call shotgun and hop into the front seat of one car, with Philip and Michele sliding into the back. We take off heading east, out of town and up toward the mountains, the energy in the car a buzz of anticipation and curiosity.

Our driver is particularly chatty, which gives me the perfect chance to practice my Spanish. He asks where I'm from originally.

"America," I say.

"Ah, *gringa!*" he replies with a big grin.

I smile, roll my eyes, and say, "Sure." He can tell I don't love the term.

In broken English, he says, "No is bad—*is funnnn-knee!*"

Gringo, in general, is usually harmless and meant to refer to a "foreigner," most often white Americans. Sometimes it refers to anyone who doesn't speak Spanish or seems disconnected from Latin culture—even people of Hispanic descent. But yeah, while not always the case, it *can* carry a bite. If you're white and treat Cinco de Mayo (not even a real holiday in Mexico, by the way) as an excuse to slam tequila shots at your local, questionably-authentic Tex-Mex spot while wearing a sombrero—well, you might just get called a *gringo*.

Shit... I'm pretty sure I have a photo from six years ago doing *exactly* that. *Sigh.*

The driver glances over. "You know de history?" he asks.

I smile and reply coyly, "Ilumíname." *Do enlighten me.*

His face lights up, animated with excitement. "Well, you sees... the story that it goeses, is dat the *gringo* meaning comes at us from the war. The wars between the Mexicans and de Americans. Hm, dees wars, they was being during 1846 to 1848, when the intruders—the U.S. men, you sees—wore big green coats! They wore dees when they march, march, march through our Mexican territory. We see this, and we Mexicans, we say so loud, we say, 'Green, go home!'"

He pauses for emphasis, his hands mimicking marching soldiers, eyes wide.

"Dees words, like a pancake, together for the locals, and the word *gringo* is borns!"

"See!" I say, pointing playfully. "It's usually meant to describe a pushy white person who's *not* wanted here."

He lets out a deep, warm belly laugh. "*Va, sí, a veces, más o menos.*" Okay, yes, sometimes, more or less. He shrugs and grins. "But for me I say *dis* with the many loves."

We climb higher into the mountains, the road still winding but mercifully smoother now. After about fifteen minutes, we pull off onto a small dirt road and begin descending into a lush valley. We arrive at what appears to be our destination, a modest driveway leading up to a handful of simple wooden buildings with red metal roofs and a single Mexican flag waving gently in the breeze beside the gate.

We pile out of the taxi, stretching and shaking off the ride. Our cheerful driver helps us unload, then with a booming "*¡Nos vemos!*" See you later. With a laugh, he hops back in his car, already down the dusty road in search of his next fare.

I hoist my backpack onto my shoulders and follow the others through a small wooden gate and diamond-patterned mesh fence, trailing like a line of ants, all of us drawn forward in unison—eager, curious, slightly nervous, each carrying some hope of revelation.

A motley crew of seekers, on the edge of silence.

The sun casts a golden sheen over the distant mountains, but one focused beam cuts through the clouds like a divine spotlight, drawing my gaze to the largest structure on the sprawling land before us. To the left, about a hundred feet away, sits what appears to be the main guesthouse—brick and wood, perched right on the valley's edge.

The property slopes gently downward, disappearing into the lush valley below. The entire retreat center is tucked into the forest, nestled so seamlessly that it feels as though the trees themselves built it. Towering pine trees rise all around it like ancient sentinels, their trunks thick with time, their giant limbs spreading out into the sky above protecting us overhead.

On the long wooden porch of the main house, facing the mountains, sits a young Black man in a simple folding chair, arms crossed over his chest, face tilted upward toward the sun. He's still as stone, bathing in the sunlight, with a soft smile playing across his full, cheerful cheeks. As he hears our group approaching, he lifts his head and slowly opens his eyes, a sparkle forming behind his lashes. A broad, white-toothed grin spreads across his face.

"Finally!" he calls out, voice smooth and warm. "I thought I was gonna be partaking in this meditation rodeo alone!"

He introduces himself as Marquis, a Southern California native, and tells us this is his first meditation retreat. I peg him in his mid-twenties—solid as a tank, built like a former college running back. His muscular frame is wrapped in a few extra pounds, and I find myself wondering how those thick legs are going to manage a classic meditation posture.

We all climb the few steps onto the wide porch behind him, exchanging smiles, soft laughter, and the gentle awkwardness of strangers becoming something more.

"Well hola, I'm Becca. So nice to meet you," I say, offering a hand. "I live in Baja California Sur—just south of the border from you. Been there the last three years. Before that, I bounced around the western U.S.—Portland, Seattle, Denver—but I'm originally from Wisconsin."

He sizes me up with warm, curious eyes—deep brown and thoughtful. "I dig," he nods. "I got here *way* too early—had my times swapped from PM to AM. Thought for a second this was gonna be a solo mission."

"Well, ironically, Cali Cowboy," I smirk, "if the itinerary's right, it really *will* be a journey of one." I wink at him.

He laughs, a deep belly chuckle that shakes the porch slightly. "True story."

Just past him, standing a few feet down the fifty-foot-long porch, is another man. He has about a week's worth of facial scruff, disheveled brown hair curling loosely around his ears, and an expression so somber it cuts through the sun like fog. He turns slowly and our eyes meet. I offer a smile, a simple nod of hello.

He blinks... then turns away without acknowledging me.

Marquis leans in a little and says quietly, "Oh. That's João from Portugal. Interesting vibe. I'm getting the feeling he's either on the spectrum, self-righteous, or going through a *very* difficult time in his life. My gut says breakup. Maybe long-term mom issues. Could be social anxiety. Or—who knows—maybe he's just an axe murderer. Hard to say. We only exchanged names and origins before he basically sprinted away from me."

"Anything else, Freud?" I laugh, shuffling my feet and glancing down.

I'm trying to stay open, to judge others less, but man—it's hard not to make snap assumptions when meeting a group of strangers. There's something hardwired in us, a pack animal instinct. In the first seconds of encountering someone new, we scan—Who's a leader? Who's a threat? Who's annoying? Who might become a friend? Who definitely won't?

"I'm sure he's just easing into silence a little early," I offer, trying to be generous.

Marquis smiles in return, and I pat him on the shoulder as I wander further down the porch where most of the group is now congregating, chatting, and dropping their bags.

Just then, a thick dirt cloud billows outside the gate. It flows in slow motion through the diamond mesh fence, announcing the arrival of our final comrade.

Out of the haze appears Mario, shuffling in with his roller bag, wearing a thin puffy winter jacket, bright red glasses, and the gentlest dark brown eyes I've ever seen.

"Hola amigos, buenas tardes," he greets us with a soft smile. "I'm Mario. I come from a northern border town in México. I am pleased to meet all of you."

Warmth radiates off him like a cozy fireplace you just want to curl up next to. His English is excellent—clear, deliberate, textbook-perfect, with that slightly melodic cadence that comes with careful second-language precision. He sets down his luggage and slides seamlessly into the small circle forming on the porch.

Everyone is buzzing, full of pre-silence energy, asking all the same questions:

"Have you done anything like this before?"

"Are you nervous?"

"What do you think will be the most challenging part?"

"Do you think you can eat vegan and give up caffeine for 10 days without going *totally* ape shit?"

The air crackles with that first-day-of-school feeling—curiosity, nerves, giddy anticipation. You can almost smell the unknown wafting through the air teasing your senses.

"Eeek! We only have a few more hours until silence!" Michele exclaims just as our teachers step—no, *float*—through the small screened wooden door of the main cabin and onto the porch.

"La, la, la, la, la, la, laaaaaaah!" she belts dramatically, laughing, squeezing out her last vocal reps while she still can.

There are two retreat hosts. Sonia flows out first to greet us, wearing a long, simple cream linen dress. Her strawberry blonde hair is tied in a bun at the nape of her neck, with two strands dancing freely, framing her porcelain face. She looks like she walked straight off the top of a wedding cake for bohemian travelers. Her movements are slow and purposeful, and she weaves between us all with a calm demeanor and a subtle, knowing smile.

Her presence is so soothing. She places a hand on my shoulder, looks me dead in the eyes, and pauses for a long moment. I don't look away. I feel seen and comforted.

"Welcome," she smiles, warm as a summer sunrise.

"Thank you." Our eyes and energy lock, revealing so much. So much in common, so many wrong turns, so many messy lessons learned. A shared knowing—the past is in the rearview mirror, we're chasing joy in the lives we're living now.

She shifts her gaze, moving on to greet the other guests, radiating calm confidence and motherly care. I'm guessing she's maybe thirty. Once, I would've judged her—too young to lead a retreat like this. But Mexico taught me better. Age is just a number. I've found friends from nineteen to eighty-seven. Younger friends bring vitality, older friends bring wisdom. Stick to your own age group, and you miss the full depth of life—the unexpected mirrors that help you see your journey more clearly.

Behind her glides out her co-facilitator, Cole. He also appears to be in his early or mid-thirties, with sandy blond hair tied in a long ponytail that meanders halfway down his back. He walks slowly, wearing simple cream linen pants and a black, oversized pullover linen shirt that doesn't seem concerned with showcasing the form beneath it. With each step, he moves with deep presence and intentional purpose.

The edges of his mouth curl upward into a warm, subtle smile that radiates peace and tranquility—with perhaps just a smidge too much effort. Or maybe that's just what extreme presence looks like when there's no rush to get anywhere. Either way, I'm not sure, but I dig his vibe and his willingness to walk his own way.

He turns his head, and I spot the gorgeous, colorful hummingbird tattoo on his neck—the one that guided me here. Just from his energy, I get the sense he's been through some shit, and this is a reset phase in life for him too.

He moves past everyone slowly, making eye contact but never speaking, then cautiously climbs the wooden spiral staircase at the end of the porch, slipping silently out of sight above us.

Sonia meets with us individually to collect our final deposits and get us fully checked in. She's lovely and kind, greeting me with a warm hug. She asks if I'd like the only private cabin, just a short path down from the primary meditation center. One final guest is still expected, she tells me, but she won't arrive until early tomorrow morning—after the retreat has already begun and we'll be in silence.

I hesitate. Being away from the bunkhouses of the main retreat center means I'll be even more alone—no background buzz of human movement to anchor me. It makes me nervous. *Lean in, Becca, damnit. You're here.*

"Sure," I say. "That sounds good."

She smiles and simply says, "Lovely."

All fourteen of us—five men, four women, two guides, two cooks, and an admin—shuffle one by one into the main building's lower level and settle ourselves into the rustic, cozy Mexican kitchen.

As I enter through the front door, I spot a typical old-school top freezer refrigerator straight ahead, about twenty feet in, against the back wall. To the left, a medium-sized kitchen opens up, with counters covered in colorful Mexican tiles and cute cream floral café curtains hugging two large square windows. The windows overlook the valley and let in generous light over the U-shaped kitchen countertop.

The entire space is wrapped in textured red brick walls and warmed by terracotta tiled floors. Just behind the open swing of the front door, to the immediate left, are two bar stools tucked against a bar-height counter that looks out over the porch and the woodsy valley beyond.

Beside the little bar dining space, a bookshelf rests against the left-hand wall, offering a thoughtful mix: Rumi, Tolle, Watts, McKenna, Buddha, the Bible—a soft-spoken menagerie of spiritual voices.

A small medicine cabinet holds the basics: Tylenol, bug spray, anti-diarrheal meds, band-aids, and throat lozenges. At the end of the wooden serving counter, a well-worn red kettle sits beside a handwritten sign: *Fresh mint tea brewing*—complete with a little heart and a smiley face drawn in green marker.

To the right of the entrance, a black wood-burning stove waits, already stuffed with crumpled newspaper and kindling.

Next to it, the main dining area spans about ten by twenty feet, centered around a navy blue cushioned daybed that doubles as dinner seating—and, in my near future, the perfect nap spot. In front of it, three small wooden café tables with folding chairs invite company.

A door in the upper right corner leads to the shared bathrooms, two small dorms (each with two beds), and two twin rooms with private terraces. The men's bunkhouse holds two hostel-style bunks, sleeping four, with a tiny ensuite bathroom.

I walk back out to the kitchen and snag a spot on the comfy daybed, grabbing a blanket to toss over my legs and tuck my toes under. It's about 50 degrees outside, and my desert-dwelling ass can no longer handle these temps without a jacket or light sweater. What in the world happened to the toboggan-riding girl from Wisconsin? She's become a sun-loving, sea-soaking devotee of warm summer breezes, that's bloody what.

We gather around, filing into every last available seat as our hosts welcome us and invite us to grab our Thanksgiving meals—already dished out and waiting for us on the service table that separates the small dining area from the kitchen space behind it. Tonight, we've got a lovely lentil soup brimming with vegetables and spices, paired with a small side of diced tomatoes and cucumbers in a light vinegar and pepper bath. The entire retreat will offer healthy vegan meals to keep our minds and bodies clear and comfortable while sitting for long periods.

This will be the first Thanksgiving since my adolescence that I won't be partaking in the usual American turkey and typical smörgåsbord of gluttonous accompaniments.

At seventeen, I switched from being vegetarian to eating poultry and fish at the advice of my high school swim coach, who nudged me to include some animal protein to boost my performance, and my chances of making it to the state tournament senior year. Until then, I'd been raised entirely vegetarian. My dad had grown up on a farm and saw one too many animals slaughtered, which he said forever changed him. He became a vegetarian the year I was born. Being a daddy's girl, I followed suit and firmly declared no meat for me, either.

A memory pops in—me and Dad going wild asparagus hunting. He'd drive us all around the countryside to our marked favorite grassy banks, with me sitting shotgun and my big stuffed ape Unga Bunga on my lap. I'd shout, "I spy asparagus!" Then I'd hop out of the car, grab my little knife, climb up the bank and cut it, proudly bringing it back. We'd pile the stalks on the dashboard in the sun until we had enough for four steaming bowls of asparagus soup for dinner.

As I look around at the new faces surrounding me, it dawns on me—this is the very first Thanksgiving in my entire life where I don't know a single soul at my dinner table. And yet, it somehow feels lightyears from any taste of loneliness. Oddly enough, for a holiday meal with total strangers, there's a feeling of closeness, openness, connectedness, and authenticity I've rarely experienced at Thanksgiving back in the States.

We all seem to share the same thread—each of us feeling like we're at a pivotal moment in life, realizing that in order to grow and evolve, we need to dive deeper within to better understand ourselves and this wonky human experience.

In honor of the American guests, Sonia tells us her mother—an adorable, short Russian woman with cropped blonde pixie hair and a kitchen presence that radiates like a guardian dove—has made a vegan apple pie just for us.

We wrap up dessert, and it's time for our guides to review the guidelines and schedule for the next ten days. I hadn't felt inclined to read the website in detail, so this will be the first time I'm hearing what exactly I've signed up for—and honestly, I love the unexpected. I feel like a kid in a candy store waiting to see what treat gets pulled out from behind the counter.

Sonia tells us the daily schedule will be nice and full. It begins at 7 a.m. with two hours of group meditation, followed by breakfast. Then comes lecture, another meditation, and Hatha yoga, then lunch. We get a two-hour rest period in the late afternoon, then another two-hour meditation session, dinner, followed by an evening Q&A. Questions will be written down on paper, and we'll close the day with one last meditation at 10 p.m.

Sneaky approach—tire us out into silence.

We're informed that everyone will have a task: either sweeping the meditation hall or ringing the sound bowl ten minutes before each session, to signal that it's time to meander to the next session. I quickly sign up for the mellow 7:20 p.m. sound bowl shift instead of a morning one. I'm most certainly a night owl, and I'd likely bring chaos to any attempt at a structured morning routine.

The rules of engagement for this silent meditation retreat, which begins at first light tomorrow, are as follows: no talking, no eye contact, no physical contact, no phones, no email, no computers, no electronics, no music, no reading, no caffeine, and no alcohol. We may journal about our experience during the rest period, but only about *our experience*—no creative writing, as that pulls us into the past or future and out of the present moment.

I knew it would be silent, but the no eye contact part catches me off guard. I'm so ridiculously expressive with my face—I figured if we couldn't chat, I could at least smile, wink, or roll my eyes to engage. Crap. There goes that.

The no alcohol part doesn't faze me. Sure, I've had my moments of excess while partying, but I've always been able to go without, or have just one and stop if I wanted. *No caffeine*, though—no morning coffee? That might be a real challenge.

Sonia explains in her soft Russian accent, "You see, the retreat was specifically created to guide people in coming to an intimate understanding of what Self-Enquiry meditation is, in order to experience the inner transformation it brings. We go to this level of isolation so the experience feels completely immersive. Our program aims to create the sensation of a solitary retreat, as if we're in a cave all on our own, with no external influence shaping our inner journey. It's about journeying far within to kindle an intense aspiration for the

Divine, and arriving at the highly focused interiorization that enables the Opening of the Heart."

We all glance at one another with bulging eyes, tight-lipped smiles, and that specific kind of excitement that has a thin layer of apprehension sitting right on top. They cover a few light principles of the Hridaya practice, but everyone is quickly fading after the satisfying dinner settles in and the long day of travel starts to catch up.

We close with a short five-minute group meditation to center ourselves. Everyone's wiped. We exchange our final words, nervous and excited glances, knowing full well we'll all feel very different on the other side of this retreat. Until then, it's just the hush of our own experience unfolding. We meet each other's eyes, offer warm smiles and hugs, and slowly drift off toward our beds for the night.

I stroll out onto the long wooden porch, my wool shawl wrapped tight around my shoulders, I'm so grateful I brought it. The night winds are strong and cold. I reach the end of the porch, where a small board creaks underfoot, and I look up at a sky almost equally filled with textured starlight and infinite black. I audibly gasp—it's simply stunning. It reminds me how small and precious I am in this human meat suit, having this gorgeous yet oftentimes gritty experience here on Earth.

Sonia's dad, who's been quietly watching from the corners and shadows, comes up behind me and gently places a hand on my elbow.

"¿Puedo mostrarte cómo funciona el calentador de la cabina?" *Can I show you how the cabin heater works?*

He's the humble helper in the kitchen and the groundskeeper of the retreat center. Short white hair, not tall, not short—he's skinny, with an incredibly kind face and a centered energy that makes you feel like nothing could ever knock him down.

I nod and smile, grateful, and follow him.

We walk down the stairs following the winding stepping stone path and arrive at my little red brick cabin, barely fourteen feet by fourteen feet. He brushes aside the magnetic bug netting on the door, pushes it open with a creak, and flicks on the light inside.

Immediately to the left is a small private bathroom with a single vanity, a toilet, and a shower just big enough for one. To the right is a small room anchored by a forest green and cream oriental rug, about four by six feet, centered in front of a large picture window that looks out over lush pines and the forest valley beyond. In the far right corner sits a jet-black gas heater designed to look like an old wood-burning stove. Next to it, a tiny wooden folding chair and table serve as a desk.

Along the back wall are two small twin beds, with just enough room between them for a little wooden crate functioning as a bookshelf. That's it. That's all there is to it.

He walks over to the heater and shows me how to open the large propane tank: turn the knob to the left, then press two sets of buttons on top repeatedly and quickly until the heater catches. He does it three or four times before the front grill lights up, and a toasty wave of warmth washes over my legs.

The smell of gas fills the room, and he immediately opens the large picture windows right next to the heater. He looks at me with kind, gentle eyes and explains, with a tender smile, that I must open the windows each time I use the heater and let the gas escape for about five minutes—otherwise, I'll make myself sick from the fumes.

I smile and nod, "Muchísimas gracias por tu ayuda." *Thank you so much for your help.*

"Buena noche," he says—*good night.* A caring smile, a slight bow of his head, and then he leaves me alone with my tiny cabin and my thoughts.

I begin unpacking my few bathroom toiletries and glance up at the vanity, expecting to catch a glimpse of my exhausted face—only to find there's no mirror. Just a small white piece of paper with black printed letters that reads: **Who Am I?**

Dang. Smacking me right out of the gate with the mother of all questions.

Who am I? Who *am* I? Who am *I*?

My name pops to mind, but that feels about as meaningful as answering "Earth" when someone asks what makes the planet beautiful. It's just a label, hardly a reflection of the wild, intricate ecosystem beneath. I decide to park that question in the garage of my mind for now. I'm too tired for philosophical spirals.

I mosey over to the bed to check out the linens when I spot it—a massive centipede, at least six inches long, clinging to the wall just above my pillow. I freeze. *Speaking of exquisite nature.* There are few things I find more revolting than centipedes. The probability of me sleeping peacefully with that thing hovering a foot above my face is zero.

I don't think it would be very zen of me to kill it, so I start looking for something to usher it out. I grab my notebook and, balancing awkwardly on one leg, lean across the bed—praying this thing doesn't have the ability to leap.

That's when Sonia walks past my open windows, still airing out the last wisps of propane. She tilts her head, her angelic porcelain face framed by strands of blond hair, silently asking: *What in the world are you doing?*

I point dramatically at the centipede, my eyes wide. Apparently, I'm already practicing silence, though that doesn't officially start until tomorrow.

Her eyes follow my point, and when she sees it, hers go wide too. "Oh, Becca... if these bite you, I'm afraid it's very, very painful. I don't know how it got in here, we check before your arrival, but I think we need to do a little more spray and get this one out. I don't think you should sleep in here tonight."

"Well, that's a bummer," I say, already half-settled in. "I don't love the smell of chemical sprays, though, so... you're probably right. Where should I go for the night?"

"Don't worry. We use something holistic for the spray, but it'll still be too strong to sleep with tonight. There's a small room off the main meditation hall with a bed, you can stay there."

I repack my toiletries, toss everything back into my carry-on, and we step out into the crisp, star-strewn night. We wind our way back up the narrow flagstone path that curls uphill toward the meditation building. As we climb the tight metal spiral staircase with wooden risers, I start to feel the retreat energy building, quietly electric.

At the top, a wide wooden deck wraps around three sides of the meditation hall. We walk along the left side and through a wooden screen door, and I finally see the space that will become my home for the next ten days.

The hall is expansive, about 1,000 square feet, with wooden floors and huge floor-to-ceiling windows. By daylight, I imagine they'll reveal a panoramic view of the valley and forest below. On the right wall, there are framed photos of meditation teachers from various traditions. In the center of the glass wall overlooking the trees stands a small brick platform with a humble altar—a simple board resting on hefty wooden blocks, draped in a vibrant Mexican tapestry, with scattered pillows for meditation.

On the far left wall hangs a striking emerald and white tie-dye tapestry, depicting a many-armed elephant goddess holding a lotus flower with the sort of serene confidence that feels ancient and rooted. I don't know who she is yet, but I'm sure I will soon.

Right now, though, my eyelids are losing the battle to stay open.

Sonia leads me to a small door set into the center of the red brick wall at the back of the meditation hall. She opens the door and I step into a snug room, just wide enough for two wooden bunk beds set across from one another, and little room to spare. She points to the bottom bunk on the right.

"Sleep well," she says, offering a hug and a warm smile. "We'll see you bright and early tomorrow."

I drop my bag on the floor and glance at my phone, just past midnight. I check my texts and emails, send a group message to let my people know I'll be off the grid for ten days, then power everything down. I tuck my phone and laptop deep into my bag—out of reach, out of mind—so I won't be tempted to peek.

Deep breath in.

I scan the room and under the bedding for any additional creepy crawlies, then sprawl onto the bottom bunk. My head barely hits the pillow before I fall into a dreamless, exhausted sleep.

Chapter Twenty-Nine

Zip it, skippy.

Day 1

"The Self itself is God." ~ Ramana Maharshi

I awaken refreshed to three slow, methodical strikes of a metal sound bowl—more gong than bowl—the long, reverberating chimes dancing their way under my cozy cabin door. The retreat has begun. Silence has begun.

I spring out of my comfy little twin bed and gather my bag. There's a note slipped under my door: **Your cabin has been fumigated and is now safe to return to.** I open the door and gasp. Sunlight pours through the towering pine trees, bathing the meditation hall in sparkling golden light. The whole room feels alive—like it sees me, knows me, and is already holding me in its gently, knowing embrace.

The morning is chilly, though, so I zip up my fleece and wrap my wool scarf around my shoulders.

Two small propane heaters hum in the corners of the hall, trying to get things toasty before our 7 a.m. meditation. I know the first gong sounds at 6:30, so I have a bit of time and head to my cabin to drop off my bag. Birds are chirping, the sun is shining brightly, and a gentle breeze rustles through the pines, creating a soft, soothing whooshing sound.

Along the path, I run into Mario—the gong ringer—and immediately forget one of the rules. I look him in the eye and smile warmly to say good morning. He meets my eyes, then quickly looks away. *No eye contact. No smiles.* Dang, this is going to be a challenge.

I make it back to my little cabin, nestled alone at the edge of the forest, and find another note on the door: **Your roommate isn't going to make it. The place is yours.**

I guess I'm really going it alone.

I drop my things and head up to the kitchen. A handwritten sign reads: **Fresh mint tea from the garden is brewing. Help yourself.** I grab a mug from the menagerie of colorful, mismatched cups and fill it to the rim, lifting it to my nose and inhaling deeply. *Delicious.*

Several others are now up and moving quietly around the kitchen, but I keep my eyes focused on my mug and don't look up.

Holding my toasty warm tea I wander back up the creaking spiral staircase and head toward the door on the left side of the mediation room—this is where the women enter. The men use the door on the right. For the duration of the retreat, we'll enter and sit on opposite sides of the hall, maintaining separation between masculine and feminine energies.

I walk inside and see four yoga mats piled with pillows and blankets on the women's side, two in front, two in back. Each mat is outfitted with a pair of rectangular foam meditation blocks, a thin cream-colored circular cushion adorned with beautiful hand-stitched flowers and geometric designs, and a small rectangular blue pillow.

I take the mat in the back left, closer to the center of the room near one of the two pillars that visually separate the two sides, and begin unfolding the blankets, testing the firmness of each pillow.

As everyone finishes trickling in, we sit quietly, facing forward towards the immense pine forest and valley below. Our teachers will rotate each day. For the first morning, Sonia ascends the spiral staircase, dressed in simple white linen, and silently slips through the left-hand door. She enters the hall barefoot and moves gracefully toward the altar. After some gentle adjustments to the pillows, she settles into a cross-legged position, her back straight, a serene smile unfolding across her face as she gazes softly toward the back of the room.

We aren't to make eye contact with the teachers while on the grounds, but during lectures, it's allowed.

"Good morning," she begins. She may speak—we may not. *Note to self: do not automatically say 'Good morning' back.*

"I hope you all slept soundly," she continues. "I want to begin our first day together with an in-depth explanation of the principles of our Hridaya practices, including Hatha Yoga and meditations for the revelation of the Spiritual Heart. As the retreat progresses, we will share techniques for cultivating awareness in daily life."

"This is a spiritual path whose purpose is the revelation of our True Self—*Atman*, or the Spiritual Heart. Developed by Sahajananda, Hridaya is rooted in traditional spiritual principles and visions from classical yoga, particularly Patanjali's *Yoga Sutras*, *Advaita Vedanta*, *Tantra Yoga*, and *Kashmir Shaivism*. The teachings present ancient spiritual truths in a clear and accessible way. They invite you to discover the divine essence of your being—not to deny the outer world, but to celebrate it, as an expression of the Divine.

"You learn how to see the divine in everything. You reveal your own nature of awareness and spaciousness. This brings freedom and peace, love and acceptance. To live in the Heart, in the Supreme Reality, in God—God experienced directly, beyond any common conceptual or religious definitions."

I glance around our spacious meditation hall, and my eyes settle on the center of the right wall lined with photos of great spiritual teachers. I smile at the beautiful variety I see. I don't recognize all of them, but a small handwritten sign beneath lists their names: Nisargadatta Maharaj, Thich Nhat Hanh, Mother Teresa, Paramahansa Yogananda, Buddha, the 14th Dalai Lama, Jesus, Papaji, Swami Vivekananda, Mooji, Adyashanti, Lurjett, Jean Klein, Jiddu Krishnamurti, Eckhart Tolle.

It's quite the crew.

Something about this mix, this reverence for many paths, feels deeply right in my heart.

Religion was used by the power-hungry to divide us—to pull us away from Oneness, to diminish our collective consciousness for the benefit of the terrible few at the top, those consumed by ego and an insatiable hunger for control. All they want is to blind us from the Truth so they can separate us. Somehow, we forgot that at the center of all these beliefs are the same inherent messages of Love.

Throughout history the founders and followers of religious movements, while ignoring the most precious creation—human life—have repeatedly massacred each other over labels.

Religion itself was born from pure, loving intentions. It emerged at a time when our ancestors needed to foster cooperation and tolerance among relative strangers, in a world with little law or formal governance. You don't have to follow Christianity, Islam, Hinduism, Buddhism, or Judaism to be considered religious. All you need is appreciation—for this existence, for the mystery of something greater in the cosmos, something beyond labels and beyond our earthly comprehension. That something would be incomplete without you. *You*, and only you, were created with profound purpose. You are irreplaceable. You were needed to make this existence whole.

Isn't that wonderfully reassuring? In our darkest moments, when we wonder whether we are needed, I hope you remember—you truly are. I truly am. We all are.

The thing is, all religions point to the same core teachings. When we look within, we find, at the heart of us all, a spark of Universal Love—what created this entire beautiful journey. Sadly, most of humanity has forgotten this. But there is hope. We are awakening to the Truth—myself included, and countless others.

Buddha, Muhammad, Moses, Krishna, Jesus—when they speak of God, I humbly understand them to be pointing toward the same sacred Source—what some might call Spirit, Love, or the Universe. They're all saying the same thing. Yet we create wars over semantics—over *brands*. Buddha was not a Buddhist. Jesus was not a Christian. Muhammad was not a Muslim. Egos claimed those titles in their names, using them to gain power.

They were all teachers who taught love. *Love* was their religion. We are all One. And we are all Love. The end.

I bring myself back to the present moment just as Sonia continues explaining the teachings in depth.

"The Spiritual Heart, *Hridaya*, is our essence," she says, "the truest part of who we are. It's not just a spark of divinity—it *is* divinity. It's the awareness behind all our thoughts, feelings, and experiences."

She explains how we can begin to feel this connection through meditation, by gently focusing on the vibration in the chest. "This subtle tremor," she says, "is the Heart's way of calling us back to Truth, to the infinite."

She describes the journey as beginning with the Heart as a focal point, then deepening into a living connection, and eventually realizing it as the very source of our awareness.

Her words flow effortlessly, but it's a lot to take in. The Heart, she says, is more than just emotion; it is a gateway to unity, to Oneness. By training the Heart to love, to witness, and to surrender, we can transcend the boundaries of individuality and uncover the infinite Self.

She weaves in the teachings of Ramana Maharshi, who taught *Hridaya Self-Enquiry*—a practice centered on the ultimate question: "Who am I?" She calls it a simple yet revolutionary path, one that asks us to turn our attention inward and observe the source of our thoughts.

This, she explains, is the heart of the meditation we'll be doing here: the Spiritual Heart as the ultimate reality, the home of pure existence.

It's a lot to process—and yet, as she speaks, I feel a warmth radiating from my chest, a quiet knowing. Old Corporate Bex would've dismissed this as woo-woo nonsense, shaking her head and thinking, *Good luck functioning in the real world.* I would never, in a million years, have imagined myself sitting here, soaking in all this consciousness talk—if it weren't for my father showing it to me firsthand.

But now? Now I've experienced the hum of energy coursing through my body. The warmth in my chest isn't just a feeling—it's a visceral knowing that the words coming from her mouth are true.

She finishes by sharing, "Hridaya Meditation is more than a technique—it's a path to uncovering your deepest essence, often called the Spiritual Heart, or atman. At its core, it invites us to connect with our true nature through three simple practices:

1. Bringing awareness to the Heart Center in the chest.

2. Noticing the pauses after each inhale and exhale.

3. Asking the timeless question, "Who am I?"

But these practices are just the beginning. A Zen metaphor describes it beautifully: they're like "fingers pointing to the moon." The techniques themselves aren't the destination—they simply guide us toward the vastness of Supreme Consciousness. For example, focusing on the Heart Center might deepen your concentration or heighten emotional awareness, but when seen as a gateway, it opens into something limitless—what some traditions call the divine dwelling within us. Similarly, awareness of the breath, pauses, and self-inquiry can move us beyond individuality into the infinite freedom of our Real Being.

Hridaya Meditation goes beyond tools or techniques; it becomes a celebration of joy and inner peace. By connecting with your Spiritual Heart through breath and presence, you can experience a profound transformation—one that lets you carry happiness and stillness into any moment, regardless of life's circumstances. This retreat offers a space to explore these practices, drawn from yoga, Buddhism, and Sufism, even if you're completely new to meditation. It's an invitation to step into silence and discover the peace that's already within you."

Sonia looks out across the room and smiles warmly. "Bueno." *Good.* She closes her eyes and stretches her long arms slowly over her head, rolling her neck gently from left to right. Tilting her head back, then returning to eye level, she opens her eyes again.

"Okay, that's enough on the practice foundations. Let us actually practice."

We all straighten our slouching backs, eager to dive into our hearts.

"Meditation," she says, "is getting naked with your mind. The first thing is to relax the body. Tension and attention relax into themselves. Don't look for anything. Seek nothing. All is enough as it is.

Rest in presence. Ego must settle down and accept. Ego wants to avoid being—it's not its nature."

After practicing daily twenty- to thirty-minute meditation sessions over the past year, I know that asking the mind and ego to settle is like asking the ticking second hand on an analog clock to pause. Still, I've been fortunate enough to experience a few deep, blissful moments of silent presence.

"We must settle our minds," she says again. "Again and again. Again and again."

I've found through my short meditation sessions that the monkey mind loves to just mindlessly blah blah blah—and meditation brings it back to center. It's the repetition of witnessing the thoughts that eventually creates a pause between thought and awareness, and it's in that pause that Truth can slide in and help us find space: from emotional reactivity, from excessive thinking, from needless stewing, and offer the ability to feel before responding.

Our first hour-long meditation session is mostly spent just trying to figure out my posture. Admittedly, I've always cheated at home, meditating with my back against a wall. But now, in the center of the meditation hall, relying on my own core strength and a few pillows, I'm finding it decidedly trickier.

I shift from kneeling, to cross-legged, to using one pillow, two pillows, three pillows, a folded blanket under one leg, then under both. I shuffle around, searching for optimal support. Simply trying to get comfortable enough to sit completely motionless with an upright back is its own practice.

It's surprisingly tricky to find the sweet spot where my lower back can soften, but my core stays engaged just enough to keep my spine tall for that ideal energy flow they always talk about. I'm tempted to use the wall at the back of the hall or one of the wooden folding chairs lining the sides of the room waiting patiently as an option for relief if needed, but leaning on them so early in the retreat feels like cheating.

And I'm definitely not going to be the one to fold on day one.

Oh, ego.

All is going fairly well, and I'm working on getting into the flow of meditating with a larger group. There are quite a few more noises compared to meditating alone—a sneeze, a shuffle, a yawn, loud breathing. Directly to my left, on the other side of the male-female invisible mid-room divider, sits English Nick, whom I've aptly nicknamed Darth Vader. He has a slow, deep inhale and a very loud exhale, like a drawn-out *Haaaaaaaaaaaaaah*, which I'm finding rather distracting.

I open one eye and peek over at him. He must have a deviated septum.

Haaaaaaaaaaaaaaah.

I close my eye and tilt my head back to my own realm, returning to my meditation practice, taking a long, deep inhale and focusing on the pause at the top of the breath, just as we were instructed.

Haaaaaaaaaaaaah, from my neighbor.

Let it go, Becca. Let it go.

We break after our first morning of meditation and return to our mats to begin our first Hatha yoga class. Cole enters the hall walking very slowly and purposefully, taking his place on an outstretched yoga mat at the front. We've gone a little long on the meditation, so he lets us know that we'll get more into the principles of yoga tomorrow. For this morning, we're simply to follow him in some slow postures and deep breathing.

We move through several rounds of deep inhales and exhales, focusing on the pauses right after each inhale and exhale—the quiet, knowing nothingness there, the vastness of the pulse of our own hearts vibrating into the stillness. We hold a few mountain poses, downward dogs, warriors, and tree poses. We move through a few sun salutations incredibly slowly, holding each pose and bend at length.

It feels wonderful to move my body after sitting all morning. We end with gratitude and silent *namaste*. I almost slip and say it out loud. I feel exhilarated, my pulse rushing—but I also begin to feel a pain in my temple. I'm not one to get headaches often, so I brush it off as an effect of my excessive focus on clearing thoughts and all the forward folds.

We break for lunch, everyone shuffling about the hall with heads bowed to avoid eye contact, easing into the flow and routine of solitary confinement in a group setting.

After a tasty vegan lunch of vegetable soup and mixed berry salad, I soak in the sun on the outdoor porch. I notice that the subtle pain has grown into a massive headache. I head to my cabin during the break and lie down, attempting to nap, but I just can't get comfortable. By the time the early afternoon session rolls around, my head is pounding. I take two Advils, then head up to our next meditation session, determined to push through. *This is day one, damnit. I'm not going to miss a moment!*

But the pounding intensifies. I can't think beyond the pain—each pulse feels like it's swelling my head. This is not my idea of discovering my Spiritual Heart.

Tears form in my eyes. I break posture and reach for a pen and a small piece of paper on a nearby table at the back of the room, scribbling a note to the teacher. I get up from my meditation cushion, barely able to walk across the room. Cole looks surprised to see me approaching. I hand him the note: **Terrible headache. I must go lie down.**

He looks up with sympathetic eyes and writes back: **If you need anything, let us know.**

I barely make it out of the meditation hall before the tears start to flow. I'm nearly 24 hours into silence, and the sound of my crying actually startles me. I don't know where to go or what to do.

The Christian Science upbringing rears its head again, I'm really not feeling well, so a lot of anxiousness begins to fill my head as well. It creeps in fast—fear around how badly my head hurts, fear because I'm not prone to headaches.

How do I get help up here, in remote Mexico? Is something drastically wrong?

I head to my cabin to lie down. *No good.* I barely make it a minute—I can't take the pressure. I sit up, but my stress is building. *No good.* I pace, then walk outside to wander a bit, but the utter loneliness and silence are chasing me. *No good.* I cry some more, but the crying causes such tension I have to stop that too.

No one is around. No one in sight. It's totally silent, except for a breeze rolling through the valley, rustling the pine needles.

I try again—back into my cabin, back into bed. I repeat this cycle for an hour or two, getting frazzled and weary.

As night falls, I step outside for a moment and see the glow of cozy light spilling out from behind the square, gridded kitchen windowpanes below the meditation hall. The session has ended, and everyone is walking in to eat dinner. My head is still spinning, and my appetite is nonexistent. I retreat back into my cabin, open the window, and light the propane heater, sitting in the small wooden folding chair in front of it.

Suddenly, my mouth begins to water—quick and unstoppable. I rush to the tiny sink and vomit. Repeatedly. Two, three, four, five times. I quickly fill the small vanity sink. I stumble to the toilet. Six, seven, eight deep, involuntary belly tremors pull out everything my stomach holds.

The pressure from vomiting intensifies the pain in my head—it's now excruciating.

Fear floods every second, every thought.

Am I going to have to get choppered out of here?
What is wrong with me?
Is this an aneurysm?
What is happening?! Please stop. Please stop. Please stooooooop.

Everything in my stomach is now in the sink and the toilet. I am sobbing.

I run out of my cabin to the one next door, where Sonia and her mom and dad live. I knock on the door. Her father answers quickly with a warm smile. His face falls the moment he sees the tears streaming down mine. He calls for Sonia.

She appears from an open-air loft above the living room, peeking down the stairs from her bed. She sees me cowering in the doorway. She grabs a shawl and comes down immediately.

As soon as she's within a foot of me, we lock eyes. I whisper desperately, "Help me."

She takes my arm gently and begins guiding me back to my cabin.

"We are in silence," she says softly.

Holy hell—childhood memories of the ear infection and being silenced from voicing my pain come flooding back in an instant. I stop. I look her straight in the eye and say again, more forcefully, through tears, "Help me!"

She breathes in deeply. "When did this begin?"

I explain—during yoga, during the forward bends. It built slowly until this.

"Perhaps this is altitude sickness?" she offers.

I can barely speak. Slowly, through gritted teeth, I respond: "I was in town two days to acclimate. It was only a short elevation gain up to here at the center. We're at 7,700 feet. I lived in Denver at 5,280 feet for half a decade. I've been to Lhasa, Tibet, and the northern mountains of Chile—both at 13,000 feet. I've never had an issue with altitude before. I don't know what is going on... but I really need it to stop."

I'm bent over, grimacing.

She looks at me, head tilted slightly, with a puzzled expression that lingers for quite a while. At last, she says she'll return shortly and slips out the door.

I can barely keep my eyes open—the overhead ceiling light is unbearable.

The rest of the evening becomes a blur of people and movement, figures bustling in and out of my cabin. Sonia, her mother, and her father enter and exit quickly and repeatedly. The sweet Danish admin, Myrtha, comes in and sits gently on the bed beside me.

They turn off the main lights and bring in a string of soft white Christmas lights so as not to worsen the pain in my head.

An oxygen detector is slipped over my finger. A pill or two is presented—I take them without question. Tea arrives, but I can't sit up to drink it.

A blood pressure cuff tightens around my arm. "A little high due to elevation," Sonia says to her mom. A thermometer is popped into my mouth. I hear someone say, "Normal."

Everyone is buzzing around me. I'm terrified. The pain is so intense I'm genuinely afraid something inside my head might rupture.

Sweet Myrtha remains at my side, holding my hand. Suddenly, a memory surfaces—a pressure point that helps with headaches.

I speak slowly, deliberately, each word a labor:
"Myrtha... will you press here... hard... between my thumb and pointy finger."

I point to the spot.

She quickly places her own thumb and forefinger there and presses.

"Harder."

She presses with all her might. And after a bit, maybe ten minutes, I feel a slight lessening in the pressure. Time loses meaning. Ten minutes or an hour—it doesn't matter. She continues, swapping hands when one tires, pressing as hard as she can.

Eventually, the pounding in my head begins to ease. The panic subsides.

Thank God.

An hour or two passes. I ask for a little food, and someone brings a small scoop of oatmeal. I eat it gingerly, and it seems to settle in my stomach.

Real relief washes over me. I look up at everyone and smile. They all return it with big, warm smiles of their own.

The propane heater burns brightly in the corner. The holiday lights twinkle. I am struck by the compassion and love surrounding me. Deep gratitude rises within.

Slowly, everyone says goodnight and leaves. Only Myrtha remains.

I thank her, tears in my eyes, for staying by my side. I explain, quietly, that my childhood upbringing in Christian Science still causes some deep fear of illness. She listens intently, nodding comfortingly, as if to say: *It's okay. It's okay to feel this way.*

She asks if I can manage on my own now. I nod and smile gratefully. "Yes. Thank you so much."

She heads out into the night to return to her own modest bed.

I wish I had received that kind of comfort growing up. Instead, there was no open communication. I carried the heavy burden of feeling like any illness made me a poor student, someone disconnected from God.

Myrtha, though in her early twenties, has the calm, knowing warmth of a grandmother who's spent countless hours nurturing others.

I glance at my little red analog travel clock, glowing in the light of the propane heater. It's 8 p.m.

It feels like I've been fighting this headache for days. I'm exhausted. I don't recall the much-needed rest or the welcome darkness falling.

Chapter Thirty

Moments of delight.

Day 2

> *"I wish I could show you, when you are lonely or in the darkness, the astonishing light of your own being."* - Hafiz

Next thing I know, I awaken to the wonderful, warm dawn light spilling through the large front window of my little cabin. The holiday lights and heater are off, and there's a definite nip in the air. Birds are chirping just outside, welcoming in a new day. I hear the gentle three rolling gong tones of the 6:30 a.m. wake-up, and I'm feeling right as rain.

Because of my little space heater, I've noticed that moisture tends to gather in the cabin. So far, the weather here seems to hover around 75 degrees Fahrenheit during the day, typically with light showers rolling in by early afternoon. Then slowly, the wind and mountain air usher the temperature down to 40–45 degrees at night.

I shuffle within my nest of blankets and feel the outside of my cocoon is damp from the moisture. A pretty harsh chill has taken over the room, but I'll take it. There's no headache this morning. My heart pulses comfortingly, filling me—and the space around me—with warmth and gratitude despite the chill and the cold tip of my nose.

I pop out of bed uncharacteristically quickly for my night-owl self to start the propane heater, warming myself up a bit before walking to the main meditation house to begin the day. I click the starter button a few times until the heater finally roars to life.

I open the windows wide to let the fumes out for a few moments, and a lovely whiff of pine needles floats into the cabin, carrying a sprinkle of light dew and wildflower notes.

The teachings from the first day are resonating, and I feel like I'm in the right place. I've noticed my ego whispering expectations for something profound to happen here, and I know it'll be a process of releasing that thought again and again throughout the retreat.

I'm already so grateful for the assistance from the hosts last night that helped me heal quickly from my headache. For the simple yet insanely delicious and nourishing food that awaits me three times a day. For my cozy cabin. For the thunderstorms followed by warm, gentle sprinkles I haven't experienced in over a year since living in Baja.

Being surrounded by silence and free of distractions is such a gift.

I turn off the heater, push my way through the black magnetic bug net covering my door, and stroll up the little stone path to the main hall for breakfast. Everyone is gathering their bowls and finding their seats, oblivious to the hellish night I had or to my absence altogether. I smile to myself, head bowed, and grab my little breakfast bowl set out on the kitchen counter. It's filled with warm oatmeal, topped with dried cranberries and spiced gently with ginger and cinnamon. On the side is a plate of ridiculously fresh papaya and lychee.

I sit on the porch and eat very slowly, deliberately, truly tasting and enjoying each bite.

A flashback hits me: those corporate days when I barely had time to eat lunch, squeezing in a quick bathroom break between back-to-back meetings before shoving a protein bar in my face on the way to the next one. I'd eat so fast my stomach would ache for the first ten minutes of the meeting.

With a bit of time and space, you really start to see how backwards it all was—that grueling, drunken dog-and-pony show we called "corporate efficiency." Constant spinning, moving so fast that no one could communicate effectively or even think for a damn second. Just action, action, action.

It is no way to live.

I lean back, letting the morning sun warm my face and savor my slightly dry oatmeal. I sprinkle a few pieces of fresh fruit into the bowl.

Across from me, English Nick is sitting at the small café table. I catch him watching me, and as our eyes briefly meet, he smiles with a kind of quiet approval. He looks down at his own oatmeal, then reaches for the fruit and sprinkles some into his bowl too.

The gesture delights me—a subtle moment of helping someone make their breakfast just a little tastier.

See, I tell myself. *With pause comes space for ingenuity and innovation.* Ah, the little things.

We all finish breakfast, and the familiar trifecta of gong rings signals us to begin moseying up the spiral stairs.

I'm the last to enter the meditation hall. Cole is already seated at the front on the altar, legs crossed, eyes closed in present silence.

Everyone has settled into their usual places on the floor. I shuffle in quietly, head bowed, and take my own seat.

Cole taps the small sound bowl on the altar once, crisply, to begin our morning lecture session.

"The principles behind our spiritual practice help us navigate the path with clarity and purpose," Cole begins. "As Nagarjuna said, *'One cannot realize the ultimate reality without relying on conceptual knowledge.'*

"Here are the key principles that ground our understanding: There is one Supreme Reality—the source of all existence. Whether you call it God, Universe, Spirit, Source or the Divine, it is ultimately the same. This Reality is Consciousness—not just mental activity, but the very essence of life, energy, and creation itself. It is the light behind all thought, the root of all movement, and the foundation of existence.

"This Supreme Reality exists as the core of our being, often called *atman* or the Spiritual Heart. Through practices like yoga and self-inquiry, we create the conditions to realize this essence. Indian sages recognized that *Brahman* (the Supreme Reality) and *atman* (our essence) are one and the same. Within us, there is a Sacred Tremor, or *spanda*—a primordial vibration that connects the transcendent and the manifest. It serves as an inner guide, bridging the personal and the infinite.

"This interconnectedness means that every moment becomes an opportunity for revelation and sacred celebration. Life is a vibrant, cosmic dance of infinite interactions, where each part is deeply connected to the Whole. By living in alignment with the Spiritual Heart, we embrace this truth and allow each experience to reveal the freedom and joy of our essence."

He smiles warmly at all of us.

"So you see," he continues, "as we start to develop an intuitive knowledge of the one universal background of existence, the understanding arises that all aspects of our being are ultimately divine.

"We also become intuitively aware that our Ultimate Nature is not limited to the physical body, or to the subtle mind, soul, or other energy structures. We become aware of the universal background of existence as being the transcendent dimension of our being."

He smiles again, gently chimes the sound bowl once, and closes his eyes to signal that we are to shift into meditation.

I wonder what these concepts sound like to those in the room who haven't yet awakened to non-duality.

Here I am, tucked in my back corner, silently and enthusiastically whispering, *Yesss, preach!*

And I wonder for those who haven't yet touched these realities through transcendental experiences, or mystical life lessons, do these words stir something deep within them when he delivers these truths with such certainty and sincerity?

I wonder—how do they sit with *you*, my friend?

We break and settle into an hour of meditation, but I haven't been able to "go deep". My core and back are working too hard to keep me upright, and it's stealing my focus. Tomorrow, I might lean on the wall or grab one of the chairs if this tension keeps up. I'm frustrated, but hey, it's only been forty-eight hours—*patience, amiga, patience.*

Lunch is a light soup of potatoes, veggies, brown rice, black beans, and carrots, with cucumbers and tomatoes in a light vinaigrette on the side. I'm not sure if it's the lack of distractions while eating or the chill in the air making me so hungry, but everything is simple and yet tastes divinely rich and complex.

At the afternoon break, soft rain showers fall through the pine trees and across the valley in the distance. I grab *The Essential Rumi* off the kitchen bookshelf and settle onto the porch sofa with my book, blanket, and a cup of fresh mint tea. I slowly peruse his poetry, really taking my time to read each line and pause before moving on. I had no idea how witty and playful Rumi's writing is—I'm loving it.

"Why do you stay in prison, when the door is so wide open?"
"If you are irritated by every rub, how will you be polished?"

One verse especially catches my eye:

"There are many ways to the Divine. I have chosen the ways of song, dance, and laughter."

I love it. Music, dance, and laughter truly are medicine. Chase what brings you joy.

My hands flip through pages, stopping randomly:

"The core of the seen and unseen Universe smiles,
but remember, smiles come best from those who weep.
Lightning, then the rain—laughter."

An incredible warmth spreads through my whole being as I soak in his words. Suddenly the rain begins to fall harder, and thunder rumbles through the valley, shaking the sky with mist that dances in the air. I smile giddily and look around to share the synchronicity with... no one. So, I share the delight with myself. My nose is chilly. I sip the warm tea and snuggle further into my blanket. His poetry is the perfect companion to the retreat's teachings, and I look forward to reading more.

I drift off into an afternoon siesta, only to be gently awoken by the gong for our late afternoon meditation session. I'm pleased to find that my back and core are growing stronger. I'm able to sit through most of the session fairly comfortably with only my feet fall utterly and totally asleep toward the end. *Success!* I give myself a little mental pat on the back. *Good job, kiddo.*

Dinner is a big, steamy bowl of sweet potato, onion, carrot, and zucchini soup with rich, earthy spices I can't quite identify. There's also a bonus side dish of small, simple cheese quesadillas lovingly made from homemade grilled flour tortillas—the kind with those delicious little bubbled, toasty, burnt spots all over them.

I sound the gong in the evening to beckon us all upstairs for tonight's Q&A session. I was so incredibly sad to miss the first night's gathering, I'm sure the questions were juicy and plentiful. Oh well, such is life. I'm just glad to be here now.

We begin seated on our mats. This time, Cole walks in and sits at the altar in a more relaxed posture, legs parallel, feet dangling, brushing the floor. Next to him is a small golden metal bowl filled with folded slips of paper holding students' questions, dropped off throughout the day in preparation for the evening session.

He lifts the bowl and tilts it gently, spilling the questions across the altar, sifting through them with his hands. One by one, he opens each folded paper, considering them in silence. The first gets a quiet chuckle. The next, a thoughtful tilt of his head to the right. Another earns a furrowed brow of confusion. The next, another chuckle. Then a slow, subtle nod. He moves through all the questions like this, reading and reflecting, before placing them in an order that feels right to him. And then, we dive into listening.

Tonight, we ask mostly about Cole himself—what brought him to teaching, his experiences in meditation, and how to bring the practice into everyday life. It's funny: in the absence of connection with each other, we're using the Q&A not so much to learn techniques, but to feel closer to our teacher.

He speaks openly about his past: addiction, being a man he wasn't proud of, spending forty-five days meditating in total darkness. He talks about how teaching meditation became the only path that didn't feel hollow or purposeless. I relate deeply to that—the soul-sucking feeling of corporate work, how for me, it was deadening my sense of passion and purpose. As he shares, I find myself truly appreciating his honesty and candor.

I love that both teachers here are just... human. Not to be idolized or worshipped, not above us—just more deeply studied in spiritual teachings, more seasoned in meditation, and eager to share what they know.

We close the session with a beautiful meditation centered on the heart space—the life force of this meat suit that we can draw upon in moments of frustration, anger, or judgment. We breathe deeply into it, feeling the vibration and energy of our hearts. It feels simple, yet powerful. I leave the session feeling lighter, yet more grounded in myself.

The immersion with nature here seems to help with that. I step outside into the chilly night and look up to see a firework display of milky white stars. Absolutely stunning.

I stroll back to my cabin, thoughts swirling. *So... what's my deal? Why have I been feeling funky, disconnected from Source and my inner calm?* I think the home invasion in Todos Santos may have thrown me more out of alignment than I realized.

I've spent the last two years searching, reading, trying to experience something greater than a career, something deeper. But money and societal pressure to re-enter a high-paying job—just to secure the future—still tug at me. That old programming runs deep. It's hard to shake.

These first few days of silence, my mind has been like a broken record, hopping all over the place—thoughts, emotions, stories from the past and present just spewing forth haphazardly. It's unsettling to witness how the mind actually works when there's nowhere else to look. Right now, it feels like my mind is at the helm, a loose cannon firing thoughts around without much rhyme or reason.

I'm trying to detach, to step back from the chaos, to be the observer rather than the participant. But right now, it's like my thoughts are having their first fashion show—and man, they are strutting. I'm not trying to stop them. I'm just trying not to let them trample me. So far, they're winning.

I haven't really thought about the boyfriend while I've been here, which is... worrisome. I feel numb about us. Neutral. I chalk it up to being present in the moment and hope the clarity will come in time.

You'll get there.
But in the meantime, enjoy where you are.

Not so deep down, I know.

Chapter Thirty-One

Savor what matters.

Day 3

> *"You have to keep breaking your heart until it opens."* – RUMI

The morning gong draws me up into the meditation hall to happily discover that I'm starting to get a little more comfortable with sitting longer, thank goodness. Which really just means the numbness isn't bothering me as much, and I have a bit more core and lower back strength slowly building. This morning was a pretty good meditation, and the group seemed to find a nice rhythm to the silence, with few disturbances.

We had a great, down-to-earth conversation—well, I should say *listening*—with Sonia about what it really means to live consciously in a modern, messy world. Sure, sometimes it sounds appealing to just disappear into a cave and have people deliver food while you meditate in solitude forever. But let's be real—that path is available to, what, maybe a couple dozen people out of the 8 billion on the planet? So for the rest of us, it comes down to this: living a heart-centered life. Letting Love be your compass. Doing your best to lift up yourself and others, even in the middle of the chaos.

Simple really, isn't it?

It means catching ourselves when we slip into reactive, programmed ego. Pausing. Stepping back. Seeing the moment for what it really is—just thoughts, just past stories, just future projections. And then choosing Love again. For ourselves and for others.

It is about seeing the joy and beauty in all aspects of life, for the highs and especially for the lows. The peaks and valleys of the meandering journey. To see that pain and loss is a part of the beauty of living this life of the universe learning through a body. Consciousness casually playing dress-up in human form for a while. We are energy, life flows in waves, and a life well-lived has the same rhythm—it ebbs and flows. Yes, pain is painful. See it, acknowledge it, allow it in. Swim in it. Don't push it aside but feel it fully—this is how we pass through the experience more quickly to heal the trauma, instead of burying it or shoving it down.

Life isn't climbing a ladder or a mountain in order to reach a certain point at the top; it is about enjoying the rhythm of each day. We have to embrace the sloppy mess of it all with love and openness. With a joyful heart. With a spirit of exploring. This is the purpose of life: to rejoice in the chance to experience all that is. To eat the damn mango!

Sonia sits cross-legged atop the altar and with three gentle taps of the sound bowl she gathers our attention, her blonde hair pulled into a casual bun, as she begins to share the essence of Hridaya Hatha Yoga. With a warm smile, she explains:

"Hridaya Yoga, developed by Sahajananda, is not just about physical strength or flexibility. Its true purpose is to reveal our True Self—*atman*, or the Spiritual Heart. Rooted in the teachings of Patanjali's *Yoga Sutras*, *Advaita Vedanta*, *Tantra Yoga*, and *Kashmir Shaivism*, this practice prepares the mind and body for the ultimate goal of yoga: the union of the individual self with the Supreme Self, the core of our being."

She pauses, letting the energy of the room settle, before continuing:

"This path is grounded in *Advaita Vedanta*, which teaches the Oneness of all creation. Everything in the Universe is a manifestation of

Supreme Consciousness, which also resides within us as the Spiritual Heart—the source of freedom, spontaneity, and profound bliss. Through Hridaya Yoga, we eliminate the tensions of dualistic thinking and aspire to experience our Ultimate Nature—the Oneness of existence."

Sonia describes how the practice blends meditation and Hatha Yoga to bring awareness of the Spiritual Heart into every moment. "We use specific methods, including a focus on chakras and energetic phenomena, to help students cultivate subtle awareness. Over time, the aim shifts from energizing these structures to transcending attachment to them. This is a journey of surrender, not control—letting go of personal limits and aligning with the Divine Reality."

She emphasizes the spirit of devotion in every pose. "Asanas are performed not with an ego-driven will but with surrender and a deep aspiration to remain connected to the ultimate spiritual Reality. Hridaya Yoga inspires harmony with the Divine, helping us let go of limited consciousness to reveal our inherent beauty and freedom."

Sonia concludes with a gentle reminder: "This practice is not about achieving the Supreme Reality—it already exists within us as our innermost essence. Instead, we purify the body, mind, and soul to express this Reality more fully. By living in the Heart, we experience the eternal dimension of each moment, where God is not a concept but a direct experience. Retreats like this offer a profound opportunity to immerse ourselves in these teachings."

With a serene smile, she stands and moves gracefully to her yoga mat, inviting us to continue the journey. I pause, a quiet smile tugging at my lips, as I realize the word *God* no longer triggers the old ache of guilt or shame from childhood. Now, it feels like something else entirely—like love, like warmth, like grace flowing through me.

We rise to begin the morning practice, beginning simply in mountain pose, hands to heart, breathing in and out deeply in unison for quite some time. We gently move our arms above our heads in a leisurely stretch, softly bending backward. All of this takes a few minutes, and then we slowly make our way into a forward fold—breathing deeply, feeling our bodies in the slow movement and stretches.

The thing I'm finding I love about this practice is that it truly is not your typical gym yoga or what-kind-of-extreme-insta-worthy-poses-can-I-show-off yoga, which in my experience have time and again induced some sort of muscle tweak or injury. This is a very slow, steady, purposeful, achievable yoga. It feels meaningful.

The poses and movements are so slow and intentional, I'm able to feel a deep connection to my breath and body that allows me to intuitively know exactly when to inhale and exhale. There is no rush. With the faster yoga flows, I end up always holding my breath—I don't feel I have time to breathe.

We continue to move through the practice, and I can begin to physically feel the energy flowing to my head, hands, and heart. There's a warmth spreading through my body. I notice that I can actually feel the rhythm of my pulse and the actual flow of blood into my veins. It's incredible and deeply grounding me into my body in an interconnected way I haven't felt before, pulling my attention fully inward.

It's funny, I had the expectation of a massive "moment" but I'm seeing the grand prize might just be the little things, like these subtle realizations and deep connections to self. The beauty is slowing in down to savor what matters most. Shocker, I know. I should know this by now.

As I flow into my forward fold I hear my mind asking me to slow down, be more intentional, and it occurs to me—in the way my thoughts will usually ask and ask and ask and ask me until I finally cave—shit, I just realized I do that to other people sometimes in order to get my way or simply to feel understood. I need to be much clearer about articulating my needs, to myself and others. Turns out, I'm a couple decades out of practice.

I remind myself, there is nothing wrong with me. Just old patterns to unlearn, wounds to tend to. And that takes time. Hate to break it to you, my friend, but you'll likely have to heal the same patterns more than once. Many times in fact. So give yourself a break. It's all part of the messy miracle of being a soul wrapped in skin, here to feel it all. Give yourself permission to get messy as you heal. That's where the real magic happens.

I am trying to grow while healing. Trying to forgive while grieving. Trying to find and let go. Trying to love others while trying to learn how to love myself. *Breathe. Give yourself a break, love.* This practice is helping me to see: I am Love. I keep coming back to Love. I am okay. I am enough. So are you, my dear friend. So are you.

These childhood patterns still run deep—judging others to protect myself, fearing I'm not enough, forcing outcomes to get what I want. I learned early on to manipulate my surroundings to meet my needs, because no one was meeting my emotional ones. When love felt unreliable, I focused on survival. If I couldn't feel safe emotionally, at least I could control the physical.

Now I recognize the pattern, and I see I don't need to play that game anymore. I can ask directly instead of trying to control or coerce. If someone can't meet me after I've lovingly expressed a need (once, maybe twice), then yes—there might be loss. And that's okay. As long as I stay rooted in what's true for me. I need to become more comfortable with loss—not clinging so tightly to everyone. Relationships shift. People change. That has to become a natural part of how I live. Differing opinions and vibes are okay. Moving on is okay. Not everyone wants to grow or evolve at the same pace. And that's okay too. Coercion isn't love—it's shoving.

What a beautiful stream of realizations, all rising as I breathe, connect, and finish the session deeply tuned inward. Safety lives inside me. And for a recovering codependent... that's a revelation.

The evening gong that calls us into meditation is swallowed by a deafening downpour—like trying to sit still at the base of a waterfall. The sound is wild, powerful, almost holy. Living in Baja, I sometimes miss the thunderstorms of the Midwest. But this? This evening feels like a homecoming. The rain wraps around the meditation hall like a spell, and I drift in and out—between the rhythm of my thoughts and the rhythm of the storm.

We end the evening silently enjoying warm lentil soup overflowing with rich curried veggies. Food is so glorious, isn't it?

I'm about to crawl into bed in my little cabin when it hits me—damn, I actually love having this space all to myself. Sure, the nights are cold and the sheets are damp, but no one's snoring, no midnight bathroom trips. Just peace. Simple. Cozy. Quiet. Mine. The main meditation house has radiant heat, but I'll trade that for a full night of uninterrupted sleep any day. I don't feel lonely at all—I'm actually craving the quiet.

Chamomile tea in hand, I write, reflect, and unwind. No mirrors anywhere—just the soft, persistent question echoing in the stillness: *Who am I?*

I have childhood stories I recognize that need to be released. I can't continue to say I'm like x, y, z because of my mom or dad or middle school trauma or my ex or blah blah blah. I see now—they were all unconscious or damaged and doing the very best they could, myself included. Not their fault. Not my fault. The experience has simply been learning on my chosen path.

I need to step away from the story, stop giving the past narrative in my mind power by reliving it, because each time I do, my mind knows no difference—it's like I'm reliving it all over again. I see my role in the suffering I've caused in my own life. Where attention goes, our precious energy flows. We won't find lasting fulfillment swimming in the stories our minds are playing.

Zoom out, Becca. Zoom out.

I vow to be better about creating my story in the current moment. Be aware it's all just a past story. See it, separate it from my identity, and let it go.

I would say meditation is going alright—decently. I am desperately trying to get physically comfy and there are lots of distractions with nine people also trying to do the same. Coughs and sneezes and sniffles and shuffles and and and and...

Ultimately, only one thing creates tension: wanting things to be different than they are.

Baby steps on the bus.

Chapter Thirty-Two

Sign received, Dad.

Day 4

"Life isn't as serious as the mind makes it out to be." – Tolle

Snot is dripping like a leaky faucet from my nose down my face this morning at meditation, as I dare not be the one to disturb the room. I've also been struggling with pools of saliva in my mouth—called *spiritual liquid* according to Cole, and apparently very common in prolonged meditations.

I'm digging in today. I've decided I'd rather feel my own snot trickling down my face than disturb the room with a loud nose blow, mainly because of the way I've judged others these past few days. The judgment I hold for others directly reflects the areas where I continue to judge myself. Same goes for acceptance.

This is your life. You decide the meaning you make, the story you write, the purpose you choose. No one else can.

The more unconscious we are of our own negative qualities, the more they show up in how we perceive others. Mirror, mirror on the wall... perhaps this is why they've removed all the mirrors.

I judged someone for sneezing, and then—boom—I was hit with a mega sneeze myself. I decide letting snot roll down my face for an hour is a fitting way to punish myself for being a Judgy McJudgerson about their mostly unavoidable bodily noises.

I'm allowing snot to coat my face and my stomach to cramp instead of disturbing others—while some rustle their jackets freely, sigh loudly, yawn audibly and unapologetically, with no care for those around them. Okay... maybe not so unavoidable.

I wonder if withholding those noises at my own discomfort is a *pleasing wound* or simply being conscientious? In this instance, I go with the latter.

I learned early on that attunement to others equaled safety. No one asked me to do it—my nervous system simply took over, scanning for problems, distress, or disconnection to avoid rejection, punishment, or abandonment. It became my unspoken job to manage the emotional temperature in every room, even if no one gave me the role.

I tried to earn love and stability by being hyper-aware, emotionally useful, and never too much. Somewhere along the way, I started to believe that if everyone else was okay, I would be okay too. That their stability somehow guaranteed my safety. It sounds a little wild when I say it now as a recovering codependent—but for a long time, that was my truth.

I've come to see that those volatile snaps in my past weren't random. They are what happens when you abandon your own needs for too long. That kind of self-sacrifice comes with a cost. Turns out, ignoring your own feelings for too long doesn't make you more loving. Just more likely to explode.

I'm learning to send loving-kindness to the most difficult people in my life—because underneath it all, we're all just trying to be seen, heard, and loved. But I'm no longer letting myself become entangled in what isn't mine. Their issues aren't mine to manage. Their healing isn't my responsibility. I no longer make their pain my project.

Despite the physical discomfort, the meditation this morning feels really good. Nothing deeply profound in terms of connectedness, but there's some solid, lengthy stillness of the mind and actual physical comfort in my body and posture—once the pesky snot dissipated. Small wins.

It took a lot of messing with my pillow setup to find that two pillow blocks under my bum and a small circular pillow wedged halfway under my ass, landing just in front of my tailbone, helps tilt my hips down juuuuust that extra degree or two. It takes the pressure off my knee joints. Delightful.

We roll into the slow Hatha yoga flow with Cole after meditation, which is quickly becoming my favorite part of each day. The slow pace, the subtle stretches—they feel like an internal hug. Our teachers continue to emphasize that this is a spiritual practice, not a physical one to be perfected. They remind us not to aim for achieving the "perfect" posture, but instead to immerse ourselves in *being* yoga.

Rather than "doing" or "practicing" yoga, the aspiration is to enter a state of yoga—to use it as a tool to sharpen our Witness Consciousness, to access the deeper layers of the Heart, and to reveal our true nature. This is about expanding consciousness. Hatha Yoga, they explain, is not just an aesthetic discipline or a physical workout. It's a practice of awareness and joy-filled openness—a method of connecting with the infinite, eternal potential of our true essence.

They caution us to avoid the trap of a rigid, ego-driven practice. Instead, this practice is directed inward. It becomes more intimate, more freely expressed, more dynamic—continuously refreshed by the subtle flow of our inner energy. As this happens, we let go of routine problems, dramas, and fears, and gain access to the extraordinary treasures found in the present moment.

These sessions are not meant to feel imposed; they're a creative invitation to witness the living energy of *now*. In the practice of yoga, we *become* yoga. Oneness is reflected within and without, as we align with the sacred rhythm of life itself. Yoga becomes a celebration—an honoring of the raw, vibrant power of being alive.

At the end of the morning session, we try something new: walking meditation indoors.

Walking meditation is more than just strolling—it's meditation in motion. We're training ourselves to be as mindful as possible, bringing awareness to our body and physical sensations with each step. Spread out evenly in a large circle, we begin walking *very* slowly, our hands either clasped behind our backs or gently folded in front at diaphragm or navel height. Our muscles are soft, our bodies move naturally and easily.

We walk with intentional poise, keeping our bodies upright, aligned, and dignified. Our eyes remain soft, slightly open, and our minds and bodies are rooted in the present. We feel each foot lift, each foot land. We notice the subtle motion of our bodies advancing through space. At first, it's tricky to maintain spacing and rhythm with the group. But then something clicks. It becomes like moving with a flock of birds—deeply soothing, almost instinctive. With my focus so fully attuned to each movement, there's simply no room for thought loops or mental chatter. I love it.

Afterward, I'm all zenned out, wrapped in a blanket on the porch during our break. I open *The Essential Rumi* again, basking in that sweet post-practice quiet. Sonia passes by and gently reminds a few of us, with a handwritten note, that we're not supposed to read during breaks.

But why are there books here then? I almost make a scrunched-up, confused face to silently ask—but catch myself. Instead, I nod gently and return my gaze to my lap.

She scribbles another quick note, as if hearing my thoughts, and holds it up:

These books are for other retreats. Go contemplate nature.

Grrrrr. Sigh.

As I slowly stand, I notice her hair is a bit thin, and I hear my mind go, *Ohh, see—she suffers from thinning hair!* I dealt with that too during the pandemic, when all the stress—the loss of my dad, the loss of my job, and, well, being stranded abroad on my own for the first time in my life—caused my hair to thin quite a bit. With some wonderful natural products and a lot of stress reduction, it finally came back to its previous fullness just before this trip.

But here I am having this mean, judgmental thought about her. Like, *Ha, she suffers too!* I catch myself in the middle of it: *What the hell is that?* Why would my mind go there? Is it trying to give me an ego boost of superiority in some twisted way after she scolded me? That's ridiculous.

Sigh.

IT'S GONNA GET MESSY

I'm starting to *really* get it—thoughts shape everything. They create our entire reality. They color our world, set the tone, and create the energy we live in. What we resist? We attract. What we criticize? We invite. So every judging thought we hurl outward? It boomerangs right back at us.

The truth I can't ignore smacks me in the face: judgment is just a mirror. The habit of judging others only reflects our own unmet desires, buried insecurities, old wounds we haven't healed.

Case in point: the hair.

Compassion, Becca. Compassion.

Because every time we catch a judgment before it calcifies, we have a chance. A chance to meet ourselves with grace. A chance to understand instead of assume. A chance to soften. Observing our judgments isn't just about being a better person. It's about tracing them back to the places we're still hurting—and choosing to heal.

I make a mental note to email her the information on the products that helped me after the retreat.

I kick aside the judgmental thought, vow to do better, and take Sonia's advice. I wander off the shaded porch into the sun and stop in front of a small bush, its thin wiry branches bursting with tiny purple flowers. I pause. I close my eyes. I come into my heart center, breathing deeply for a few minutes. With full presence and sincerity, I ask the Universe:

It would be so lovely to see a hummingbird.

I open my eyes and gaze out into the valley beyond. Calm. Centered.

Not ten seconds later, zooming in from the trees below, comes the largest and most stunning hummingbird I've ever seen in my life.

My eyes widen. I stifle a gasp so I don't scare it away. It has a sleek metallic black head, a radiant emerald chest, and fluorescent turquoise flashing outward toward its wings. A magnificent royal purple flows across its tail, wings, and the lower half of its body. The energy it carries—the vibration, the presence—is the embodiment of *Pure Presence*.

It hovers just a foot in front of me, pausing above a flower, then darts to another bud, and another, and another—each just a foot or two from where I stand. Then, impossibly, it comes and hovers right in front of my face. Six inches away.

I don't dare move. I am filled with joy. A huge smile spreads across my face.

Time dissolves.

I'm mesmerized by its rhythm: stillness and motion, perfect and alive. The sound, the vibration—its wings carry the force of a box fan, yet it carries the sacred stillness of deep nature. That kind of beauty pulls you instantly into the spectacular silence of the now.

Then, just as suddenly, it darts away—back into the sea of pines.

I close my eyes, sun drenching my face and body. And in that moment, I am profoundly grateful for Sonia's redirection.

Sign received, Dad.

Chapter Thirty-Three

The monkey mind.

Day 5

> "*The mind is a battlefield, and we must learn to control it.*"
> –Buddha

Wow. I am somehow halfway through the retreat already. Time actually does fly.

Sun streams in the meditation hall this morning as Sonia offers a timely lecture on the power of separating from our thoughts—letting them pass without grabbing hold or giving them our energy. What we resist tends to persist, so the invitation is to recognize our thoughts simply as thoughts... and then let them go.

Living from the heart isn't passive. It's a form of action that generates energy and awareness, with the power to awaken others and uplift humanity. The real goal, my friend, is to be present. To love, to feel joy, and to connect from that heart-centered place as often as you can. Follow what lights you up. Let go of what weighs you down. Love freely, without expectation.

Goooooong.

After morning meditation, we try a walking meditation—this time outside, on the freezing wet grass still covered in morning dew. A construction truck drives by, and I look up to see two men leaning far out of their windows to catch a glimpse of this motley crew, slowly walking in a circle, staring at the ground, in the middle of the forest, in our simple clothes, contemplating life...

Yes, Corporate Becca, I am now *that* lady.

I laugh. Silently, of course. And I give myself some credit. I can be so hard on myself, constantly thinking I'm not making enough progress in my growth—but if I pause and look back, I *can* see how far I've come from the codependent, pleasing, emotionally repressed, materialistically driven, Corporate Becca. I'm beginning to understand healing isn't a straight line—it's a spiral staircase. We circle back to the same wounds, again and again, not because we've failed, but because we're ready to meet them with deeper awareness. Each return is not a setback, but an invitation. This is integration. This is how we heal.

I say a silent prayer to myself: *Thank you for continually trying, showing up, and simply giving your all to do better.*

Food continues to be ever so deliciously vegan and healthy. Portions are so plentiful that I actually have to write a note to Sonia's mom, the chef, to ask for smaller portions so I don't feel overly stuffed or like I'm wasting food.

In meditation after lunch, I struggle a bit with Mario, who I've nicknamed Sighing Shuffle Bear. He shuffles and moves a lot. He yawns like a lion—audibly and rather loudly. Which, in a café or movie theater or library or literally anywhere else in life, wouldn't bother me in the slightest.

But when you're in a small room trying to silence thoughts and distractions and go deep within, any small sound or movement can pull you right out of the journey inward. Perhaps not for seasoned, long-time meditators, but for me as a beginner—it definitely does.

I get so annoyed. I get so distracted. Why is that?

Do I honor my annoyance and ask politely for him to try and be quieter? Or do I send love and compassion? Likely the latter. I need to accept what's outside of my control, even something as simple as this, and practice giving it no more energy or power by focusing my attention in its direction.

I decide I'll ask at the Q&A tonight what their thoughts are on the matter.

I practice seeing the goodness in me, and the goodness in all. To simply not allow my thoughts to make someone else's movements a distraction or form a judgment—just send them love.

It is *so* much harder to do than one would think!

Whelp, I hoped it wouldn't happen. I suppose it was somehow bound to happen. But after I finish lecturing myself that morning about releasing judgment and containing my thoughts, during the evening meditation I mentally snap in such anger as all the distracting noises continue.

I write a note—er, maybe a novel—for the Q&A session tonight as follows:

"**Bear with me, a question is coming... I am so embarrassed to say I mentally lost my ever-loving shit during meditation this afternoon. I have wanted to do a retreat like this for years, getting away from my phone and inbox was damn near impossible. I deeply desire to connect to Source. I sit with my legs falling asleep, thirsty, aching back, and only move or make a sound for absolutely necessary involuntary bodily reflexes like a cough or sneeze. Yet there are excessively loud yawns, sighs, gulping water, slamming down water bottles, and yes... zipping of fanny packs during a walking meditation!?!**

I wanted to scream. Why aren't you trying?! Why don't you care?! Why are you not being considerate?!

So the question is: How to be?

I'm sad because I'm allowing distractions to affect me. I can't not hear them. I can't seem to just let them go. Do I send love and compassion and keep trying? Is it a fault in my own mind that this bothers me so? I could put in the damn earplugs, but you can't walk through life with earplugs.

I truly care for everyone here. I think all are good, caring humans... but. Thoughts on how to be? Or maybe the problem is me. Maybe I should just fucking drop it."

Three hours later, I look at my ranty note just before the Q&A session begins. We drop into a short mindfulness meditation beforehand, and a bomb of *knowing* goes off that feels like it wasn't even my own. My reactivity is just pure mind chatter. The anger is the result of these reactive thoughts—and really nothing more. I can choose to give them power... or just let them go. The choice is mine.

I sit here and cry as people shuffle about, making noises that my mind is telling me are ruining my experience—and in that same moment, I realize: They have no bad intent in their hearts. They simply don't see or realize how they're being distracting to others. They are simply deep in their own experience.

Man, I have *got* to get to a point where my mood doesn't shift based on the insignificant actions of someone else.

This is how a silent meditation retreat goes, my friend, at least for me. An epic yin and yang of mind vs. presence. I'm feeling huge swings of emotions and thoughts, from bliss one moment to judgment the next, presence to annoyance. They just keep purging uncontrollably, skipping about like a broken record, killing the harmony of a perfectly good tune. This is a front-row seat—insanely up close and personal—to the madness of the human mind. It's a bit shocking to witness, honestly.

We never really have time in our daily hectic lives to actually look at and analyze why we react the way we do, to see that beneath every behavior there is a feeling, and underneath that feeling is a need. When we get the rare chance to understand that need, rather than focus on the upset behavior, we can begin to work with the root cause beneath the surface, not just the emotional symptom that's showing itself.

For me, the underlying need that wasn't being met—the one causing the anger—was that those noises kept affecting my ability to go deep. That I couldn't control the situation. That's why I was so frustrated.

Three hours later, does it matter? No. Did I need to melt down over it? Also no. Why was I trying to control my environment so much, and those around me? I had in my mind a certain way this retreat was supposed to go. A certain way people would behave. A certain way people would follow the rules. But that simply isn't how life works, now is it?

I get annoyed when people don't follow the rules or basic logic—but let's be real, humans aren't exactly logical. Most of us are just operating inside our own little universes, largely unaware of what's happening outside our own minds. Simple as that. *Breathe. Release. Let go. Don't sweat the small stuff you can't control.*

A theme keeps circling back to me, the desire to control my environment. It started in childhood, a way to feel safe in a world I couldn't influence. Now, I see the grown-up version: fixer energy. Micromanaging outcomes. Trying to mold situations or people so I feel valued, secure, or needed. But really? It's just fear in disguise.

Control, I'm realizing, is often a stand-in for safety. When we don't feel safe within ourselves, we try to manage everything outside of us. And when that doesn't work, we sometimes turn inward with something even trickier: self-sabotage.

Self-sabotage is when we act, consciously or not, in ways that undercut our own success. We stall. We shrink. We withhold effort or over-attach to perfection. Because if we fail on purpose, at least we're in control of the crash. We turn our inner wounds into self-fulfilling prophecies. It's painful—but familiar, and our nervous systems are wired to return to the familiar.

Cough, cough, cough. A good chunk of my adult life in a nutshell.

In the quiet of this retreat, I can't hide from it. I'm face to face with the truth: I've been my own worst enemy more times than I care to admit. And yet, even that awareness is a gift. A gift to witness my repeated cycles, and choose to respond differently.

So now I'm learning to let go—daily, imperfectly. I remind myself: I am safe in stillness. I am safe when I respond with love instead of reactivity. I am safe when I trust the flow, not force it.

Because in the end, most people aren't trying to hurt us. We're all just walking around with old wounds and tangled beliefs, bumping into each other. Underneath it all, we're made of the same Love. The same breath. The same light.

And the more I soften, the more I see it—everywhere.

I crumple my ranty note, dropping the repetitive mental victim track playing in my mind.

And the irony in all of this?

The very last comment before we close for the night from the teacher:

"I know it's challenging to sit this still for this many hours a day, but if you can all take care to limit your coughs, shuffling noises, yawns, and any unnecessary sounds, it would be appreciated."

So there's that. I could just... let whoever is responsible for this environment *manage* it.

Sigh.

Meditation isn't self-improvement—it's self-acceptance work.

I silently laugh at myself and the absurdity of it all, then head off down the rock stepping-stone path to my little cabin for the night.

If you're reading this and thinking, *Ummm Becca, I hate to point it out, but you're sort of all over the place right now. You're zenned out, then you're an ass. You're connected to Oneness, then you're deep in judgment. You're blissed, then you're frustrated with yourself and others. This hot mess is hard to follow...*

Well, you'd be completely correct.

If I'm honest—and if you've noticed—that's exactly how this is unfolding. These first few days, I realize I'm feeling totally overwhelmed by my yo-yo mind.

I just turned 42 two months ago, and I realize I have *never* sat with my own mind, in silence, with absolutely zero allowed distractions, for... an hour, let alone five continual days.

There's a reason we all distract ourselves with TV, podcasts, packed schedules, drinking, video games, shopping, hobbies—the list goes on. We're all part of this human collective neurosis of sorts. Mind is mind. And we're all battling something it has to say.

Of course, I did zero research on what to expect before plopping myself into a silent retreat. I barely know the curriculum, the focus of the content, the format—hell, I didn't even know before I arrived that I couldn't listen to music or look anyone in the eye.

I simply trusted. I let go of control and let the Universe take me where I was supposed to be.

And now I know—I am exactly where I need to be.

It is time to listen to my mind. To hear what it has to say.

IT'S GONNA GET MESSY

And it turns out, if you don't listen to it for a few decades...it's got some shit to throw down.

And so it is.

And I'm glad for it. Glad to recognize its patterns, its nuttiness, so I can get ahead of it, see when it's running the show, and just let it pass on through. I was experiencing the strongest ego death of my life—my mind was completely flailing.

These early days of the retreat feel like I'm releasing some of my mind's programmed malware, clearing the cache, clearing the cookies, if you will. It's like training a puppy—right now it's pissing and shitting literally everywhere, chewing up my favorite shoes, rebelling because it's not allowed on the sofa. Next thing you know, we're snuggling in bed, sharing two ends of a croissant for breakfast until we meet in the middle for a smooch. That's the goal anyway—that's the hope.

But in these moments, right now, I can't remotely feel that peace with my ego yet. I'm just, sort of, vomiting out all the contents of my mind. Finally becoming conscious of all my unconscious, programmed thoughts. Witnessing them firsthand.

I'm experiencing, for the first time, that my brain truly is a memory bank—a repository of epic capabilities. Every person, place, feeling, emotion, and experience from my life is somehow stored in there.

It's funny, isn't it? We make sure our phones, apps, and computers get software and malware updates constantly... yet we never do that for our own minds? Insane, right?

As I'm falling asleep, I notice the ache in my right foot that's been building up, getting worse, making it really uncomfortable to get into a proper Zen meditation folded-leg posture. I've had some pain in my right foot tendon from sitting cross-legged—and from a little surf tweak injury before coming to Chiapas.

Before leaving Baja, I got a short YouTube video from a girlfriend in my conscious lady lunch group—a group that meets once a month to discuss all things spiritual. I had this visceral feeling I *had* to watch it before going into silence, and it ended up being the last thing I watched.

It was a video of Joe Dispenza being interviewed by Lewis Howes. Lewis was talking about how he was raised Christian Scientist, like I was, and how he was exposed to the power of the mind and healing from an early age. My whole body buzzed with resonance.

Joe recounted the journey of healing his spine after a catastrophic biking accident that doctors feared would leave him permanently unable to walk. I listened intently as he described how he imagined healing energy scanning over his body, bringing it back into resonance and health through the power of the mind.

Laying here with my foot aching, I decide to put it into practice.

I focus all my positive thoughts and energy on my tendon. I imagine bright, healing white light emanating deep from within, radiating over the injury. I have never done anything like this before in my life—but what the hell, I figure, why not give it a go?

I do it with my full attention, belief, and heart-centered love for over an hour... until at some point, I drift off into blissful sleep.

Chapter Thirty-Four

Surrender your ego.

Day 6

> "*The heart is a mirror, and the world is its reflection.*" – Attar

Things are starting to shift. I awake to a beautiful sunny day and bask in the sun like a seal out on the porch before our first meditation, soaking up the warmth to chase away the morning chills. Today, all the noise disturbances—I'm letting them go. I remind myself to chill out. *Remember your learnings from your mushroom journey, Becca.*

After a delicious breakfast of fresh fruit and oatmeal, I'm standing outside before yoga when, uninvoked, a teeny-tiny baby hummingbird zooms past me, chirping cutely. It stops right in front of my face for a moment, as if to say good day, before darting off in search of a blossoming floral buffet.

I soak in the rapid flutter of its delicate wings—such power and gentle grace in perfect harmony. An overwhelming sense of contentment washes over me as I flow into yoga. With limited sighing and coughing joining us today, we move together in a silent, cohesive rhythm of pure delight.

Later, during our afternoon break, I decide to finally take the hiking trail down into the valley below the retreat center. During morning meditation, I noticed something: the soreness in my foot tendon is *completely gone*. Not a trace of ache or discomfort.

I can hardly believe it! Was I really able to help it heal with my thoughts?

Just a few days ago, I struggled to cross uneven ground, and now here I am—no mobility issues, no pain—completely fine.

Absolutely amazing. I am *so* elated.

Go figure, everything my parents tried to show me growing up with Christian Science is now showing up as *Truth*.

You see, the core concepts of Christian Science, I now realize, are totally sound. But expecting a young child to grasp the nature of our spiritual essence to realize the power to heal oneself, well, that's quite the task. It's too much to ask of any child—hell, even an adult—to grasp that level of spiritual awareness: to *know* we're ultimately spiritual beings having a human experience. These meat suits we're all wearing still need maintenance sometimes.

Thanks, Dad. You knew you'd show me the way one way or another, didn't you? I just wish we could have had some of these deep spiritual chats while you were still here. I know you are here. I just can't see you.

And that knowing will have to be enough in this lifetime.

I step outside my cabin and spot the small dirt path just a foot wide leading from my door. I shuffle down the steep bank in tiny, mindful steps, conscious of each movement. I zigzag deeper into the forest.

The tall pines slowly give way to leafy trees, and the path is padded with pine needles, still slightly damp from the rains earlier in the week. It feels like walking on a bouncy, comfy cork floor. Nature's very own trampoline.

As I descend into the valley, a wonderful melodic sound reaches my ears, the flowing of a stream. Such a rare and precious sound in all my Mexico living and travels.

I follow the beckoning sound, grinning when the path crisscrosses the water. And at their meeting point, I catch my breath—a massive, stunning, thick palm tree stands right at the stream's edge.

Golden sunlight pours through the trees and lands directly on that very spot where stream and palm meet, bathing the leaves in gold and turning the running water into a river of sparkling diamonds.

It might as well be a palace. It *feels* like a palace.

I walk slowly to the stream, smiling from ear to ear, and find a rock right in the center to perch on, right below the palm. The sun bathes my face. I'm truly as giddy as a kid in a candy store.

In pure awe of the incredible beauty of nature. The vivid, intricate details that have somehow always been there, hidden in the background of my life—I finally *see* them.

With presence, they come alive, joining each living frame. Time slows down.

I feel free from the old stories my mind has been chattering at me in the meditation hall each day.

I realize that in order to free them, I have to first be comfortable *sitting with* them.

By walking through the valley of my own shadow.

I close my eyes, standing on the rock in the center of the flowing stream, and simply listen.

Soaking in all the healing sounds of nature. All the sights, scents, and moments in nature feel more vivid and alive. The incredible beauty and magic of the everyday begins to shine a little brighter. This creation, this planet, this natural splendor... it's all a slice of pure Love.

My body relaxes, like it's been chilling on the sofa of a dear friend—you know, the kind you can walk into their home unannounced, kick off your shoes, and lie down without a second thought.

I inhale deeply.

I am in the Kingdom of Heaven.

It's amazing how wondrous the world is, even amidst all its imperfections, evil, hate, wars, and destruction.

Some people in this life are deeply called to participate in those wars, to watch the news about them, to funnel all their energy into conflicts of borders, race, religion, and politics, in the hope of helping make them cease.

Bless those people, truly.

That is not my calling. It's never been my calling.

You're not a bad person for not pouring your time and energy into those conflicts.

Where attention goes, energy flows. You are free to fuel whatever constructs, passions, topics, and people you wish.

I realize now how much I have loved walking my path of spiritual awakening—and all I really want to do is share it with others, to help lift them up. Help lift myself up. Help lift the planet up.

I wonder how I will do this. Yet I trust: if I put the intention out there and follow my passion, the path will unfold.

Breathe. Inhale. Trust.

I look up and spot the arched wooden bridge I glimpsed earlier from above. I make my way down the path, passing a fresh water pool big enough to claim as a personal hot tub.

Wooden bridges over streams are so damn storybook perfect.

I step onto it, feeling the wood bend and creak, welcoming me aboard. I walk slowly, reaching the peak of the small twenty-foot bridge, and sit down.

To my right, a gorgeous, huge lily. To my left, lush emerald foliage, bright mustard-yellow flowers, birds chirping enthusiastically, moss covering the rocks below, and sunlight dancing through the leaves.

I close my eyes.

I notice I can feel my own presence—a small, centered spot where I am meditating from, right behind my eyes. The Third Eye chakra. I learn a little trick: I gently slide that point of awareness down from behind my eyes, into my throat, and then further down my throat until I land it right around my heart center.

My chest feels warm. Calm. My awareness feels so much more relaxed resting there—somehow protected from ego, from my racing mind.

I take several deep breaths, following the inhale and exhale, focusing on the pauses in between.

My presence now sits cradled in the warmth and calmness of my heart. *In and out. In and out. Again and again.*

And then—I am gone. Into an altered state, losing my connection to time and space.

I hear a loud bird squawk, and my eyes pop wide open. I blink, realizing where I am—and that I'm oh so late for meditation. But

I don't care. I linger for a moment, soaking in what was the most profoundly deep meditation I've yet experienced. It feels like I was resting deep in... simply put, home.

I check my watch. Hah! What? Only ten minutes have passed. That's when you know you've connected to who you really are: time stops in infinite beauty.

Nature has a way of reminding us that all is okay as it is. Maybe the trees are here to show us that growth requires patience. Flowers, to show us that beautiful things don't always have to be blooming. Clouds, to remind us that when things feel too heavy, it's time to release. Growing, living, dying—it's all okay as it is.

Trees don't tell other trees how to grow better. They don't whisper, "Hey buddy, gosh, your branches are looking a little, well... limp. Maybe try some volumizing leaf spray?" They simply follow their purpose, beautifully and without question or comparison.

Granted, our lives are a little more complicated. But are they really? Vacations, rush rush rush, see see see. I realize how many places I've visited in my life so far—but also realize I've rarely *truly* seen them.

New rule: no AirPods while hiking! The melody of nature guided me home, back to the beauty and abundance all around me—and also within me. Nature is perfect. So are you. The rhythm of the earth, the cycles, the light, the dark, the rebirth, the death. It all belongs.

I return from the forest for our final afternoon meditation session. Meditations are now stretching close to two hours at a time, three times a day. I find myself getting a little loopy and restless during this last session, especially after just stretching my legs out in the great outdoors.

Afterward, as I wander into the dining hall this evening with the sun slowly setting behind the towering pines, we are served our first lackluster meal of the retreat. I'm handed something that looks suspiciously like soup, basically a few green sprigs floating in water, as our entire evening meal.

I turn to grab a seat in the little crowded kitchen dining area and end up sharing a small wooden café table with Philip. As I sit down, I catch his eye just as he's making a ridiculous face, clearly questioning whether the soup was a joke—or maybe some kind of lesson after all the incredible meals we've had so far.

We catch each other making stupid faces, and then Philip takes a loud, exaggerated slurp of his "soup," and that's it—the laughter begins. Out-of-control, ridiculous, can't-pull-it-together laughter over the mysterious "green water" meal.

Eventually, we manage to collect ourselves and finish eating.
But later, during the evening meditation, one of the aides, Myrtha—the same woman who helped me during my headache and held my hand—passes a note to the teacher, Sonia.

We're scolded. Sonia reminds us that we're supposed to feel solitary during this retreat, but there's no compassion in her tone. No acknowledgment of what our experience really was. We were like two blissful children, and now I'm sitting there, annoyed. I've just been scolded for feeling joy.

I hastily scribble a note back to Myrtha: **"I've been wanting to come to a retreat like this for over a year. We're six days in, and I've been attentive and eager to learn. Meditation just increased in time, and today I'm physically uncomfortable and a little loopy. Philip slurped his soup, and like two five-year-olds, we giggled uncontrollably for 30 seconds, feeding off each other until we pulled it together. And that's a reason to tattle to the teacher? Where's the love and compassion for a spontaneous emotion like childlike joy? That one action managed to zap my enthusiasm for this whole darn retreat in an instant... I ask myself, 'Why is that, Becca?'"**

Myrtha's written reply: **"I think it is very beautiful to look at why this takes your enthusiasm away. We also love you all being cozy. It was for that reason that a point of doubt to speak to Sonia arose. Eventually, we thought it better because we noticed the whole group—including us—was getting too communicative with facial expressions and sound. You will, in the long run, get more out of this experience if you stay in your own lane. It was not about laughing, not aimed at you specifically. It was a general observation, and it was shared from love. Plus, instead of worrying about this, there's a lovely lecture happening upstairs right now! I hope this calms your mind a bit. It was honestly for you all. Personally, I would rather have a talking retreat. Don't be**

too hard on yourself. I understand it came across that way. Just believe my pure intentions."

Sigh. Failed again. Surrender your ego, Becca. They laid out the rules. Trust the process. Get your ass up to the night lecture.

Each day I was witnessing, little by little, all the pieces of myself I didn't really like. And that's a wonderful thing—because witnessing allows us to see ourselves fully, which is what's required to love ourselves fully, and to let go of the behaviors that no longer serve us.

We finish the night lecture and have our closing meditation. The room has melted into silence, everybody grounded, breath steady, stillness thick in the air.

Then—THUD! A loud crash shakes the whole room behind me.

I pop open one eye and peek over. Philip has fallen asleep sitting upright, and toppled right off his little pile of cushions, smacking his full limp body weight onto the wood floor.

It takes every ounce of willpower in my entire being not to burst out laughing. I snap my eyes shut, whip my head back toward the front of the room, and clamp a giant Cheshire cat grin across my face.

Not a peep. Not a single peep. Buddha would be proud.

Chapter Thirty-Five

Nothing is lost.

Day 7

> "*Only that which cannot be lost in a shipwreck is yours*" - Al Ghazzali

I find myself waking just a few minutes before the 6:30 a.m. gong goes off, which is shocking to me. I thought this schedule would be the most challenging aspect for me as a lifelong night owl, but shockingly, I find I'm quite perky in the mornings. Plus my body and bum are fresh, so I tend to like these morning meditation sessions the best.

Today there are lots of random thoughts of childhood flashing through my mind, and I find myself reliving a traumatic event from when a friend's finger got pinched badly in the metal on the upper part of a teeter-totter while he was trying to manually push me higher. He ran inside to show his parents, blood gushing everywhere. They didn't say anything to me, just yelled: "Go home!"

I thought it was my fault. Oh no. Oh nooooooo. *How will they pray that much blood away?*

I cried the whole way home on my pink and purple banana seat bike, my colorful handlebar streamers offering little comfort, and promptly hid when I got there.

The next day, they came over—his finger wrapped in a huge white bandage.

His parents said twelve stitches were needed, but he was okay.

I still felt it was my fault. They said he had to go to the doctor. *How terrifying*, I thought.

He must have gotten in so much trouble. Until I was about eight, I thought everyone avoided doctors and hospitals at all costs. But around that age, it started to sink in just how unusual my family really was in that regard.

Breathe. Center. Find stillness. Let go. *Sink in, Becca. Slow your mind. Get comfy on your cushions.*

I'm shocked at how vivid the memories are showing up now, like I'm right there.

Ahhhh. *Shoot, I forgot to send that email....*

Breathe. Seriously. Attention, thoughts, and ego: *please, for the love—chillax.*

Here is some imaginary popcorn I have made for you, and I've bought you a ticket to this epic blockbuster movie. You are trying to control my experience by weighing me down in past stories that no longer exist. Instead of doing that, here's a blanket if you get cold. Now please just sit your ass down, zip it and watch the movie.

It's a long one—1.5 hours of negotiations with my mind. I try to loosen my lower back, which is cramping. Breathe. Connect...

A huge horsefly dive-bombs my face and I jump a foot, letting out a tiny, "Ah!!" *Shit! That was not silence.*

I get back into it. Memories flood in one after another, deep from my subconscious hard drive, all day long.

Something has broken free, deep in the recesses of my mind where everything is stored. I flip between vivid scenes like an old-school record player at will: forgotten childhood moments, flashes of marriage, random trips, warm embraces.

Rapidly and repeatedly, they come—which is amazing to me, given my limited childhood memories.

Turns out, it's all stored away, stacked high in the subconscious like an old used bookstore, shelves packed to the ceiling, ladders swaying as you reach for stories hidden deep in the corners.

All is there. Nothing is lost. Only repressed, waiting to be brought to the surface.

We move into Hatha yoga and I get deep into the slow pace, and I just love it *so* much versus the rapid, gym-like variety where I usually hurt something and end up with no connection to my body or breath. This version feels just amazing. Holding each pose deeply, pausing with a simple sequence. Nothing complicated. Simple. Clean. Pure.

I know exactly when to inhale and exhale. With the next forward fold, I can feel my pulse and blood flowing from heart to feet—my God, these bodies are insanely complex and magical. I feel the ending sound bowl chime ripple in my chest, and happiness floods in through my heart. If we slow down, there is so much beauty and so many gifts we are missing in the hustle. I think back on my old life. Man, being overly busy does not equal success.

I look out at the massive pine trees just outside our full glass window, covered in raindrops from the early morning shower. With the sunlight streaming down, the branches look more elegant, gorgeous, and brilliant than any of the biggest, fanciest, most expensive hotel crystal chandeliers I've ever seen.

Stunning.

Heading into the evening Q&A, the wind is absolutely howling and it's damn chilly. I wrap myself in my scarf, pull my woolen hat over my red ears, and pile on all the layers I brought with me. I stop into the cozy little kitchen to fill my huge mug, grateful for the endless fresh hot herbal tea. I think I've been drinking a gallon daily.

I got a nice handwritten note today left on my meditation pillow: **"It's been noticed you have been less communicative."**

A gold star! Hah. Definitely from Myrtha. Such a kind gesture. I send her a silent thank-you.

I know my emotional freakout last night was simply me not following the rules and getting caught. I'm just saying—thirty seconds of uncontainable childlike laughter should have a little wiggle room, that's all. But today, with no eye contact, no sly expressions, I'm being good.

Our teacher Cole says, *"The ocean is silence; the little fish swimming around are sounds. Let the sounds sink into the silence and become part of the rhythm."*

He speaks that evening about anger and how, despite its reputation, it can actually be a helpful guide. When anger arises in response to someone's behavior, it's often a signal: a boundary has been crossed, a fear has been activated, or a core need isn't being met.

The key is to slow down and tend to the vulnerability underneath—the pain, fear, or powerlessness we often cover with volatility. When we express our needs clearly, we can prevent that buildup. Because anger isn't just an emotion—it's a defense. It surfaces when we've swallowed too much, suppressed too long, or felt unsafe for too often. And when our boundaries are crossed or our needs ignored, it comes forward to protect. To show buried pain.

I think back on my marriage, where all the volatility came from—a mountain of needs not expressed, and reactivity to protect ourselves in an unsafe environment. We both did a really poor job of expressing our true desires and admitting our vulnerabilities.

Cole also talks about how common it is for the debris of your subconscious to rise to the surface during silent retreats—thoughts, emotions, memories, and dreams.

He says it's not uncommon for dreams to become incredibly intense, along with memories. We can use the tools we've learned here, such as yoga, breath, silence, walking, eating, and sitting meditations, to stay grounded in the chaos of everyday life. This is a practice in trusting yourself through a difficult experience. Surrendering to your inner compass, your heart space. Finding stability within. Your breath is your anchor in all of life's storms. Keep breathing.

He asks us to consider:
How might this experience change what you're capable of?
How might this change alter what you value?
How might this shift how you define yourself?

A deep pause allows us to get clearer on who we are at our very essence: not our job title, our marital status, our achievements, or our possessions. This is when we learn to disconnect net worth from self-worth.

We think we are our personality, our thoughts, our thinking mind—yet those are simply filters. If we can pause and step back as presence, you can feel that you are the awareness perceiving the dream.

You *are* consciousness.

Your highest presence and safety are within yourself.

Lean into yourself first and foremost for security, acceptance, and confidence.

Trust the flow of life that moves through you—lovingly—and with your best interest at heart, guiding you on your journey here in Earth School.

As I walk back to my cabin, I think about how in the past I made a lot of idiotic decisions. Thank gawd I'm learning that dwelling on past decisions is also idiotic, better to focus on my current direction.

I pause, just for a moment, to offer myself a little grace. For the distance I've traveled, the ways I've stretched and softened, the becoming that's still unfolding.

The lessons—some learned the hard way, some learned twice—and likely, I'll learn again. And again. And that's okay.

Cultivating calm, cultivating clarity, it's like tending a sacred garden. It asks for patience. Presence. A quiet kind of devotion.

And dare I say... I'm proud of how my garden is growing.

Chapter Thirty-Six

Forever and always.

Day 8

"*What you are looking for, is what is looking.*" -St Francis of Assisi

In this morning's meditation, I'm extremely calm and ready to go deep. Which, of course, means I am greeted by lots and lots of shuffling from the group. *You know what? Fuck it. I'm going to try the damn earplugs.*

I squish, twist, and pop one bright orange cone into my ear, then the other—the ones that have been tempting me from a little jar like candy this entire time. Holy sweet surrender, the silence hits immediately.

I play a few seconds of Sarah McLachlan in my mind. I can't help it. I miss music.

Focus, Becca!

Okay. One, two, three, four, five, six, seven, eight... deep, long breaths in and out. Silence.

I'm gone. Into myself, into timelessness, into bliss, into who we are. I am content, calm, serene. All the distractions cease to exist.

I come out of the depths for a moment to reposition my complaining hips. I'm so happy. I think that's the deepest I've ever gone in meditation, besides my solo bridge escape in nature.

Hey, sometimes we need some training wheels, and that's okay.

I drop back in and open my mouth ever so slightly to relax my jaw, which softens the spaceship sound the earplugs had been corralling inside my ears. Instead, as my jaw relaxes, it creates a hum—a low, steady vibration, like the sound of the Enterprise moving through space on *Star Trek*. I used to watch every dang episode with Dad growing up. I was a little Trekkie. Of course, space makes no sound, but you know what I mean.

My jaw relaxes even further, and that spaceship hum disappears. Suddenly, I can feel and hear my heart beating—each steady beat, like a brand new baby coming online on a sonogram.

Bliss. I'm gone again.

I lose all sense of time. My heartbeat pulses: *Love. Love. Love.*

I come out of the depths again for a moment. The room is so silent I have to open one eye to check if everyone is still there. I see Sighing Shuffle Bear off to the left, five feet in front of me completely still, unmoving. You can tell he's incredibly deep in his meditation.

A tear rolls down my cheek for him.

That's the magic of this life, right there—the joy is for him, not for me. I see that he has struggled, just as I have, and he too has reached a nourishing depth today.

The unified field of Creation, alive in each of us, getting a chance here on Earth to help itself, to cheer itself on—recognizing our shared struggles. Simply gorgeous.

I begin to realize I really had no self-awareness of who I was or what my inner child had gone through—until now.

Silence has had an incredible way of helping me take an honest survey of how I need to move forward with this new information and adjust my actions.

Perfection is not possible—but progress is.

The beautiful outcome of silence is that patience blooms—with myself and with others. If you can't see yourself, you can't truly see others. That's why self-awareness is so critical to a fulfilled life: it leads to compassion.

Understanding the hot mess of emotions and fears that shape your own identity lets you see—you're not the only one who feels so much. You start to notice: the way you struggle with your mind, others struggle too.

Breakfast today is just as divine as the morning meditation, toasty warm oats with cranberries and nuts, a side of local guanabana and pineapple.

I was going to grab one of the coveted bananas (they go so fast), but they're all gone. Sigh.

Sighing Shuffle Bear must have seen, or maybe felt, my heart sink. As I walk past him, he leans out, head down, and holds out the extra banana he had grabbed in his big bear paw, offering it to me.

My heart warms with love.

I smile, looking down, and happily accept it. I can tell he feels wonderful offering it.

Gratitude makes everything taste better. It's the best banana I've ever had.

After breakfast, I contemplate nature outside. The baby hummingbird comes back now that the wind has died down—second sighting. So damn chirpy, adorable, and enthusiastic. Just like dear 'ole Dad.

***

As the sound bowl strike drifts off slowly into the morning light, Sonia shares a story before our yoga session begins.

She tells us about her mind being deeply annoyed by sounds during a retreat she once attended for her own growth in Oaxaca. *"Why am I so annoyed?"* she silently asked her mind.

And her mind answered: *"You gave up on your school career—you are a failure. You gave up on a potential wealthy husband—you are a failure. You gave up a marriage—you are a failure. You will build this retreat center, where there is construction noise—you will be a failure yet again. You need to do something important and worthy and big in this life to be successful. Or you will be a failure."*

She said she had to fully listen to that voice—*all* of it—before she could release it. And when she did, she could finally relax and simply let her path unfold. We all struggle. No one is free from the petulance of the mind. It's just a matter of learning how to recognize it, accept it, and let it go—with greater and greater ease.

Having a community, or even just a dear friend, where you can ditch the filter of perfection and share the raw, unfiltered truth... That's where real healing starts to unfold.

For lunch, we have Ajapsandali—a rich eggplant stew from the country of Georgia, filled with potatoes, onions, tomatoes, zucchini, nuts, and warm spices. I love how they leave the recipe cards out for us, sharing the origin and ingredients of each dish. I've been writing down all my favorites.

As the tasty meal settles in my stomach, I take advantage of the afternoon break for a little siesta. With the chilly weather, I find I'm ravenous lately. I drink extra tea to try to make myself feel full. I'm so grateful for the fresh food, three times a day, without lifting a finger—magically appearing after every session, delivered by Sonia's mom with so much love and kindness.

As we begin the afternoon session, I'm hoping, of course, for the same tranquility I had in the morning. But instead, I find myself restless.

The young teenage cousin of the retreat family, who's been volunteering in the kitchen, joins us for meditation—and sniffles. Again. And again. And again—for the entire hour.

I can't quite express how loud it is, except to say: it is impossible to meditate with that constant disturbance.

Finally, João—the stoic, incredibly quiet Portuguese guy, who rarely moves or makes a sound—suddenly bounces up to his feet. You can almost see the frustration built up in each heavy step. He crosses the entire room, grabs the toilet paper roll from the little wooden table where our pens and tiny Q&A slips are kept, crosses back in earnest and shoves it into the kid's hands.

Silently saying: *For fuck's sake, just blow your nose, kid.*

Clearly, none of us could focus during this session.

For the evening meditation, the wind picks up again—loud and wild—but this time the rustling trees become comforting, like white noise.

I try to settle my mind, but it's a mishmash of repeated thoughts that just won't simmer down.

And then, out of nowhere, a scene bubbles up... A vivid, visceral memory.

I'm with Dad, out at the rural house where I grew up. We're in the family room. The fireplace is roaring, like it always was in winter. I'm curled up on my little foam plaid sofa that folds out into a sort of bed, snuggled under a pile of blankets, my favorite stuffed animals surrounding me.

I have a big red bowl of buttery popcorn—Dad's favorite snack, naturally mine too. He always popped it fresh on the stove for me.

We're watching the movie *Contact*. It's that scene: when Jodie Foster's character is standing on a beach in deep space, face to face with her father who had already passed away. His image and voice are projected by a universal intelligence, a gentle way of convincing her that life continues beyond Earth.

They have a beautiful conversation that finally makes her rigid, scientific mind believe in something bigger.

I look up at my dad, firelight dancing on the walls, and in a small, sweet voice, I ask: "Will you come for me on the beach too, Daddy? When you... go?"

He smiles down at me from his green suede recliner, that big warm reassuring smile of his. "If it's in any way possible," he pauses, "you betcha I will, kiddo."

The memory had been long buried in my subconscious. But now, it bursts forward, fully alive.

In that instant, I understand—truly understand—the depth of my father's love for me. It explodes in my chest in a wave of unseen light. For a moment, I can no longer tell where the boundaries of my body end and where the energy radiating from me begins. My physical form dissolves. I become pure, radiant, magical love.

Tears. Endless tears of joy, stream silently down my face. My heart connects to Source, like a key turning in an ancient lock. Something opens deep within me—something I didn't even know was closed.

I feel my heart actually bursting open.

Suddenly, I remember where I am. I try not to sob out loud, perhaps I was, I'm not sure anymore. Tears of joy and pure, stunned disbelief overtake me.

My God, he did it.

A soul agreement, a promise spoken aloud on that wintery night in Wisconsin, thirty years ago—

Fulfilled.

He came for me, on the beach in Mexico. Just as he promised. He came to unlock something sacred within me, to transform my life forever. To show me that this life is only a beautiful dream... A fleeting moment in infinite time.

That our love, our essence, are truly endless. That this strange, precious journey through Earth is just a curious expression of the Divine we are all part of. A quiet knowing moves through me: our souls chose this path, our parents, every joy and every wound—not by accident, but with intention. To learn, to explore, to grow into who we came here to be.

I sit here in the meditation hall, long after everyone has stacked their cushions for the night, filed out the doors, and clattered down the spiral metal stairs to their bunks below.

I stay.

Moonlight pours through the windows. I smile, tears still flowing silently, soaking in this sacred moment for as long as I can.

I realize: I am achieving what I set out to do here. To connect with the Universe in a way just as powerful, more powerful, than plant medicine could ever provide. To find that depth within myself, through breath and silence alone.

That memory, and its impact on my body and mind, feels as profound, as eternal, as the moment he came to me on that other beach... to show me the Truth.

I hear his words again—not in my mind, but from somewhere deeper, reverberating from inside my heart: It's him.

He whispers, and the message flows through me like an eternal river of Love: *"You're beginning to understand, aren't you? The entire Universe is inside you. To find peace, you must be at peace within yourself.*

To enjoy life, you must enjoy who you are. When you are alone, you will never be lonely. Find a home within yourself."

I breathe in—a slow, deep, profound breath—and sink even deeper into my heart space.

Silently, soul to soul, I send my reply: "*Soul agreement fulfilled, Dad. Thank you. A million thank-yous. I know you are off having the most grand adventures. I'll use what you've shown me to make the most of this grand adventure on Earth—this incredible dream. I'll see you again soon. I love you. Forever, and always.*"

Chapter Thirty-Seven

Choose with care.

Day 9

"In the infinite ocean of myself, the mind-creation called the world takes place. I am supremely peaceful and formless, and I remain as such." -Janaka

I am beaming from the beauty of last night's meditation, but this morning it's noted that this will be our first time doing a two-hour meditation stretch without a mini break. That goal gets into my mind. I set an expectation before I even begin that it could be challenging.

Fifteen minutes in, my hip flexors and knees get incredibly achy. I've gone nearly an hour and a half before and been fairly comfortable up until now. Simply knowing it was going to be a long session, I find it's a battle my body has unknowingly already signed up for—because my mind is at the helm.

If you're familiar with the mind-body connection, then you know that our thoughts, feelings, beliefs, and attitudes can positively or negatively affect our health.

I try to make my way through the meditation with micro subtle shifts. I straighten up a bit. I pull in my stomach a bit. I unfold my legs an inch less. I fold my legs up an inch more.

For two hours straight, I fidget. This one is physical torture.

I want to make it the full two hours and am being stubborn, refusing to simply take a five-minute stretch. By the end, I'm yelling in my mind: *"Ring the fucking sound bowl! Ring the fucking sound bowl, por favor!!"*

Sigh. Mind over matter.

Turns out, changing a lifetime of behavior is damn hard. It's not a one-retreat fix. Nothing of real value in life is a quick fix.

But—I've made a huge dent in facing, understanding, and releasing some of my old programming, and I forgive the session. I also finally recognize that all emotions, pleasant or unpleasant, hold equal value in meditation. The goal isn't to favor happiness over frustration, but to cultivate awareness and presence with whatever arises. Real freedom in practice comes from allowing each moment to be exactly as it is, without judgment or resistance.

Funny how the freedom we find in meditation mirrors the freedom we long for in life. I sink into a quiet wave of gratitude—for the growth, the clarity, and the journey itself.

I'm rewarded with a breakfast of fresh, crunchy muesli right out of the oven, followed by a vegan baked apple tart in the shape of a pie slice, with cacao almond milk poured on top.

It's delicious and divine. I'm finding food just keeps tasting better and better—even vegan food, smirks the Wisconsin cheesehead native.

Hatha yoga today is lovely, flowing, with quite a few salutations—more than we've done up until now. My body feels stretched, centered, and good after nine days straight of an hour daily. My hips feel so loose and limber, where before they were usually so tight. On my planks, I feel completely solid—no wobbly arms. My mind and body feel connected, clean, and calm. I feel like my roots are deeper, my internal and external structure more grounded.

For our morning lecture, Cole talks about integrating these teachings into everyday life. Tomorrow is our last day, I can hardly believe it. As with most things in life that take you out of your normal routine for a while, it feels like it went incredibly slowly, and also miraculously fast. You know, like life.

He speaks of inner and outer purpose, of aligning this feeling with outer doing. How easy it is to get distracted with money, societal scripts, and external pressure. But purpose can be a quality of action, a presence in anything you do—not necessarily achieving some milestone. To look at whatever it is you're doing: what is your intention in the moment? Is it pure of heart? Or driven by ego or expectation?

"The joy," he says, "of experiencing life is simply to be, to exist." To find a little joy in each day. To simply experience life in this material form—what a challenge for infinite beings, right? "We believe we are material, and so, we are. We are here to learn from this existence out of our own infinite curiosity."

I think so many are sleepwalking through life in a program built for the masses instead of following their own internal compass—myself included, until my father jolted me awake to a larger perspective.

Cole shares the story of Shiva and Shakti—the story of the feminine vs. the masculine, Yin vs. Yang, Zero vs. One, possibility vs. actuality. As energy, the Universe is referred to as Shakti; and the Father, that which is an identity in the formless, is referred to as Shiva.

He says, "All conscious beings embody both these aspects. Some have a dominant Shiva energy, typically men. Others have a dominant Shakti energy, usually women. Some might be a perfect balance between these two energies, and they are often less driven by sexuality and do not care so much about finding a wife or husband in life. They tend to be the travelers, the explorers, the artists.

The path of enlightenment is the path of bringing together the two parts of this identity until form is no different than formless. A being who has merged into that identity—clinging nowhere to form, neither here nor there, to neither this nor that—is said to be realized. Which is the ultimate union of the Mother and Father. The process of bringing about that union involves working with Shakti, the Mother, directing and using the energy in form, in order to transcend that form and merge with the formless."

The lecture ends and we all trail down the spiral stairs to lunch. I silently ponder my overzealous Shiva energy over the years and how

Baja and presence have really shown me how to bring in more of my Shakti energy.

I stare off into the forest with an amazing salad in front of me, overflowing with fresh tomato, cucumber, basil, mustard, sesame seeds, pepper, ginger, olive oil, and salt. The veggies and spices, as always, brought in from the garden just outside. A side of dahl with some brown rice.

I do believe I'm going to terribly miss this homemade, delicious food made for me three times a day. I'm pretty sure I've put on a decent chunk of weight. Oh well. Happy belly, happy heart.

In the afternoon the wind picks up mightily, and I hunker in my cabin for my last afternoon nap, snuggled up with my gassy propane heater. The first hour of the afternoon meditation is calm, the room peacefully quiet, we all seem to go deep in a unison of surrender.

In the second hour, everything suddenly shifts into a shit show—wind crashing doors shut, super loud gusts, the building rumbling. This time we all surrender to just sitting, and being. Listening intently to the story the wind wants to tell.

Life is full of radical shifts, highs and lows—it's all in how you react to them that provides the power they have over you. The gong fights with the wind to be heard, signaling our break into dinner.

We head into the final evening Q&A after a tasty dinner of rice noodles, homemade peanut sauce, carrots, onion, broccoli, with peanuts sprinkled on top. Dear Lord, holy hell, I love to eat and taste food. It was so cold I took the full portion, then stuffed myself with seconds. I can't help it, I have to ask. I walk up to the Q&A bowl and drop my paper in before the sound bowl rings to begin the session.

He opens my question: **If God/Source created all, then why did we as reflections of God create ego, mind, thoughts to torture ourselves with?**

He chuckles out loud, his laughter filling the room, and thinks for a few minutes.

"Everything is made of Love, flowing through all. Torture is a perception. Eventually Love wins. The mind is a confused kid, forgetting its essence. We must teach it so it no longer torture us. It's a powerful tool in a veil of forgetfulness. The mind is filled with greedy mind programs trying to get things for ourselves, or keep us in fight or flight survival from hunt-and-gatherer days—it is no longer a useful program. Ego isn't really a thing. It's like the moon, no light but simply reflecting the light of the sun. There is beauty in this dance we have created, but the rules of the dance aren't comprehensible. Life will show us what it wants us to do, if your intentions are pure. If you are following a deeper purpose, guided by your heart, you're on the right path. Trust."

I let his words wash over me and feel so deliriously happy to not be asleep in the game of life anymore. No longer running on autopilot. No longer living as a programmed, following a playbook that was never mine in the societally scripted machine.

They don't call it TV "programming" for nothing. Where you put your attention and what pulls your focus—is where your life force flows. We become what we consume. Not just the food or the screen time, but the thoughts we replay, the voices we absorb, the noise we let settle into our minds. So be mindful of what you consume, not just with your eyes and ears, but with your time, your thoughts, your emotional space. Allow for stillness. Make room for what uplifts, expands, and grounds you. We can't block out every low vibration, but we *can* choose what we invite in and what we dwell in. Your attention is powerful. Choose with care, my friend. It shapes everything.

There is a question on falling in love. He replies, "Falling in love is intoxicating because it takes us away from mind, into Diviness. Over time, the mind takes control, ego, and it becomes an eye for an eye. Another person can never give one the stability we can find within. Asking a human to provide that is asking the impossible. No partner can complete you. Find someone who compliments you. All the love you need lies within."

We listen a little more—on compassion, timeless Buddhist stories, about how some ruling this planet simply want to destroy others and get as much money, power, and control as they can. The majority of us simply want to be. What most don't realize is your precious attention and energy—and where you invest it—gives those other forces their power.

We close the evening session with a beautiful ceremony about transmuting pain into love, where we take on a loved one's pain and transmute it for them. Release it for them, silently asking the

Universe to take the burden off their shoulders and put it onto our own to help them heal.

I think of my mother—how much she is hurting to now be alone after losing her partner of fifty-seven years. To now have to sit at home, alone. In a home now so silent, with the ghost of my chatty, positive, caring father lingering still in the air.

I think of her, deep in my heart. I hold space, and I ask with all my being for that pain to be taken away. Tears roll freely. I send her infinite Love. I send her what she already carries within—for it to awaken, and nourish her.

I can feel it—new software upgrade, complete. Adios, cookies; adios, malware. At least, for this precious moment. They may build up again—and when they do, I will give them my attention with curiosity and not judgment.

I'm a blank canvas, reset, open to all the wonderful infinite possibilities this one precious Earth life can offer.

Chapter Thirty-Eight

A simpler way.

Day 10

"Let life be beautiful like summer flowers and death like autumn leaves." -Tagor

It is the final morning, and we all share a lovely, rather distracting meditation. I find I am in total acceptance of all the sounds. I'm not sure what is happening in my being, but this morning, all bullshit aside, I love the loud yawns. I love the truck screeching outside. I love the dog barking. I love the sneezes.

I want to bottle up this feeling so I can crack the cap open and guzzle it whenever I choose.

Ten days of breathing into my heart center, of nourishing it, the energy in my chest is radiating in a way I simply can't explain. My heart is so full. Everything seems to radiate. I am feeling everything—every emotion, every presence, every experience—so profoundly.

I feel like I'm floating throughout the day's meditation and yoga. I cry heartfelt tears the entire morning. I can't help it; my emotions are gushing out of me. My heart feels so full and open.

I feast and savor each and every bite at breakfast. Childlike glee overcomes me, fresh eyes drinking in the pure wonder of this existence. Deep gratitude for this path I have been guided down.

The afternoon meditation is so very chill—calm, centered, filled with gratitude. When the teachers explained that centering in the Spiritual Heart induces a feeling of sacred interconnection with our true home, where we find ourselves together in the radiance of Pure Presence, I think I am feeling a glimmer of that lightness.

At sunset, we gather for our final silent Q&A ceremony. Our teachers talk about death—how Western culture ignores death, leaving us thinking we have forever. There's often a sense of mystery and dread when a person dies. Confronting one's mortality is uncomfortable, but realizing the truth brings us greater presence.

In the US, the body is quickly picked up and taken to a morgue or funeral parlor, remaining out of sight of the grieving family until the wake or funeral. This is another reason why I love Mexico so much. The concept of death in Mexican culture is so wonderful—as they mourn death, they also celebrate it with humor and joy.

One of Mexico's biggest and most widely known traditions is *Día de los Muertos*—the Day of the Dead—where they celebrate and face death instead of silencing and ignoring it. They are filled with and exude so much color, joy, dancing, and remembrance on this day. It's a time when good spirits are welcomed to join us once again and are remembered through gorgeous altars of flowers and candles, designed by those they've left behind.

There is no desire to stockpile treats or frighten each other, just the sharing of a rich heritage and warmth that spreads from person to person as they share their beautiful creations, costumes, and memories.

The States, by contrast, is about snagging all the unhealthy sugary goods and moving from house to house as fast as humanly possible, sans interaction with those around you, to amass the most goodies you can. Sigh. A broken holiday. Just my two cents.

In Mexico, death is seen as an extension of life—just another chapter in the journey. A transition from Earth School to whatever comes next. There's something beautiful about that... well, truth. When you hold a broader view of life beyond this existence, it softens the edges of grief.

Sonia shares the story of a mother told she has 30 days to live. She immediately quits her job to be with family. She finds herself at the grocery store before heading home to share a favorite meal she wants to cook for them, but she notices the cashier has overcharged her $17. She is told to wait to get the manager to resolve the matter, and she does.

And then she starts to laugh to herself. She smiles, leaves the store, and lets the matter remain unresolved—knowing now that her time with her family is worth so much more than righting that wrong.

Look at how we could live differently from this example—if we embrace the knowledge that our time here on Earth is limited. If we get out of the accumulation mode of material goods and invest instead in experiential goods.

If we invest in connection and giving, instead of getting.

We're all dying—the urgency should be influencing where we spend our time and energy, yet we ignore it.

Please don't.

For our closing circle in the meditation hall, we have the most glorious hour-long sound bath—sound bowls, didgeridoo, rain sounds, drums, tambourine, and incredible music. My entire body hums. I feel like I'm leaving my body. It is sublime.

Of course, our speaking silence is also ceremoniously ended with a sound—our last sound bowl ring of the retreat.

And then, we all go up to the altar at the front of the room and share our experiences one by one. My heart is so full; what each of my comrades shares is so special to this very moment. Everyone is grateful. Everyone feels more aligned with what matters. Everyone vows to value the little things, to let more meaningless worries go.

I will say—it is absolutely hilarious to hear everyone speak after so much time in silence. I forget everyone has unique accents and expressions from all over the world. In the past ten days, there were no borders, no countries, no man-made labels to separate us.

I get up to share, hearing my voice—which sounds so bizarre. "Hello. Helloooo. Hello." I smile. "Hi there. Gawd, I sound weird. The word *hello* sounds weird."

I share about my journey on how I came to be here at the retreat—the story of my dad, my rebirth, and the memory that came to me during this retreat—the gift of his soul to my soul. Pure LOVE.

Lots of little miracles—like my foot tendon, the hummingbirds, feeling the immense love of strangers. I'm excited to share and maybe go on and talk a little bit too long because it feels so good to share. To create space for my soul to finally learn to speak.

I thank everyone from the bottom of my heart, crying, smiling, gushing. "Thank you. Gracias."

I hug our teachers, our chefs, our assistants—all helping to keep the retreat grounded, welcoming, and nourishing.

Sonia offers a simple small piece of folder white paper, I open it to reveal lovely handwriting in blue pen covering the page:

> **Even**
> **After**
> **All this time**
> **The sun never says to the Earth,**
> **"You owe me."**
> **Look**
> **What happens**
> **With a love like that,**
> **It lights the**
> **Whole**
> **Sky.**
>
> **Poem by Hafiz, (1320-1389)**

Beautiful.

Later that evening, I find myself sitting around the roaring fire, chatting away with everyone, expressing our love and gratitude for the shared experience.

You know, in finding your purpose, it's important to remember—there is only one you. One fingerprint. One voice. One path meant for you to walk, one calling only you can express—no matter how big or how small.

It could be to make the best bread on the planet, or to share your art, or to fight for the freedom of others—or it could be simply to lift others up in the best way you can, to support and teach those around you each day, in simple ways. Using passion in service of others, that's purpose.

If you follow your curiosity regardless of where it leads, you might just discover your passion in the process. Whatever calls to you, lights you up, *do it*.

We live under the Law of Attraction. When you follow what truly lights you up—day by day, step by step—Source rises to meet you. It's a game. And if you're not having fun, you might be playing someone else's. Most of us are guilty of that to some extent, at least for a while. So learn. Play. Reflect. Ease up on yourself. This was never meant to be perfect. Especially not by tomorrow. Experiment.

It's hard not to get pulled along with the societal scripts.

But if you're feeling bogged down by bills? Downsize. Don't have enough resources? Find a community to help you and pool resources. Hate your boss or career? Shift direction—drastically, if you feel called to.

I share with the younger attendees around the campfire that I ditched a model home with a gourmet kitchen to live in a casita with an outdoor hot plate as my kitchen, and I have never felt happier.

Their eyes glow with relief, a glimmer of knowing—there may be another path forward.

A simpler way.

As a solo woman, I'm aware I have a bit more luxury to choose to live this way—but I've seen families with children on sailboats, in RVs, in yurts, and in communes. The only thing holding you back is the worry of what society has told you life *should* look like.

Let those stories go.

Collecting things won't make you happier. Real connection is what makes you rich.

Life is about embracing the joy of playing this game—no destination to get to, no prize to attain—simply the joy of being in these physical bodies. The joy of a dip in the salty, fresh ocean. A nice cup of coffee. A warm embrace. All the emotions—good and perceived bad. Taking a lover. Squeezing your furry friends.

We are in a special place in infinite time—and you are the architect. Isn't that just so incredibly magical!?

It's the way that we live—the way we connect with those around us—that matters.

If your job has you tired and stressed at the expense of your family and your mental health, set your intention. Change direction. You're one decision away from a different life.

Chase your joy—and work your ass off for it. Ask for help.

Don't strive for balance. Find work-life harmony. Find your rhythm.

I feel more than ever, sitting up here by the fire offering my two cents to these younger travelers, that my deeper purpose is simply to be more grateful, peaceful, joyful, and loving to myself—so that I can offer that to those around me.

Daily doses of these elixirs are the strongest medicine in our cabinets.

I begin to embody this new awareness, giving myself a taste of how life *could* be lived. My eyes and body are opening up to a new way of walking through life—in Love, not fear.

As we give our long hugs and warm goodbyes, we leave the retreat, heading back into town the same way we came—via taxi—but this time, I ride back in humble, pensive silence with Philip and João.

On the drive, I am struck by the beauty of nearly everything and everyone. The crumbling, colorful buildings. The sun through the palm leaves. Even the stoplights are beautiful.

I am deeply living in my heart-centered space.

I reimagine what a vibrant, meaningful life can look like. I want to continue to shake things up. To create a life that makes me hop out of bed, instead of sinking into the mundane.

Chapter Thirty-Nine

And so it is.

I spend a few final days in San Cristóbal de las Casas reintegrating. Everything is magical—the lights, the sounds, the food, the people. I dine out, and at each dinner, I find someone in the restaurant dining alone and buy their meal. The waitresses desperately wanting to let them know who it's from, I smile and say, "Please don't."

At one point, though, I guess the waitress can't resist sharing who the culprit is, and the gentleman chases me into the street. "Miss! Why did you buy my dinner?" he asks urgently, confused, needing to know.

My face lights up, I tilt my head. "Why not?"

He stares, not sure what to make of that statement. "Well... um, thank you. That made my night, thank you so very much. How can I repay you?"

I can't help but smile warmly, sincerely. "No need. If you would like, simply pay it forward."

I turn, and continue on my way, leaving him looking grateful and somewhat dumbfounded. My heart could explode with joy in lifting him up unexpectedly, in offering a bit of light to a stranger on a chilly, dark night. When you radiate love, you get that reflected back to you. Why don't we all do these little acts for others without expectation more often?

Smile big. Open your heart. Express your emotions. Be unapologetically you. If it makes you happy, warms your soul, helps you grow—choose that. Breathe deep, love hard, really live your precious life how you desire to. There is but one.

It's nearly the holidays, and the town plaza is filled with a stunning nativity scene and a massive Christmas tree light sculpture in front of the city's white, classical history museum. The adorable plaza takes up one long city block and is filled with palm trees, paths, benches, and street vendors. The lightness and playfulness of the notes streaming out of the pavilion are so welcoming. I sit on a park bench below a palm tree covered in a string of multi-colored lights and allow my ears to linger for a while.

Happiness is circumstantial—it's chasing shiny objects, only to hold them in your hand and seek another. Joy is a state that bubbles up from inside of you, independent of what's outside of you.

The next day, a holiday begins—when Mexicans celebrate the anniversary of the apparition of the Virgin of Guadalupe to a humble Indigenous man, Juan Diego. Although Catholicism in Mexico has fallen from where it was a century ago, many Mexicans still participate in the annual parades, which begin four or five days before the December 12th anniversary date. There are fireworks, loud parades of cars honking, and dancers down the street blasting music, twirling, intertwining.

I float, taking it all in, in bliss.

I am finally ready. I purchase a journal, find a cozy café, and as the days in Chiapas come to an end, I begin to write the beginning of these very pages.

I decide to have a drink to celebrate, and I notice how much my relationship with alcohol—and how it affects my body—has shifted. This evening I push myself and have several glasses, and I find that I hate the feeling of being buzzed. That warm sensation that used to make me feel relaxed, happy, and playful now makes me feel a little anxious, and I see it's a gateway to negative thoughts and feelings. Interesting, and about damn time I noticed this.

In the months that follow, I find I still enjoy a drink, but my mindset shifts. I become intentional about why I'm having it. Alcohol used to be a gateway: for numbing, for releasing suffocated emotions, for helping me connect more freely. But I no longer need it for that. Now, when I choose to imbibe, it's merely one or two, paired with my favorite foods and savored with appreciation. I'm very conscious of why I'm consuming it. Sometimes the answer isn't cutting out every coping mechanism, but understanding the need that led to the dependency—because once we do that, we no longer have to be ruled by it. That's where balance lives. Not in control, but in inquiry.

I end my Chiapas trip with an epic boat ride through the breathtaking Sumidero Canyon—a place I hadn't even heard of before, yet one that rivals the Grand Canyon in its own wild, majestic way. Gliding on the water at the bottom of the canyon, breeze in my hair, sun on my face, staring up at the cliffs towering a few thousand feet above me, all on my own, I realize that I actually love myself to my core. I don't *think*—I *know*—I am lovable. I am enough. I am so worthy, in all my labeled good and bad behaviors.

I am delighted to discover I am able to be alone without being lonely. I am releasing what drains the life out of me. In my solitude, I am reenergized. So creative. So *me*—and I love her.

As I think about returning home to Baja on the plane, I can feel the changes taking seed within me. Yet the reality of human interaction, and matters of the heart and emotions outside of my little solo sanctuary, prove challenging as I flow back into the noise of everyday life.

The following week is Christmas Day, and do you know what happens when you take the monk out of the monastery? Well, turns out they have to encounter other humans—like the idiots in traffic, for instance, that ride your ass. And dammit if those triggers aren't hard to shake.

Mastering yourself solo is relatively easy; add other humans into the mix, that's where the challenge lies. This time, though, there is progress because I am able to pause and observe my reactions instead of simply responding to the triggers of the past. I'm able to see the root of my reactivity clearly. That is progress.

So, after my high-flying enlightenment escape from reality, I find myself out of my safe cocoon, with Danny, having just an epic fight that leaves him at the bar on Christmas Day and me at home alone crying. I fall from grace. We had the entire argument over text—which should never be done, as complex emotions, voice inflection, and energy are impossible to portray in text. It is awful, and we both know, just a year into our relationship, that this is the end.

Does this mean my retreat failed? Hell no. Presence takes practice; growth takes patience. It is consciously trying each day to break free from your old self, the emotions and thought patterns you're addicted to, and start molding the new version of yourself you wish to become. Day after day.

Flawed and fabulous.

Love just asks that you show up, do your best, stay present, and feel fully. You're not pure, you're not spotless, you're not perfect. It means continually coming back to yourself with a heart of love and compassion despite your imperfections as a human being.

Spiritual paths are not about love, light, and smiling through it all. That's toxic positivity—not allowing yourself to feel and process your emotions. This path means getting to know all the parts of yourself, the light, the dark, so you can heal what hurts. It means working on settling your ego and really witnessing your repetitive behaviors. It's a deep dive into the depths of your soul. It's raw. It's vulnerable. It's messy. Most importantly, it involves speaking your truth.

You see, people will make up stories about you regardless, based on their unique life lens. Our job is not to change their perception—it's impossible. Do you see how much we all live in our nutty heads? Their reality will never match yours. Release that external worry and live your truth.

Doing so can be deeply uncomfortable at times, and that means you're on the right path of undoing your programming by coming back to your soul. That's brave. You may feel lonely; you may have woken up while many around you still lie asleep. That's okay—let them sleep. Keep going, keep walking your path, and shine on like the divine being you are. That we all are. They'll wake up when ready, and by simply walking your truest path, you help show them the way.

What I know is ending this time with Danny, however, is just a label. Our connection is rare and profound, and to this day, he remains a beloved friend. When boundaries are crossed in romantic relationships, we often feel like we have to stay and fix it together, to heal side by side. But staying isn't always the answer. Repair takes deep maturity and a shared willingness to grow. Not everyone arrives there at the same time. If you constantly have to defend your boundaries or fight to feel worthy, that's not love—that's a warning. When words don't match actions, when promises go unfulfilled, you're off course. The only real apology is changed behavior. I'm finally learning to embody that truth.

We often know the answers far before we're ready to admit it. But listening to our heart at the end of a relationship takes radical self-trust—like, cellular-level trust. Relationships will stretch us, yes. They'll reveal our blind spots. But they're not supposed to break us. They're meant to enrich us. To remind us of our innate wholeness.

Ignore the red flags long enough, and what could've ended gently often burns to ash. Sometimes, there's more healing in letting go early than dragging it out when deep down, you already know the relationship is not aligned. Yes, so many teachings say, "stay in the game" because, in our culture, we often throw in the towel far too early. We project our fears and wounds onto the other, bounce from body to body, chasing a fix instead of doing our work.

But here's the uncomfortable truth: We have to let go of the childhood fantasy that one day someone will show up and love us *exactly* how we want it, in the exact way we crave. We have the right to our boundaries. To emotional peace. To fulfillment. All of it. Authentic connection is built on love, trust, and honest authentic communication. It doesn't feel like chronic pain or anxiety. It will certainly stretch you, but it's supportive. If feels safe. It feels settled. So I'm taking the uncomfortable steps. No one else is responsible for saving me but me. I'm healing. I'm slowly mastering myself. And really—what could be more valuable than that?

I find myself in a place I never imagined could be possible. Despite the hardships, heartaches, I am taller and stronger than ever before. I am more content and at peace within myself, having learned to find joy and fulfillment in the simple pleasures of life. I find myself renewed, with a sense of optimism and possibility for how life and love will continue to surprise and delight me.

I want to make each moment count. I am grateful for each challenge that has shaped me, for the blessings that have helped me grow, and for knowing that tomorrow is always a new beginning.

No regrets—just lessons. The plot twists, the so-called painful life chapters, have become the fuel for future wisdom. Each detour was quietly shaping me, leading to new opportunities for growth. All along, I was building the confidence I'd need to finally trust myself in love.

Finally, I had uncovered the love of my life I was seeking all along—*me*.

On this journey to healing, you will lose a lot of the people you thought would be with you forever. Most of those people were only meant to be with you for a season. Sometimes you have to accept that some people only enter your life as a temporary happiness or a lesson.

It has taken experiencing a lot of loss to realize that not everything in life is meant to have a lovely ending. Not every person we feel a connection with is meant to stay. Some people come into our lives to teach us how to love—and sometimes, how we desire not to be loved. In that learning, we're shown how not to settle, how not to deny ourselves ever again. Sure, sometimes people leave—but that's okay, because the learning remains, and that is what matters. Their lesson was a gift to you that you'll carry always.

The biggest lesson I've learned is how to let go of things that no longer serve me. It's hard. It gets lonely at moments. But I have found that when I clear away all the background noise, only then am I truly able to be me. And only then do I realize: I still have so much more healing to do.

Whatever it is your soul longs for, give yourself permission to go after it. The way we show up in the world—the way we speak to ourselves, how we treat others—creates our personal reality. So to change your personal reality, you need to change your personality. You need to see the good in yourself and in others. To embody positivity. To create a positive reality.

As my perspective shifts, the people I once felt good around, and the environments I was drawn to, are shifting too. I'm peeling back my vulnerabilities, seeing my ego, and the drama I create for myself. I'm getting more and more comfortable crying, no longer burying my emotions but sharing them vulnerably. Those who can lovingly hold space for me, who hear me without judgment—those are my people.

I'm embracing my deep sensitivity and realizing I need to be more cautious with my energy. The people and places that used to numb me, like excessive drinking, spending time with people who never ask how I'm really doing, don't feel magnetic anymore. I don't feel the pull to win anyone over. I'm okay being me.

I'm craving solitude, and to balance that, I'm craving deeper, more authentic connections. I want to nourish my body, mind, and soul. My internal world is shifting. It's amazing and it's scary. It's so foreign to me, yet it also feels like coming home.

Ya know, I'm not sure if in Earth School I'll ever graduate to "healed completely"—whatever that may even mean. Maybe that diploma doesn't exist. Maybe my heart is too soft, my scars too deep. Maybe I'm supposed to stay a little messy, a little sensitive, a little chaotic.

Either way, I'm enough.

I'm enough just showing up and trying my best. That goes for all of us—it's inherent in this nutty human condition.

To honor my journey into silence, I get a hummingbird tattoo hovering over a lotus flower on my left arm—the divine feminine side of my body. Hummingbirds, or *colibrí* in Spanish, are known as messengers of joy. They symbolize intelligence, beauty, devotion, and love. The hummingbird in my tattoo is the exact shape and size of the last sticker my father ever gave me. Tiny stars and a faint moon above it, a quiet reminder to trust the direction of the Universe, and to remember that Dad is always with me. To know I'm being guided, if I just pause, ask for help, and listen.

There are deep, hidden parts of myself emerging, and I just want to keep letting it all show up. I want to fully show up. I want to let go of whatever doesn't help me evolve. I want to trust my co-creation with the Universe.

The little nudges, the pull inside your heart, the feeling of rightness guiding you forward—that is the entire Universe flowing through you, with you. You are never separate. You are an incredibly important part of that magic energy, always.

Isn't that a grand relief? As you awaken to your true nature, only to spend the second half of your breathwork session wondering if your ex watched your story... then spiral-scroll Instagram for an hour trying to fill the void.

I sure hope so.

It's so easy to feel like you're losing some invisible race in this digital world, but most of it isn't even real. It's a false narrative of people's lives—you're only seeing 1% of their full story, so you aren't really seeing them at all.

True happiness has nothing to do with how many followers you have, your relationship status, or your external achievements. The real qualifiers are: Are you being kind to yourself? Are you loving toward others, and allowing yourself to be loved? Are you letting life guide you into your heart?

Don't spend your life comparing from the outside in. Step into it. Let Love, and your unique inner knowing, be your guide.

The minute you decide you want better for yourself is the moment the Universe shifts in your favor. Really live your life as you desire, instead of being a slave to society's expectations.

This shared human experience is universal. No amount of money or celebrity allows you to escape it. In fact, those paths are often burdened with even more pressure and pain. It helps us wake up to all the societal conditioning we never asked for. Through self-awareness, you come into contact with your genuine preferences and aspirations—not what society tells you to strive for, but what actually feels nourishing for your soul to spend your energy on.

As we heal, it means: deeper self-awareness, self-acceptance, self-compassion, taking responsibility for our actions, living intentionally, setting boundaries, giving ourselves permission to be who we are, breaking detrimental patterns, and offering kindness to ourselves and others each and every day.

We have to forget the essence of what we are to experience this world fully—the sun on our face, the warm cookie on our tongue, the ocean enveloping our toes, the fresh flowers blooming under our nose—along with the inevitable pain of being human.

This is what our souls have chosen. We are here to experience it all.

You are not meant to follow anyone else's path. Don't limit yourself. But also—don't push yourself into exhaustion.

Don't label yourself. You're too big, too bright, for that box.

This wonder within you—this Divine spark—exists to help you find your own unique path. It knows you better than you know yourself. It knows what's meant for you and what isn't.

It speaks by withdrawing your energy from what isn't meant for you, and flooding you with excitement for what is. It wants you to grow, to expand, to shine.

Think of it like a giant disco ball, and we are each an individual ray of light emanating from it—separate enough to dance and explore on our own, yet deeply connected to, and a part of, the same radiant Source.

This energy is rooting for us—in every single cell of our bodies, in every single particle of the Universe. It is on our side, always.

Tap into it. Let it guide you.

Never abandon that voice within, that intuition, that flutter in your chest, that pull in your stomach. That is your perfect compass. And it will never fail you.

I think most people realize that the ultimate goal in life is contentment. Notice I didn't say *happiness*, because happiness is just a slice of the human experience pie.

Without the peaks and valleys of emotions, you wouldn't even know you're on the damn mountain. You'd have no compass at all. And without a compass, there's no present moment to experience.

The living is in the whole range of emotions—feeling, sharing, and expressing them all. We don't get to be happy all the time. That's not the journey. That's a false destination.

The real goal? To be who you want to be. To love who you want to love. To make a difference without needing to broadcast it to the world on social media. To live in a way that brings some satisfaction each and every day.

Don't force vibes. Go where your energy is loved, welcomed, and respected.

Life brings enough anxiety on its own. The people meant to journey with you will not be the ones causing you to feel uncertain. Invest in people who make you feel at home.

Home isn't a place; it's a frequency. If you breathe, if you feel deeply around that place in your heart where your compass lives, and if you listen—you will not be misled. I promise you.

Will I love again? You bet your sweet sexy ass I will.

Look at all I have learned from Love. But at this moment, I don't need to flail about seeking it in a partner. That will come naturally when it should, and if it's in my best interest, in perfect Divine timing.

You are your own soulmate. Look no further than your own being within. All the love you need beats right within your chest.And when you feel lonely, come back to this truth.

Trust me as someone who has moved—okay, literally—*thirty-seven times*. You don't have to move towns, or states, or sell everything you own and hop countries. You can find this knowing exactly where you are.

You will never rise above the opinion you hold of yourself. There has to be a conscious effort to nourish yourself from within—and no one else can do that for you. Only you.

If you keep trying to feed your soul with the opinions of those around you, you'll keep eating... but never feel nourished.

Self-love is the highest frequency there is—it attracts everything you desire.

The more fulfilled you feel within, the less you need from the outside world.

The secret has never been out of reach. It's always been right here—within. Wishing. Hoping you'll notice.

These guides live deep in our hearts, in our inner world.

Can you live from the heart? Can you trust that pull is the exact thing you've been searching for?

Because it is—if you have the courage to follow where it leads you.

You are never alone. That's an illusion, my friend.

We may carry a million labels on Earth separating us, but at our core, we are One.

Finally, I not only see it, but fully feel: I am enough, because I am Love.

And you, my sweet friend—you are Love too. You are already enough. Our worth isn't conditional on a damn thing.

We are here to experience this messy human path—and if you find yours rather messy, congrats. You're living.

You are the one you've been waiting for.

I hope you dream. I hope you listen to the little calling in your heart, even if your mind doesn't yet understand how it's all possible.

It would be easy to give in to fear. Instead, quiet those voices. Share your gifts.

Loving yourself unconditionally, and doing what you love, isn't selfish—it's your right.

It's your life's intention.

It is your purpose.

This isn't the Matrix.

Everyone is Neo.

You don't need to travel anywhere, take any colored pill, or change who you are.

You just have to remember.

You are pure eternal magic.

Own that shit.

You have everything you need, right now, at this very moment.

The only question is:

Will you pause, and listen?

Epilogue

I'm back at my mother's house the following summer when I hear it clear as day, the whisper: *Go through the box again.*

I know exactly which box it means. I have one small storage bin, tucked beneath the stairs. Inside is a collection of old cards—mostly from Dad.

I listen to the voice and pull open the storage door, dragging out dusty boxes and other long-lost treasures. There it is, tucked away at the back: my bin. I slide it to the center of the room, sit cross-legged on the rug, and lift the lid.

There are a hundred cards, maybe more. I sift through them slowly, reverently, until one seems to pulse with warmth in my hand. A folded card, watercolor landscape on the front. I open it.

His handwriting. From 2008. A letter falls out.

Dear Becca,

The enclosed typed letter is an exact copy of the cover sheet addressed to you in the ring-bound book, *Dream Time 33*. **It's in our 'archives' closet (nope, actually, moved to filing cabinet)!**

When I wrote this letter, I thought you'd only read it once I gave you the bound book. But I'm giving you this letter early to give you a preview, because by the time you *do* **fully read** *Dream Time 33*, **it might be 10 or 20 or 30 years from now. So when you open it someday, this letter will refresh your memory.**

Dear Dad, silly as ever!
Love, Dad. xoxo

Chills. Everywhere.

I have no memory of this letter, just a vague mention of the book. I was 28, I read the letter and forgot about the book entirely, too busy with my Denver adventures to read it. Hint: I wouldn't even be *close* to ready to understand its contents.

I rush to their closet. On his side—still untouched—rests a stack of poetry, musings, manuscripts, research notebooks. Then I see it: a thick, royal blue three-ring binder. On the cover, in his handwriting, are the words *Dream Time 33*. I gasp.

I pull it off the shelf and dust it off. Inside, I run my hands over the 500 pages typed on his old-school typewriter, meticulously assembled, one keystroke at a time with occasional white out dabbs and all. I see the first page cover letter addressed to me, a duplicate of the one that just fell out of the notecard.

I scan the letter and halfway down a sentence grabs me-

"...Be all this as it may, I doubt you will read any of this until after I've left this world..."

Turns out, a father's greatest gifts don't always arrive in his lifetime.

Acknowledgements

I feel like this is Monopoly and I'm passing Go, collecting $200. At the same time, I'm collecting a lifetime of learning that could never equate to any form of currency. I still can't quite believe I'm fortunate enough to actually write an acknowledgements page in a book. Honestly, I never thought I'd make it this far.

This has been the most challenging and deeply rewarding project I've ever taken on. I now have a whole new level of respect for writers—and for every single book I now see on a shelf. The work that goes into creating each and every story is immense.

I'm beyond delighted to be here, writing this, but also a little worried I'll forget someone important. I even asked my editor for a few extra days to gather my thoughts. And here I am, hoping I can do this moment justice.

What better place to start than with Q'Harina, editor extraordinaire and the person the universe led me to. I'm so deeply grateful. There are absolutely no words that can express what it means to have someone who has turned from editor to mentor to friend to therapist to mirror... to a greater expansion and awareness of myself. There's just no greater gift than someone who can be so new to your life and hold all those places. I am eternally grateful for all that you have done for me in bringing to life this most precious story.

Thank you to Katelynn and Christian for shaping the arc, asking the right questions, and carefully nudging my meandering sentences into clarity. To Tiffany, for custom-designing this absolutely stunning cover. I'm in love. A special thank-you to each of you, too, for your profound patience with me throughout this lengthy process as a new writer. Let's just say... bless you all.

You'll recognize these next few by the names I used in the story—private names, chosen with love. To Danny, for holding space from start to finish. You witnessed me lose confidence countless times and helped me step back into it with care and encouragement, again and again. Thank you, Dawn, your support was endless and heartfelt, and your unwavering belief in me reminded me to keep going on the most challenging of days. Nikki, thank you for your fabulous photog library that helped me with precious details, for showing up with steady support, and for the occasional afternoon tea that grounded me more than you know.

To the Former, and the former lovers. It was beautiful. It was messy. But each one of you taught me something essential that helped shape this journey. In that way, it's all been perfect.

The Hridaya teachers and my motley crew of retreat mates, I carry your kindness with me for sharing such a magical moment in time with me that I'll always cherish.

To my Ladies Who Lunch, Cabo Mastermind Crew, Tenacious Twelve Team, and my surf lineup family—you've not only inspired stories in these pages but also stood beside me in so many meaningful ways. Randi and our whole lovely garden tribe, thank you for cheering me on with heartfelt check-ins and words of encouragement that stayed with me more than you all probably realize. Nicholette and Miss Mila Moo, thank you for walking this transformational Baja path with me. Being part of the beautiful Baja conscious community has changed me forever. Thank you to everyone who's walked alongside me, helping illuminate the way—especially the healers who have held me so gently in ceremony.

Lindsey, Mary, Cory, Anneliese, Debra, Katie, Leia, Ani, Catherine, Lacy, Jen, Carrie, Hillary, Anna, Nettie—thank you for your sisterhood. Ashley and Tyler, thank you for your guidance on this new writer's path. Megs, Misti, and Lindsey L., for lending the very first eyes on my story and offering the tender guidance to keep going. Susan, Bev, Heather, Jackie, Caroll, Sandra, Erin, Alexa, and Christina—thank you for your support during such a pivotal season. Your encouragement helped shift my course and open the door to this next chapter. I'll always be grateful.

A special squeeze goes out to my dad's dear brother—my favorite uncle, Jerry. Profound gratitude to my brother—thank you for loving me, for helping me remember those small but meaningful details from our childhood, and for always showing up with your big heart. I love you so much.

Mom, thank you for being exactly who I needed, right when I needed it. You have been both a guide and a teacher in this lifetime, and I'm so grateful for your love and support.

I wish I could just thank *everyone*. So, I will. To all my friends and family and dear ones who have supported me along the way on this precious path—thank you times a million.

And last, but never least, to my dad—thank you for making this book possible. Your love and belief in me have been a steady force, infinite in a way I'm only just beginning to understand. I love you. To the moon and back, and beyond the bounds of time and space.

If you've made it this far, dang, thank you *so* much. Your support means more than you know. I put my whole soul into this book, and although I don't have the mega audience or the flashy PR team, I do have *you*. If you feel compelled to share this story with friends, family, community, on social media, or by writing a heartfelt review—those are literal gold—it would mean the absolute *world* to me. I'm deeply grateful to everyone who generously helps me share this story.

Finally... I hope, with my whole heart, that these words offer comfort and guidance to someone, at the exact moment they need it most.

Sending you all so much love.

About the author

Becca Eve Young is a soulful storyteller and former corporate strategist turned guide for those navigating the wild terrain of healing, reinvention, and radical self-worth. After years spent building brands for huge corporations and climbing ladders that turned into cages, she escaped the noise to rediscover her own voice—one sunrise, meditation, surf session, and psychedelic journey at a time.

Her writing blends grit and grace, grief and humor, with an uncanny ability to make you laugh, cry, and see yourself more clearly. Whether she's chronicling the awkward beauty of modern love, the tender ache of loss, or the unfiltered magic of spiritual growth, Becca brings raw honesty and grounded wisdom to every page.

Based in Baja when she's not roaming the globe, she coaches soulful entrepreneurs out of the corporate matrix, guides others through their messy middle, writes from beachside cafés, and stays devoted to living a life that's slower, deeper, and undeniably her own. This is her debut book.

www.beccaeveyoung.com

www.ingramcontent.com/pod-product-compliance
Lightning Source LLC
Chambersburg PA
CBHW032146080426
42735CB00008B/607